M000106234

Power and MADness

Power and MADness

The Logic of Nuclear Coercion

EDWARD RHODES

COLUMBIA UNIVERSITY PRESS New York

COLUMBIA UNIVERSITY PRESS
NEW YORK   OXFORD
Copyright © 1989 Columbia University Press

All rights reserved

Library of Congress Cataloging-in-Publication Data

Rhodes, Edward Joseph.
  Power and madness : the logic of nuclear coercion /
    Edward Rhodes. p. cm.
  Bibliography: p.
  Includes index.
  ISBN 0-231-06820-4
  ISBN 0-231-06821-2 (pbk.)
  1. Nuclear arms control—United States.   2. Nuclear arms control—
Soviet Union.   3. Deterrence (Strategy)   I. Title.
JX1974.7.R497   1989
327.1'74—dc19   89-594
                 CIP

Book Design by Charles Hames

Casebound editions of Columbia University Press books are Smyth-sewn
and printed on permanent and durable acid-free paper

Printed in the United States of America

c 10 9 8 7 6 5 4 3 2 1
p 10 9 8 7 6 5 4 3 2 1

To Anne Case

CONTENTS

ACKNOWLEDGMENTS

I HAVE been fortunate. It has been my luck to discover that the qualities of charity, wisdom, and good counsel are, like the quality of mercy, not strain'd. Consequently, my task in acknowledging and thanking all those individuals and organizations whose support and assistance moved this project forward is a large one.

My debt to five great universities—Princeton, Cornell, Stanford, Harvard, and Rutgers—is perhaps most obvious. Both intellectually and financially these institutions nurtured me and my research. The intellectual debt is impossible to describe adequately; the financial debt is somewhat easier to specify precisely, though the list of debentures is a long one. I must note my gratitude to Princeton University's Woodrow Wilson School for its University Fellowship; to Cornell University's Peace Studies Program for its Peace Studies Fellowship; to Stanford University's Center for International Security and Arms Control for its Arms Control Fellowship; to Harvard University's Center for International Affairs for its Paul-Henri Spaak Fellowship in U.S.–European Relations; to Harvard University's Centers for International Affairs and European Studies for their Ford Program Fellowship in Western Security and European Society; to Rutgers University's Research Council for four separate research grants; and to Rutgers University for its Henry Rutgers Research Fellowship. To the various foundations whose financial support made these fellowships possible, I express my deepest thanks and my hopes that this book begins to justify their investment. In addition, I am grateful to the U.S. Arms

Control and Disarmament Agency for its Hubert H. Humphrey Fellowship in Arms Control and Disarmament.

Columbia University Press' confidence in this work and Kate Wittenberg's skill, tact, and efficiency in overcoming every obstacle I managed to create are appreciated far more than I ever led them to suspect. Paul Carroll undertook the dreary task of checking footnotes. To the *Review of International Studies* and its editor, R. John Vincent, I wish to express my thanks for permission to reprint portions of my article from the January 1988 edition.

In the pantheon of saints in this project, Richard Ullman deserves pride of place. No young academic ever had a wiser or better mentor. Without his advice, support, and trust this book would have been impossible. His counsel was critical at every stage. Kenneth Oye's support has been similarly invaluable throughout the many years this project has taken. Richard Ned Lebow provided not only invaluable advice on dealing with the issue of irrationality, but friendship and backing whenever it was needed, which was frequently; our discussions greatly sharpened my thinking and my wits. Klaus Knorr read the bulk of this manuscript twice, each time opening my eyes to the logic and implications of my own argument.

This work and I have benefited from contact with an impressive new generation of international relations scholars. On behalf of the readers of this volume, I wish to express my particular thanks to Anne-Marie Burley and David Petraeus, who selflessly worked through draft after draft of this work with me, helping me to understand what I meant and showing me how to communicate it. Matthew Evangelista and Scott Sagan read the entire manuscript and kindly, but thoroughly, exposed the errors in my argument. William Drake, John Duffield, Joseph Grieco, Stuart Kaufman, Charles Kupchan, Richard Moss, Mark Schaffer, Michael Shafer, Jonathan Shimshoni, and James Wirtz all exceeded the ordinary call of friendship in providing comments on all or portions of this manuscript. Only pure stubborness on my part can account for the errors of fact and judgment that remain.

Throughout the course of this project, senior colleagues have also been generous with their time—and, in many cases, their skepticism. I fear that most of them will not be disappointed by this work, for they anticipated its faults and weaknesses long ago. For their willingness (frequently despite their inclinations or better judgment) to look over this manuscript or portions of it at various stages in its development and for their advice, however little I have heeded it, I am grateful to Robert Art, Alexander George, Robert Jervis, Roy Licklider, Richard Mansbach, Patrick Morgan, and Barry Posen. For their patience and comments early on, when I was attempting to formulate the inchoate questions that motivated this study, I remain indebted to Douglas Arnold, Avinash Dixit, Gerald Garvey, Robert Gilpin, Stephen Van Evera, and Julian Wolpert.

During the early stages, my thinking also benefited a great deal from contact with a remarkable interdisciplinary group of scholars at Princeton. David Bennett, David Wilcove, and the other members of the weekly "sherry hour" group provided a stimulating setting for exploring questions of rationality and irrationality.

My family provided not only the customary support and encouragement, but real substantive advice and suggestions as well. My parents, Mae and C. Harker Rhodes, Jr., and both my brothers, Harker and James, read this manuscript at various stages and provided helpful comments.

Beyond doubt, however, my greatest debt is to my wife, Anne Case. She has participated in this project from before its beginning, serving in every necessary capacity: as advisor, sounding board, critic, supporter, editor, and inspiration. To her, with great appreciation and, if possible, even greater love, I wish to dedicate this volume.

Power and MADness

INTRODUCTION

Though this be madness, yet there is method in't.
—Polonius, in *Hamlet, Prince of Denmark*

T

O UNDERSTAND nuclear deterrence is to comprehend the curious relationship between power and MADness. It is a relationship in which the rational and the irrational are inherently linked. It is the logic of this linkage, and of the corresponding linkage between power and MADness, that this volume begins to explore.

The study of nuclear deterrence starts with two inseparable observations. On the one hand, nuclear threats create the potential for significant political power—even if, as is frequently claimed, only the power to maintain the status quo. On the other hand, the mutual vulnerability in the U.S.-Soviet relationship that stems from the existence of capabilities for Mutual Assured Destruction—MAD—threatens to make the actual execution of nuclear threats quite mad, at least for a state that values its own survival. What, then, makes nuclear threats credible? Where, in a MAD world, does power come from? What capacities or incapacities make it possible to employ nuclear threats to achieve desired outcomes in a world of mutual vulnerability?

This volume explores the logic of power in a MAD environment. It focuses on the ability of a state to create credible commitments to effective nuclear threats. Ultimately, its conclusions are quite optimistic, if books on nuclear deterrence can ever be said to have optimistic conclusions. In the great and never-ending policy dispute between those who think nuclear deterrence requires more (more weapons, more capabilities, more options) and those who think it requires rather less, this volume provides strong support for the latter group. The logic it uses in doing so, however, is likely to be distasteful to many of that group's adherents. For the logic developed below differs from classical explanations of deterrence by avoiding classical assumptions of rationality and by frankly exploring the implications for deterrence of more reasonable behavioral assumptions. Such an exploration, after considering the fragile and transient nature of rationality and the necessary and sufficient conditions for coercive power, inevitably wanders into the taboo logic of Doomsday Machines and the discomforting notions of contingently irrational behavior.

The approach to deterrence theory taken in this volume is logical-deductive rather than empirical. This approach is dictated by the fortunate paucity of empirical case material on nuclear deterrence. In its method and concerns, this volume thus clearly follows in the path of Thomas Schelling and other classical deterrence theorists whose work has informed U.S. policy and guided policy debates since the early 1960s. The incorporation of new behavioral assumptions grounded in bureaucratic politics and political psychology, however, dramatically alters the conclusions of deductive models of nuclear deterrence and points policy in very different directions from those suggested by classical theory.

Classical deterrence theory, this volume concludes, is fundamentally limited by its exclusive focus on the rational elements of nuclear deterrence. Nuclear deterrence policies, as a consequence, have been caught in a blind alley for the last quarter century. To move forward, it is necessary to understand better the logic of nuclear coercion, and particularly to face up to the role played by irrationality in that logic. Indeed, a more reasonable understanding of the relationship between power and MADness suggests that U.S. deterrence policies are wasteful and counterproductive. While the costs of maintaining our deterrence commitments are not so high as today's debate suggests, these costs—and the dangers and risks inherent in particular nuclear deterrence policies—are different from those predicted by classical theory.

Consequently, this volume's logical-theoretical exploration of nuclear deterrence should be of interest not only to social scientists interested in the phenomenon of power but to policymakers as well. Indeed, for policymakers the concern is immediate, if enduring. What weapons to procure, what declaratory policy to adopt, what arms control measures to pursue: given the costs of a failure of nuclear deterrence, today these are among the most important decisions a state must make. Policy journals overflow with arguments for various capabilities and options; readers familiar with this only slowly changing literature will recognize that this volume's rethinking of nuclear deterrence lends support to the side of the policy "MADvocates" who argue that power is not directly related to the capacity for "flexible response." Rather, this volume concludes, in a MAD world MADness and irrationality are necessary and sufficient to maintain U.S. nuclear deterrent commitments.

POWER, MADNESS, AND U.S. POLICY

The principal challenge for U.S. nuclear deterrence policymakers in an era of mutual assured destruction capabilities has been to use the threat of nuclear war to deter Soviet actions that, however aggressive, do not directly threaten American national survival.

The United States has built and maintained its nuclear arsenal for deterrent purposes. In an effort to deter the Soviet Union from undertaking military actions against fundamental U.S. interests, the United States threatens to wage nuclear war. In a MAD era—in an era when the Soviet Union, like the United States, possesses an invulnerable capability to inflict massive damage on its rival's society—there are two categories of fundamental interests.

In the first place, fundamental interests involve the physical survival of the nation. The United States seeks to deter an unlimited Soviet attack which might destroy American society. It is generally accepted as inherently credible that the United States would mount a nuclear response to an all-out Soviet attack on U.S. cities and industry. The United States has nuclear forces that would survive any conceivable Soviet attack, and it would experience considerable provocation to use them if a massive Soviet nuclear attack had reduced American cities to radioactive rubble, inflicting perhaps 100 million casualties and destroying the United States as a functioning society.

Beyond this, however, fundamental U.S. interests also involve political and economic survival. Limited Soviet military actions which avoid a massive attack on American cities may still directly or indirectly threaten U.S. sovereignty, "way of life," or prosperity. Some such Soviet military challenges to U.S. political freedom and economic well-being, though not threatening the physical survival of the American nation, may be severe enough to be judged to engage "vital" U.S. interests.

As a consequence, the U.S. nuclear arsenal bears a far greater burden than that of merely deterring massive attack on U.S. cities. History, economics, and politics have dictated a central role for nuclear weapons in protecting vital U.S. political and economic interests as well. This role imposes two additional, more difficult, tasks for nuclear deterrence.

First, nuclear weapons are also counted on to deter attacks on close U.S. allies. Vital national interests may be jeopardized by attacks against the United States' most important allies as well as by direct attacks on U.S. territory. In the post-World War II period there has been a general consensus in the United States that fundamental economic and political interests would be endangered by Soviet military actions that threatened the existence of a free and independent Western Europe. American and European leaders have consistently affirmed that the best and perhaps only acceptable way of protecting Western Europe from Soviet military intimidation and attack is through a collective defense effort; further, American and European leaders have repeatedly concluded that to obviate the need to match the Warsaw Pact in conventional military capabilities this collective Western defense effort must envision the possibility of nuclear escalation. The U.S. threat ultimately to use its nuclear weapons, if necessary, has been and remains a cornerstone of the NATO alliance.

Second, nuclear weapons are counted on to deter limited nuclear attacks on targets in the United States. Because the United States relies on its military forces—particularly its nuclear arsenal—and on its domestic industrial capability to protect its national survival and political sovereignty as well as to deter attack on close allies, the preservation of those military forces and key economic assets also represents a vital, though instrumental, interest. No adversary must be allowed to think that it could gain a significant political advantage, either in terms of undercutting U.S. commitments to allies or in terms of being able to dictate U.S. national policy, by destroying or threatening to destroy critical U.S. military and economic assets. Ironically, therefore, nuclear weapons must deter an attack on the nuclear arsenal itself as well as deter other limited nuclear blows against the continental United States.

Questions and Debates

But why is it credible that the United States would use its nuclear weapons in response to any provocation less than an all-out attack on its society? Given that Washington and New York are held hostage by the Soviet Union, why would U.S. nuclear weapons deter the Soviets from attempting to seize Bonn or Paris? And given that Washington and New York are held hostage, what gives credibility to U.S. threats to attack targets in the Soviet Union in the event of a Soviet "surgical" nuclear strike against military targets in the United States? For that matter, given that Washington and New York remain hostage, what makes credible U.S. threats to respond to a limited nuclear blow against a carefully circumscribed set of industrial targets (such as oil refining capabilities in Texas and the South), aimed at crippling U.S. military-industrial capacity while leaving U.S. society largely intact?

In short, the question that this book addresses is: *In a MAD world, what qualities of the U.S. nuclear force posture make it possible for the United States to use the threat of nuclear response to deter not only massive Soviet nuclear attacks on American cities, but also carefully limited Soviet nuclear attacks on U.S. targets and major Soviet nuclear or conventional aggression against close U.S. allies?* This question cuts to the heart of three continuing policy debates, representing three decades of unresolved concerns about nuclear deterrence.

The first and oldest of these debates, long a point of contention in the NATO community, stems from anxiety within the Alliance over the "coupling" of Europe to the American nuclear deterrent. This debate centers upon what U.S. nuclear capabilities are necessary, in Europe and the United States, if the U.S. nuclear arsenal is to deter Soviet aggression in Europe. America's geographic separation from Europe makes coupling difficult. The Atlantic Ocean provides the United States with a measure of safety in the event of Soviet aggression in Europe as well as with an interest in avoiding escalation: so long as any conflict remains purely European, the American people will be spared the horrors of modern war. But any use of American nuclear weapons against Soviet targets, even the use of U.S. weapons based in Europe, increases the danger of an escalation of hostilities that perhaps could not be halted before American cities were destroyed. How, then, can the United States make a convincing pledge to treat an attack on its NATO allies as an attack upon itself? Does the current U.S. nuclear umbrella, which has been the cornerstone of the NATO alliance, involve—as Henry Kissinger suggested in 1979— "strategic assurances that we cannot possibly mean or if we do mean, we should not want to execute because if we execute, we risk the destruction of civilization"?[1] Are the steps which are necessary to make the U.S. nuclear pledge credible so difficult or unpleasant that the Alliance needs to find some military or political alternative to the American extended nuclear deterrent? In recent years, worries about coupling have produced heated public and political discussions within the Alliance over enhanced radiation (neutron) warheads for tactical nuclear weapons, over the December 1979 "two-track" decision on intermediate-range nuclear weapons, over possible pledges of no-first use of nuclear weapons, and over U.S.-negotiated treaties limiting the deployment of nuclear weapons in Europe.[2]

The second debate concerns U.S. need for "counterforce" nuclear capabilities—for weapons such as the Peacekeeper (MX) missile and for a flexible and survivable command-and-control system that would permit the United States to destroy military targets, especially "hardened" ones such as Soviet missile silos and command bunkers, throughout the course of a nuclear war. Are U.S. counterforce nuclear capabilities necessary, given the range of Soviet activities that the United States seeks to deter? Or are such capabilities unnecessarily provocative and destabilizing, creating pressures for each side to strike first during a crisis? Debate on this question has raged since the mid-1970s. Although the arguments have been extraordinarily detailed, highly politicized, and at times arcane, the central issue has been the range of U.S. options for limited nuclear retaliation required to deter the Soviet Union from launching a limited nuclear attack on the United States—an attack that, while leaving U.S. cities intact and U.S. military forces with a residual capacity to devastate the Soviet Union, would undercut U.S. ability to carry out a sequence of carefully graduated nuclear strikes. The key question in this debate has been whether the United States needs to be able to match the Soviets tit for tat in ability to destroy "hardened" military targets.[3]

The most recent of the three policy debates which have demanded more careful scrutiny of the relationship between power and MAD-ness is the one concerning the role of strategic *defenses* in maintaining deterrence. While the first two debates revolve around questions of what offensive nuclear forces are necessary credibly to threaten retribution for Soviet aggression, this last debate questions the need for a shield against the opponent's nuclear forces. Although brought to life by President Reagan's 1983 announcement of a Strategic Defense Initiative (SDI), this debate plainly has its roots in an older, dormant argument about the relationship between effective defenses and the credibility of nuclear threats. Though Reagan personally presented a vision of a world freed from the threat of nuclear weapons by technological progress, because this revolution is at present unfeasible the real discussion has been about the impact of substantially less-than-perfect defenses. The Reagan administration has argued that

> The United States' conception of the role of nuclear weapons in
> defense strategy emerged in an era of American nuclear superiority.
> Now that Soviet nuclear forces are at least equal to our own, and in
> many dimensions superior, some earlier ideas are outmoded. . . .
> The President's SDI is not only a natural extension of the search for
> alternative ways to ensure deterrence; it is the logical culmination
> of that search.[4]

Given the potential costs and risks of using nuclear weapons in response to limited Soviet attacks, do credible nuclear deterrent threats
require that the United States be able to defend its homeland and
strategic nuclear forces at least partially? Similarly, does the credibility of the U.S. nuclear pledge to NATO ultimately demand the construction of strategic defenses that would offer at least some protection to American cities in the event of nuclear escalation? Are the
"earlier ideas" of deterrence "outmoded" because of the development
of MAD?

The three debates are, of course, logically linked, although this
linkage frequently goes unacknowledged. It is principally in the context of a conflict in Europe that a limited Soviet blow against the
United States becomes plausible. The consequent connection between
counterforce and coupling is cemented by the U.S. pledge to NATO to
initiate controlled escalation, including carefully limited strategic
blows, in response to Soviet aggression that cannot be halted by other
means.[5] Thus, it is the American extended deterrent guarantee to
NATO, as interpreted in the Flexible Response doctrine, that drives
the need for U.S. strategic forces that can be used in a controlled and
highly selective fashion—strategic forces that must themselves be
protected from counterforce attack. This protection, in turn, requires
that the Soviet Union be convinced that the costs of such an attack
would outweigh its benefits; costs and benefits can be manipulated
both with credible threats to respond to a limited Soviet attack and
with strategic defenses that make such an attack more difficult. Thus,
while each of the three debates has its own intellectual and political
history, each centers on the same logical problem: given the ultimate
mutual vulnerability entailed in a MAD situation, how can nuclear
threats be made to yield political power? Consequently, satisfactory
resolution of these debates requires an accurate appraisal of those
qualities of the U.S. force posture that are critical to the maintenance
of deterrence. An oversimplified understanding of what makes nuclear
deterrence work may yield incorrect or dangerously misleading policy
prescriptions.

Objectives

The goal of this book is to change the nature of the coupling, counterforce, and strategic defense debates, to move them beyond the same oft-repeated arguments and to circumvent the current intellectual impasse by substantially altering the assumptions and theory that lie beneath policy discussion. To this end, the book focuses on "policy-relevant theory," rather than on "policy" itself. Thus while this book is motivated by concerns about policy and, in the final chapter, will explore some of the major policy implications for U.S. nuclear force posture, what follows is not a collection of proposals for how to make the world safer or better. On the contrary, this book is a logical treatise on the phenomenon of nuclear deterrence; proceeding in an informal deductive manner, it refines and expands the classical model of nuclear deterrence.

As noted above, the answers implied by this book are quite optimistic. The logic developed in the following chapters suggests that the actual requirements for maintaining extended nuclear deterrence in Europe are quite moderate and that neither counterforce nor strategic defense capabilities are necessary for nuclear deterrence. These conclusions follow from the argument that the classical theoretical model of deterrence is based on unrealistic behavioral assumptions. A more reasonable theoretical model, employing more reasonable behavioral assumptions, results in a very different assessment of what aspects of U.S. nuclear force posture are critical in yielding deterrent power in a MAD world. It is to theory that we must turn our attention.

POWER, MADNESS, AND NUCLEAR DETERRENCE THEORY

Although the vast outpouring of books and articles on U.S. nuclear strategy would seem to belie the fact, for roughly twenty years the United States has been living off accumulated intellectual capital in dealing with the fundamental question of how nuclear deterrence works. There have been no significant conceptual breakthroughs in nuclear deterrence theory since the early 1960s. The detailed elaboration of official U.S. targeting and procurement strategy and the criticism of official policies that have appeared have, in general, been unrelated to any new theoretical examination of what makes nuclear deterrence work.[6]

Such a new examination is now possible, however. Insights about international behavior derived from research in related fields and disciplines can fruitfully be applied to the study of nuclear deterrence. More realistic behavioral assumptions can improve the predictive and prescriptive modeling of the classical nuclear deterrence literature produced during the late 1950s and early 1960s. To understand the opportunity that now exists for new theory-building, however, it is necessary to understand the history of work in the field and the work's peculiar characteristics.

Classical Nuclear Deterrence Theory

The decade from roughly 1954 to 1964 was, from today's perspective, the golden age of nuclear deterrence theory. During that time pathbreaking research on the subject was conducted and the principal canons were produced.[7]

The methodological approach employed during this period, in the formulation of both positive-predictive and normative-prescriptive theory, was deductive. The workings of deterrence were deduced from basic assumptions about the behavior of individuals and states rather than induced directly from historical cases. To the extent that history was used at all, it served more as a source of anecdotal support for deductive propositions than either as an independent source of propositions about state behavior in deterrence situations or as a means of rigorously testing the validity of deductively derived propositions.

The principal insight of the period came from the application of the "Chicken" game model to the problem of nuclear deterrence.[8] The "Chicken" analogy led nuclear deterrence theorists to explore notions of denial and punishment and to develop the concepts of commitment, credibility, crisis stability, and arms-race stability.[9]

Study of nuclear deterrence waned in the mid-1960s. The improvement of Soviet-American relations and the escalation of American involvement in Vietnam undoubtedly contributed to the general shift in attention to the problems of limited conventional conflict and counterinsurgency. The reduced interest in nuclear deterrence theory was also due, however, to the extraordinary success of the deductive work of the late 1950s and early 1960s, both in identifying expected relationships between nuclear capabilities and political outcomes and in suggesting basic guidelines for U.S. nuclear doctrine and policy. Given the usual assumptions of the time—particularly that of unitary rational behavior—the authors of the late 1950s and early 1960s pushed deductive theory close to the limits of the possible. The field of nuclear deterrence theory appeared exhausted from heavy tilling, and there seemed little left for additional research to yield.

Critical, Normative, and Empirical Studies

Nuclear deterrence theory was not, of course, entirely abandoned as a field of study after the early 1960s. Somewhat sporadically, work proceeded along three distinct lines: critical, normative, and empirical.

A handful of important critiques produced during the late 1960s and the 1970s succeeded in identifying weaknesses and oversimplifications in the earlier works. In particular, these critiques questioned the assumption that one state's evaluation of an opponent's hostility had no effect on the opponent's behavior; the relative importance of intrinsic interests and commitment; the willingness of state actors to take risks; and—most importantly—the rationality of state actors.[10] These critiques constituted a valuable challenge to accepted wisdom; they did not, however, provide a systematic and applicable alternative vision of how deterrence works.[11]

Classical deterrence theory and the policies based upon it also stimulated normative criticism of nuclear deterrence. Questions concerning the ethics and morality of deterrence—particularly regarding the proportionality and discrimination demands of the *jus in bello* requirement of traditional just war theory[12]—have been extensively debated. Not surprisingly, given the irreconcilable philosophic differences between the consequentialists and deontologists engaged in it, the debate has been inconclusive, though rich. Perhaps slightly more surprisingly, this debate on whether nuclear deterrence can be engaged in morally has triggered little new examination of what is actually involved in nuclear deterrence.

During the last decade of lean years, however, the special problems of conventional and nonstrategic deterrence and compellence, including coercion in the periphery, coercion involving low levels of violence, and coercion aimed at preventing political adventurism and resolving crises, have received attention. Research in these areas has drawn on empirical case studies to produce insight into the workings of coercion in settings other than the central Soviet-American one. Such inductive work has yielded improved understanding of the particular problems involved in employing threats of conventional force and in exerting coercive pressure in conflicts in which vital interests are not directly at stake.[13]

Research into conventional deterrence and crisis behavior has been encouraged by the existence of a large body of empirical evidence and by the possibility of using an inductive approach to theory-building. No such opportunity exists, however, for convincing empirical research on nuclear coercion. Not only has the historical time span of mutual societal vulnerability been very short, but the evidence available from cases in which nuclear coercion may have played a significant role—evidence on the values at stake, the threats issued and perceived, and the decision-making processes used—tends to be highly ambiguous. To be sure, this has not entirely prevented scholars from occasionally attempting empirical research into cases of possible nuclear deterrence, and for a quarter of a century the interpretation and reinterpretation of the events of the October 1962 missile crisis has been a disciplinary pastime. Quickly, however, observers attempting to discover the impact of nuclear weapons on behavior encounter the limits of the evidence, as well as the difficulties of drawing conclusions and lessons that are both generalizable and applicable to the present.[14] In short, the unavailability of empirical data for use in focused comparisons or in quantitative correlation studies has made the empirical derivation or testing of nuclear deterrence theory a dubious exercise.

As a consequence, however thought-provoking, this empirical work has yielded little that is directly applicable to the problem of understanding the credibility of the nuclear umbrella which covers the United States and Western Europe. Indeed, the *direct* extrapolation from historic cases of conventional deterrence to future situations of nuclear deterrence must be considered *a priori* suspect and potentially dangerous. The possible speed and destruction of nuclear war and the existence of mutual assured societal vulnerability are logically likely to affect both patterns of decision-making and the values at stake. This suggests that the probability of rational unitary action by either a defender or an aggressor is likely to be different in nuclear environments than in conventional ones, as is the behavior that a rational unitary actor would choose. At a minimum, as Bernard Brodie, thinking of the role of nuclear weapons in the superpower relationship, noted in 1966:

> the world is utterly different now from what it was in 1939 or 1914, when deterrence, however effective temporarily, had the final intrinsic weakness that one side or both did not truly fear what we would now call general war.[15]

Indirectly, however, empirical research does contribute to a re-thinking and reformulation of nuclear deterrence theory. Lessons learned from empirical study of behavior in conventional deterrence situations improve our awareness of the domestic political and organizational incentives that make resort to war particularly attractive (or unattractive), as well as of the types of psychological and organizational obstacles to rational decision-making that may arise.[16]

Bureaucratic Politics and Political Psychology

Rather than following directly from the critical, normative, or empirical work of the last two decades, however, the new ability to push beyond the deductive theory of the 1950s and 1960s reflects two broader developments in political science. The incorporation of insights from these developments into the deductive framework of classical nuclear deterrence theory yields a synthesis far richer than could have been imagined even a few years ago.

The first development was the production of a theory of bureaucratic and organizational behavior which drew heavily on the earlier economic "theory of the firm" literature.[17] Research, largely at Harvard, led to publications by Graham Allison, Morton Halperin, and others in the early 1970s which explored the impact of the organizational structure of decision-making on state behavior, particularly in foreign policy.[18] This bureaucratic politics and organizational behavior research emphasized the effects of internal conflicts, interests, and operating routines on state behavior. It suggested, first, that while individual or organizational participants in the state's decision-making process may still make "rational" decisions—intelligent decisions aimed at maximizing their consistently calculated expected utility—their utility calculations may involve not only national interests but organizational and personal political incentives as well.[19] Second, this research emphasized that it may be rational for organizations to establish "standard operating procedures"—predetermined behavioral routines to be carried out when specific circumstances arise. Scholars noted the bureaucratic origins of these routines, their sometimes unexpected impact in unusual situations (such as crises), and the difficulty encountered by central authorities in trying to alter these routines rapidly, particularly during crises.[20]

The incorporation of these insights into the realist model of state behavior which presently informs nuclear deterrence theory leads to the recognition that the credibility and effectiveness of threats will be influenced significantly by the organizational environment in both the attacking and defending states. Ability to communicate and ability to act intelligently to maximize expected national interest may be constrained in some situations by bureaucratic players with parochial interests. Thus, the structure of decision-making and policy implementation, and the incentives of key individuals and organizations within states, matter. Similarly, organizational operating routines may critically limit the ability of states to act in a unitarily rational fashion during crisis or conflict. Responses to deterrent threats and especially to aggressive actions are likely to be significantly influenced by bureaucratic contingency plans.[21]

The second set of developments that has permitted progress beyond classical deductive theory involved research into how individuals and small groups actually order values, deal with information, and make choices. Most obviously relevant in this regard has been the recent study of behavior during international crises, especially of how leaders' values evolve and how they deal with information, ambiguity, uncertainty, and the need for decision. Empirical research into crisis behavior has yielded substantial insight about how decision-makers react to threats and dangers as the likelihood of war increases.[22]

In addition to this empirical research into crisis behavior, however, a far larger body of new work has emerged in social and cognitive psychology suggesting that even in the absence of bureaucratic and organizational politics—that is, even if state actors could accurately be modeled as unitary actors—state behavior would not necessarily be rational. This research on the effects of stress—of "the anxiety or fear an individual experiences in a situation which he perceives as posing a threat to one or more of his values"[23]—and on the effects of reliance on cognitive heuristics has suggested that human psychology may lead to irrational behavior even when "abnormal" or psychopathological personalities are not involved in decision-making.[24]

In sum, then, scholarship since the 1960s has provided solid theoretical explanations for why the assumption of unitary rational action may result in failure correctly to predict actual state behavior: not only is the state not a unitary actor, but even at the disaggregated level, behavior may not be rational because individuals involved in decision-making may suffer from cognitive failures and the effects of situational stress. The resulting implications for any deductive modeling of nuclear coercion have not, however, been fully incorporated into the deductive deterrence theory that has served as the basis for American deterrence policy of the last quarter-century.

Classical Nuclear Deterrence Theory and Rationality

To be sure, the nuclear deterrence theorists of the 1950s and 1960s, particularly Thomas Schelling and Glenn Snyder,[25] explicitly recognized not only that irrationality might exist, but that its existence would critically affect the outcome of deterrence efforts. It was apparent to the early deductive theorists that their conclusions about the ability of the deterrer to establish a credible commitment and about the coercibility of potential aggressors were extremely sensitive to the "rational actor" assumption that states use information intelligently and make choices aimed at maximizing some consistent set of values. After issuing this caveat, however, deterrence theorists focused on the special case in which actors were manifestly and inalienably rational; they tended to assume the existence of "not just intelligent behavior, but of behavior motivated by a conscious calculation of advantages, a calculation that in turn is based on an explicit and internally consistent value system."[26]

In part, this focus derived from the realist tradition within which deterrence theory developed. Realist analysis emphasizes the real conflicts of national interest inherent in the structure of the international system. It therefore focuses on the rational use or avoidance of war by states to further their fairly constant national interests. Since challenges to the status quo are seen as reflecting structural imbalances in the international system rather than as reflecting foibles or internal or domestic political imperatives of national decision-makers, it is natural to think of deterrence in rational actor terms.[27]

More importantly, though, assumptions of rationality offered a great deal of predictive, and therefore prescriptive, power in game theoretic modeling. Schelling made this point clearly:

> The advantage of cultivating the area of "strategy" for theoretical development is not that, of all possible approaches, it is the one that evidently stays closest to the truth, but that the assumption of rational behavior is a productive one. . . . The premise of "rational behavior" is a potent one for the production of theory.[28]

The advantage of assuming rationality when modeling nuclear relationships was that it made behavior highly predictable given a few basic assumptions about the values of the adversaries, such as the importance of preserving cities and industry. Since values could be estimated only grossly, behavior was predictable only within broad limits; further, since rational strategies might be probabilistic, behavior was only probabilistically predictable. Nonetheless, in some meaningful sense, behavior was predictable, and this made the modeling of strategic interaction possible.

The last two decades of study of bureaucratic and organizational behavior and of psychological processes now permit some general, probabilistic predictions about behavior even while allowing deviations from rational unitary action. Although unitary rationality remains the ideal case, it is now possible for deterrence theory to recognize variable pressures in the real world that may significantly compromise a state's ability to behave as if it were a rational unitary entity. We have acquired some of the analytical tools to deal with the fact that, as Klaus Knorr has put it:

> In the real world . . . the actor is only more or less rational. His rationality may be degraded by factors of personal character or by such adverse circumstances as time pressure, fatigue, and anxiety. It may be hemmed in by ideological beliefs about the outside world. . . . Because these doctrines are deeply ingrained, they tend to resist ready adaptation or burial when the tests of reality indicate that their validity is vanishing, and they often end in a sterile reign of jargon that, nevertheless, traps people in postures too rigid to permit new perceptions and innovative action. . . . There is a final dimension of conditions liable to bound rational behavior. The policymaker is not a unitary actor. Ordinarily he must reconcile his own evaluation of options with that of other leaders who may express conflicting perceptions and value commitments at large in society.[29]

A key observation here is that these pressures that may degrade rationality—personality disorder, situational stress, cognitive failure, and organizational dysfunction—are *variable* across time and situation.

POWER, MADNESS, AND IRRATIONAL BEHAVIOR

The revision of deterrence theory to take into account variable pressures that may lead to departures from rational behavior has dramatic implications for the answer to the question: "In a MAD world, what qualities of the U.S. nuclear force posture make it possible for the United States to use the threat of nuclear response to deter not only massive Soviet nuclear attacks on American cities, but also carefully limited Soviet nuclear attacks on U.S. targets and major Soviet nuclear or conventional aggression against close allies?" Working through the logic of deterrence while explictly recognizing the existence of these pressures leads to the inescapable conclusion that the critical capabilities are very different than those suggested by classical deterrence theory and assumed by participants in the coupling, counterforce, and strategic defense debates.

Both classical deterrence theory and U.S. policymakers have equated coercive power with the existence of rationally executable nuclear threats. Because deterrence theory and policy debates have tended to assume (logically incorrectly) that, in Richard Nixon's words, "A rational deterrent cannot be based on irrational responses,"[30] the United States has sought nuclear weapons, plans, and command-and-control systems that might allow it to make rational wartime decisions to begin and escalate the use of nuclear weapons despite the vulnerability of American society to a riposte. Notwithstanding the considerable effort devoted toward this end since 1961, however, the U.S. attempt appears to have been unsuccessful: the risks of escalation to all-out destruction still loom too large.

The logic developed in the following pages explores the fact that *nuclear deterrence can rely on credible threats to behave irrationally—at times or in circumstances in which a rational decision to use nuclear weapons would be incredible.* Obviously, the observation that the propensity for irrationality may be useful is not a new one. In 1960, Schelling recognized that

> an explicit theory of "rational" decision, and of the strategic consequences of such decisions, makes it perfectly clear that it is not a universal advantage in situations of conflict to be inalienably and manifestly rational. . . . It may be perfectly rational to wish oneself not altogether rational, or—if that language is philosophically objectionable—to wish for the power to suspend certain rational capabilities in certain situations.[31]

If deterrence rests on the threat to behave irrationally, however, then it becomes imperative to explore, rather than assume away, those variable pressures that may degrade rationality—personality disorder, situational stress, cognitive failure, and organizational dysfunction—and to examine their implication for both the coercibility of an opponent and the ability to establish a credible commitment to an effective threat. This exercise is particularly important because irrationality is not an exogenous variable. A state's rationality or irrationality in future contingencies is likely to be critically affected by the decisions it makes *in advance* about the acquisition of decision-making resources and the structure of the decision-making process.

Just as states may, before the event (*ex ante*), structure their incentives so that they will find it rational after the event (*ex post*) to carry out their threats and promises—hoping that by so doing they will alter the behavior of their opponent—they may also, *ex ante*, structure their decision-making so as to cast doubt on their capability to act in a rational fashion *ex post*.

Unintentionally, this is what U.S. decision-makers have in fact done. Despite efforts to make nuclear war controllable and rational, the risks of uncontrolled escalation remain unacceptably large. A rational decision to use nuclear weapons is incredible; the potential for an irrational decision to use nuclear weapons *in certain highly specific contingencies*, however, makes U.S. nuclear commitments both actual and credible. U.S. nuclear deterrence thus rests on the threat of *contingently irrational behavior.* Those Soviet actions the United States seeks to deter are likely to interfere with a U.S. decision-making process that otherwise retains rational central control over nuclear forces. To evaluate this state of affairs it is first necessary to understand it fully.

What Follows

Perhaps the best way to approach the task of incorporating these insights into deterrence theory is by examining briefly why they are particularly relevant. Chapter 1, therefore, reviews the problems that MAD has posed for U.S. nuclear deterrence policy. It focuses on the difficulties for policy created by a theory of deterrence that assumes the United States will necessarily and manifestly behave in a rational fashion.

Chapter 2 develops the concepts of rationality, irrationality, rational behavior, and irrational behavior; explores the notion of irrational war; considers the sources of irrationality; and discusses the advantages of remaining within a traditional analytic paradigm rather than abandoning it for a cognitive/cybernetic one. Although such logical concept-building may seem unrelated to the problem of nuclear deterrence, it is essential to what follows.

Chapter 3 sets out the necessary and sufficient conditions for deterrence and explores the first of the two necessary conditions—the existence of coercibility—in greater detail. To this end it considers the various logical modes of coercion and the types of resources required for each.

In many respects, chapter 4 constitutes the heart of this book's argument. It considers the second of the necessary conditions for deterrence—the ability to create a credible commitment to an effective coercive strategy—and explores modes of commitment, developing and examining the concepts of commitment-through-rationality, commitment-through-denial-of-choice, and commitment-through-irrationality.

Chapter 5 examines the particular implications of nuclear weapons for coercion and commitment by exploring what is logically novel and different about the task of nuclear deterrence. As part of this effort, some attention is devoted to developing notions of conflict limitation necessary for understanding nuclear conflict.

Chapter 6 explores the logic of Doomsday Machines, particularly probabilistic, organizational Doomsday Machines. These ideas are used to explain the sources of U.S. deterrent power.

Chapter 7 builds on the logic developed in the five preceding chapters in its exploration of the idea of contingently irrational behavior. It focuses on the implications of contingently irrational behavior for the establishment of commitment-through-irrationality to a threat of punishment. Of particular interest is the discussion of the possible sources of such behavior in a nuclear setting.

Chapter 8 is less a conclusion than an attempt to suggest some of the interesting policy implications of the preceding analysis for the coupling, counterforce, and strategic defense debates. It does not suggest that policy choices are self-evident as a result of a better theoretical understanding of nuclear deterrence, only that the important trade-offs are different from those suggested by classical deterrence theory.

1

MAD AND THE NUCLEAR DETERRENCE PROBLEM

THE CENTRAL military reality confronting American practitioners of nuclear deterrence—the reality that underlies debates over coupling, counterforce, and strategic defenses—is the mutual societal vulnerability which has resulted from superpower development of invulnerable capabilities for inflicting mutual assured destruction. Excellent accounts of the development of Soviet and American nuclear arms programs and of the evolution of nuclear thinking are available elsewhere;[1] the aim of the present discussion is simply to examine the logical deterrence conundrum posed by MAD.

Beginning in the mid-1950s, it became clear to American planners that the Soviet Union would soon possess the ability to respond to U.S. use of nuclear weapons by destroying American cities and that, even if the United States struck first and attempted to blunt Soviet retribution, the United States would be unable to prevent substantial damage to its society in an all-out war between the superpowers. By the early 1960s, the risk of millions of American casualties in a nuclear exchange was large enough to constrain U.S. options for using nuclear forces during times of heightened tensions.[2] By the time the Soviets achieved rough nuclear parity with the United States in the late 1960s, both sides had arsenals more than large and secure enough to guarantee each an invulnerable ability to devastate the other's society.

While MAD thus meant that the United States had the ability to devastate the Soviet Union no matter what steps the Soviets might take, MAD also raised the possibility that the United States might be *deterred from executing its deterrent threats:* so long as U.S. cities are held hostage by the Soviet Union, the United States may be unwilling to initiate or respond to the use of nuclear weapons. The hostage status of American cities—and the concomitant possibility of enforced U.S. restraint in situations short of total war—is important because the United States has in fact threatened to use nuclear weapons in response to provocations other than an all-out attack on American cities. Since the early postwar period, implicit and explicit U.S. pledges to use nuclear weapons in response to an overwhelming Soviet conventional or nuclear attack in Europe have served as the cornerstone of the Atlantic Alliance. Additionally, since Soviet development during the late 1960s and early 1970s of forces sufficient for undertaking limited strategic nuclear options, the United States has relied on the threat of nuclear response to deter a limited Soviet nuclear attack on the United States aimed at destroying militarily or economically significant targets while leaving American society intact.

Reviewing the implications of MAD for threats to employ nuclear weapons in response to limited Soviet nuclear attacks on the United States, Albert Wohlstetter has mused:

> If you believe that any nuclear exchange will almost surely destroy Western civil society and bring on universal ruin, you may say you would respond to a limited nuclear attack, but if you are even moderately thoughtful, you will almost surely not really mean it. Even if you had so awesomely suicidal and homicidal a *conditional* intention, you would be unlikely, in the event of an adversary's limited use of nuclear weapons, *actually* to be willing to reply by ending the world. If your adversary understands that you believe a nuclear reply would be suicidal, he may count on your being unwilling to reply, even if you say you will.[3]

If U.S. decision-makers have serious doubts that the United States can exercise its nuclear options—either in response to a limited Soviet nuclear attack on America or in response to aggression in Europe —without incurring suicidal consequences, then so long as rational control is maintained the United States will be deterred from executing its nuclear threats.

Such doubts are in fact legion. Arguing in 1983 against any U.S. policy involving the threat to initiate nuclear war, either at the tactical or strategic level, former Secretary of Defense Robert McNamara stated bluntly:

> It is inconceivable to me, as it has been to others who have studied the matter, that "limited" nuclear wars would remain limited—

any decision to use nuclear weapons would imply a high probability of the same cataclysmic consequences as a total nuclear exchange. In sum, I know of no plan which gives reasonable assurance that nuclear weapons can be used beneficially in NATO's defense.[4]

Despite such concerns about the absence of nonsuicidal uses for nuclear weapons, then Secretary of Defense Caspar Weinberger argued that:

To maintain a sound deterrent, we must make clear to our adversary that we would decisively and effectively answer his attack. To talk of actions that the U.S. Government could not, in good conscience, and in prudence, undertake tends to defeat the goals of deterrence.[5]

Taken together, these statements illustrate the nature of the United States' theoretical nuclear deterrence problem. In summary, the logical dilemma inherent in official thinking on deterrence runs as follows. If one believes that nuclear war is unacceptably likely to escalate to a cataclysm, then it is logically irrational to initiate or engage in it. U.S. decision-makers are in fact likely to conclude that nuclear war does indeed have an unacceptable probability of escalating. But deterrence cannot rest on threats to behave irrationally. If each of these propositions is correct, then not only is current U.S. nuclear deterrence strategy logically bankrupt, but *any* attempt in a MAD world to use nuclear weapons for any purpose other than deterring all-out nuclear war is likely to fail.[6]

This book argues that the mistake is to assume that deterrence cannot rest on threats to behave irrationally: to the contrary, effective deterrence can in fact be based on nuclear responses that could not "in good conscience, and in prudence" be executed. Before developing the logic of this argument in the chapters that follow, however, it is useful to examine how the nuclear deterrence strategy adopted by the United States has attempted to deal with the problem of mutual societal vulnerability. To understand where the coupling, counterforce, and strategic defense debates have gone awry and why they have proven both barren and misleading, it is necessary to grasp the basic logic underlying official U.S. nuclear deterrence strategy, a logic that has gone largely unchallenged in these debates.

Such an undertaking involves a review of the evolution of U.S. nuclear deterrence strategy from threats of massive retaliation to threats of controlled nuclear response. It also requires a brief, though careful, consideration of the logical flaws in a nuclear deterrence strategy based on controlled nuclear response and an examination of the alternatives to such a strategy. Finally, and most importantly, it requires that we begin to explore the tremendous, though overlooked, power inherent in threats to behave irrationally. The possibility and credibility of such threats are key to explaining why nuclear deterrence works and how policy debates about coupling, counterforce, and strategic defense can be resolved.

INVULNERABILITY AND MASSIVE RETALIATION

The central premise of official U.S. nuclear deterrence strategy has been that effective deterrence requires the existence of a net U.S. interest in carrying out the threats it makes. The credibility of deterrence threats—and therefore the effectiveness of a deterrence posture —has been seen as resting on a congruence between what the United States *threatens* to do with its nuclear weapons and what would be in its best interests *actually* to do with its nuclear weapons. For as long as the United States has had a distinctive, articulated nuclear deterrence strategy, U.S. nuclear force posture and targeting strategy have been driven by the belief that deterrence requires rationally implementable options.

Of course, during the first years of the nuclear era, when nuclear forces were relatively scarce and their implications had not been fully recognized by the defense community, a distinctive, articulated nuclear deterrence strategy did not exist. As John Lewis Gaddis has noted:

> The Truman administration had never worked out a clear strategy for deriving political benefits from its possession of nuclear weapons. The devices figured prominently in war planning, to be sure, and their implied presence remained prominently in the background of diplomacy during that period. But.... [C]ertainly the administration was at no point willing deliberately and publicly to threaten their use.[7]

Within the U.S. Air Force, nuclear weapons were viewed simply as more powerful devices for the conduct of strategic bombing operations similar to those undertaken in World War II.[8]

It was left to the Eisenhower administration to articulate the first distinctive nuclear deterrence strategy.[9] Its approach to nuclear weapons and nuclear war distinguished between "tactical" nuclear operations and "strategic" nuclear operations;[10] its principal intellectual departure involved the latter.[11] The administration concluded that strategic weapons not only offered a means of destroying the Soviet Union's capacity to wage war in the event of a general conflict but also gave the United States leverage over Soviet behavior. Instead of defeating Communist aggression in a limited war as the United States had done in Korea, the United States could threaten to go to the brink, and over. Thus, rather than stopping Communist expansion by crushing it on the battlefield, the United States could stop it by threatening to destroy the Communist homeland.[12] First articulated in 1954, this strategy of explicitly threatening nuclear escalation came to be known as "Massive Retaliation."

In practical terms, Massive Retaliation involved posing the Soviet Union with some *risk* that limited aggression would be met with a deliberate U.S. decision to respond massively by destroying Soviet military and economic potential. Massive Retaliation explicitly threatened that the United States might respond by deliberately "knocking out" the Soviet Union as a functioning society and state. As Samuel Huntington has put it:

> Since massive retaliation was never ordered, it cannot be said that American policy was *to retaliate* massively against aggressions in the gray areas. On the other hand, with the speech of Mr. Dulles on January 12, 1954, it did become American policy *to declare* that we might respond by massive retaliation in such contingencies.[13]

The idea, Eisenhower announced, would be "to blow hell out of them in a hurry if they start anything."[14]

The evidence suggests that Massive Retaliation did not alter what a nuclear campaign, if it occurred, would have looked like. Rather, it represented a departure in how the United States thought about nuclear weapons and in how it might use them in times of peace or crisis to gain political leverage. Actual targeting plans did not change significantly with Massive Retaliation. As it had under Truman, the military planned to strike as quickly and forcefully as possible, destroying an optimum mix of military, political, and industrial targets. As it had been under Truman, the immediate military objective of actual nuclear use remained the defeat of the Soviet Union and the destruction of its political and economic capacity to wage war. The novelty of Massive Retaliation was that it marked the first time the United States explicitly threatened nuclear response in order to *deter* the Soviet Union from undertaking aggression.

Because, for a short period, the Soviet Union lacked the capability to inflict massive urban-industrial damage in retribution, what the United States threatened with Massive Retaliation was fairly consistent with what it might reasonably have wanted to do if war did arise, at least in a critical theater such as Europe. A massive nuclear strike against an optimal mix of Soviet military and industrial targets might very well have offered the best prospect of ending the war quickly and cheaply for the United States. As one student of U.S. nuclear strategy has summed up the original credibility of Massive Retaliation:

> The fact that the U.S. could with assurance attack and decimate the Soviet Union, that it could retaliate massively while the Soviets lacked a similar capacity, was a critical element in the strategy's credibility and made massive retaliation *both a deterrent strategy and a potential war-fighting plan.* Since the United States would not face the prospect of a devastating nuclear counterattack against the American homeland as a consequence of bombing the Soviet Union with nuclear weapons (assuming we initiated nuclear hostilities, a contingency that was not ruled out), it was at least conceivable that *we might rationally decide to do so in a grave crisis.*[15]

Even in 1954, however, events were already overtaking Massive Retaliation: the evolution of military technology and of Soviet military posture was creating a situation of mutual societal vulnerability that made massive retaliation to limited provocation at least potentially suicidal. The movement to a MAD world, critics of Massive Retaliation argued, meant that the threat of "unlimited war" could be used to deter only "the most outrageous kind of aggression."[16]

The inevitable retreat from a strategy of Massive Retaliation began even during the Eisenhower administration.[17] By 1959, speaking before Congress, Secretary of State-designate Christian Herter was able to announce that he could not "conceive of the President involving us in an all-out nuclear war unless the facts showed clearly that we are in danger of devastation ourselves, or that actual moves have been made toward devastating ourselves."[18] If the survival of American society could not be guaranteed in an all-out nuclear war, the deliberate initiation of such a war was unacceptable as a deterrence strategy.

MUTUAL VULNERABILITY AND CONTROLLED NUCLEAR RESPONSE

The Kennedy administration's reaction to the development of mutual societal vulnerability had two elements. On the one hand, the administration sought to build up U.S. conventional forces and thereby reduce the range of contingencies that nuclear weapons were called upon to deter. Aggressive Soviet actions in the Third World which clearly did not engage vital U.S. interests were to be deterred by U.S. capacity to mobilize superior economic and conventional military resources on the ground rather than by U.S. ability to escalate a "brush-fire" war to global holocaust. Nuclear threats were reserved to deal with only the most severe (and least likely) Soviet threats: an attack on the territory of the United States itself or on that of its European allies.

Second—and more interestingly for the story told here—the Kennedy administration devoted its effort to making these remaining nuclear threats credible by developing the strategy and force posture necessary for waging *limited nuclear wars.* As Michael Mandelbaum has put it, while the task of military planners in the past "had been to find ways to *increase* the force that they could bring to bear upon the enemy, Kennedy and his men sought to *restrict* the violence of warfare."[19]

The Eisenhower administration's strategy of Massive Retaliation had threatened to punish Soviet aggression by destroying Soviet society; it called for an all-out "Sunday Punch" spasm of strategic destruction aimed at an optimal mix of military and industrial targets. The Kennedy administration's strategic revolution was to threaten to use nuclear weapons in a carefully *controlled* fashion. The United States threatened, in the event of Soviet aggression, to use its strategic and tactical nuclear arsenals to retaliate, to increase pressure on the Soviet Union, thus compelling the Soviet Union to halt its aggression before an escalation to city destruction occurred.[20]

For the first time, nuclear war was conceived as part of an ongoing bargaining process with the adversary, one aimed at both compelling him to halt his aggression and deterring him from undertaking attacks on American cities. Where the Eisenhower administration had threatened to use nuclear weapons to defeat and destroy the Soviet Union if deterrence failed, the Kennedy administration threatened to wage a limited nuclear war that would convince the Soviet Union to make peace on terms acceptable to the West. This doctrinal revolution involved not only a change in public rhetoric, but a change in actual military planning as well: in 1961 the United States began to alter dramatically its actual plans and forces for nuclear war, adding flexibility and limited strategic options.[21] True, the smallest of the Kennedy administration's limited strategic options would still have involved more than a thousand nuclear weapons in attacks on principally military targets. But this was a substantial change from the Eisenhower administration's targeting plan, SIOP-62, which had been expected to result in 285 million immediate deaths in the Soviet Union and China alone.[22]

The logic developed by the critics of Massive Retaliation and adopted and implemented by the Kennedy administration in 1961 has remained the foundation of U.S. nuclear deterrence policy. Since 1961, American practitioners of nuclear deterrence have accepted that the way to make nuclear threats credible in a MAD era is through proliferation of options for limited nuclear wars. Limited nuclear options might be rational even when all-out use of nuclear weapons would be suicidal.

Two factors, the Kennedy administration and its successors have argued, combine to make the execution of a controlled nuclear response rational. On the one hand, rather than targeting Soviet cities in a first blow the United States would continue to hold them hostage. The Soviets would therefore presumably have an incentive not to escalate the conflict. On the other hand, the damage caused by limited use of either tactical or strategic U.S. nuclear weapons would raise the cost to the Soviet Union of continuing its aggression. The threat of additional nuclear blows would further encourage the Soviets to seek terms. As Secretary of Defense McNamara explained in 1962:

> We may seek to terminate a war on favorable terms by using our forces as a bargaining weapon—by threatening further attack. In any case, our large reserve of protected firepower would give an enemy an incentive to avoid our cities and to stop a war. Our new policy gives us the flexibility to choose among several operational plans, but does not require that we make any advance commitment with respect to doctrine or targets. We shall be committed only to a system that gives us the ability to use our forces in a controlled and deliberate way, so as best to pursue the interests of the United States, our Allies, and the rest of the Free World.[23]

Although MAD meant that the United States was unable to *defend* its cities against Soviet nuclear attack, the United States might still be able to *convince* the Soviets not to attack American cities, even after U.S. use of nuclear weapons. This dissuasion might be accomplished, the reasoning ran, by applying nuclear force selectively and continuing to hold Soviet cities hostage.

Thus, in an era in which nuclear invulnerability had been lost, the quality of the U.S. nuclear force posture which gave the United States deterrent power was the U.S. ability rationally to fight a controlled and limited nuclear war. Official thinking on this point has remained unaltered since the Kennedy administration. Most recently, Reagan administration Secretary of Defense Caspar Weinberger summed up the officially accepted logic on the need for controlled nuclear response options as follows: "If we are forced to retaliate and can only respond by destroying population centers, we invite the destruction of our own population. Such a deterrent strategy is hardly likely to carry conviction as a deterrent, particularly as a deterrent to nuclear —let alone conventional—attack on an ally."[24] Weinberger's immediate predecessor, Harold Brown, had expounded on this theme in greater length, noting:

> Unfortunately, however, a strategy based on assured destruction alone no longer is wholly credible. A number of Americans even question whether we would or should follow such a strategy in the event of a nuclear attack on the United States itself, especially if the attack avoided population centers and sought to minimize the collateral damage from having targeted military installations. . . . Our allies, particularly in Europe, have questioned for some time whether the threat of assured destruction would be credible as a response to nuclear threats against them.[25]

The implications of this for potential Soviet behavior and for U.S. policy were clear to U.S. decision-makers. As Secretary of Defense James Schlesinger bluntly concluded in 1974:

> Since we ourselves find it difficult to believe that we would actually implement the threat of assured destruction in response to a limited attack on military targets that caused relatively few civilian casualties, there can be no certainty that, in a crisis, prospective opponents would be deterred from testing our resolve. . . . In any event, the actuality of such a response would be utter folly except where our own or allied cities were attacked. Today, such a massive retaliation against cities, in response to anything less than an all-out attack on the U.S. and its cities, appears less and less credible. . . . What we need is a series of measured responses to aggression which bear some relation to the provocation, have prospects of terminating hostilities before general nuclear war breaks out, and leave some possibility for restoring deterrence.[26]

The idea of controlled and deliberate use of nuclear weapons has found two distinct applications since 1961. The first application—to the problem of deterring aggression in Europe—was responsible for provoking the continuing coupling debate. The second—to the problem of deterring limited nuclear blows against the United States itself —has provoked the counterforce debate.

"Flexible Response" and "No Cities"

Despite Secretary of Defense McNamara's interest in purely conventional options in Europe, the perceived absence of NATO forces sufficient to provide a high-confidence conventional defense against the Red Army meant that in Europe, unlike in the Third World, the United States would continue to rely on nuclear threats. NATO's strategy of "Flexible Response," pressed by the United States on its unenthusiastic allies during the early and mid-1960s, was (and still is) aimed at ensuring that escalation in Europe would remain as limited as possible while preventing Soviet success. Flexible Response reduces as much as possible, consistent with an ultimate U.S. nuclear guarantee to the Alliance, the risk that American cities will be incinerated if deterrence fails. By doing so it increases the conceivability that U.S. leaders might stand true to their peacetime commitments to the defense of Europe—above all that, if necessary, the United States will use nuclear weapons to prevent Soviet conquest of Western Europe.

The adoption of Flexible Response had important planning implications for both tactical and strategic nuclear operations. As tactical nuclear weapons became available during the mid-1950s, they were incorporated into U.S. military units and deployed in Europe without much thought about the implications of their presence. It was simply assumed that they would be used, as conventional weapons would, in the most militarily effective manner. In the event of a major Soviet attack on NATO, use was expected to be widespread.[27]

The growth of Soviet tactical nuclear capabilities and the realization by NATO members that an effort to use tactical nuclear weapons to defend NATO might cause millions of civilian casualties were responsible for a substantial shift in NATO's view of tactical nuclear operations. Any optimism that the "enhanced firepower" of tactical nuclear weapons would permit NATO ground forces to hold the Soviet Union in check until the superior industrial and strategic power of the United States could make itself felt was generally replaced by a well-grounded pessimism that a full tactical nuclear defense would turn central Europe into an uninhabitable wasteland and destroy the society it was supposed to protect. Although in the late 1950s the idea of deterring Soviet aggression by threatening an effective tactical nuclear "denial" had been toyed with, the Flexible Response strategy rejected this conception. Under Flexible Response the use of tactical nuclear weapons was explicitly viewed as a way to signal NATO resolve and impose increasing costs on the Soviet Union.

Flexible Response called not only for an initial attempt at conventional defense without the use of tactical nuclear weapons but also for a second, theater nuclear, phase before the U.S. strategic arsenal came into play. Even within this theater nuclear phase, nuclear response would be carefully controlled and, if possible, limited. The use of tactical nuclear weapons, while important for affecting the situation on the ground, was seen as part of an integrated bargaining and communication process that would convince the Soviet Union to halt its war as soon as possible. It was not presented as a high-confidence means of defeating the Soviet Union or as an alternative to reliance on the U.S. strategic arsenal for deterrence purposes. By limiting types of targets, areas of use, and size of weapons, the United States hoped to encourage Soviet restraint in the use of nuclear weapons; by avoiding attacks on Soviet command facilities, at least during the earlier stages of conflict, the United States hoped to give the Soviets the ability as well as the incentive to exercise restraint.[28]

Closely related to Flexible Response's plan for carefully controlled escalation within the European theater was Secretary of Defense McNamara's "No Cities" strategy for strategic nuclear targeting. First publicly articulated in 1962 at Ann Arbor, Michigan, the No Cities strategy envisioned deliberately withholding attack on Soviet cities. In adopting it, McNamara rejected—as his successors would—the idea that, in the event that deterrence failed, the role of U.S. strategic weapons was to maximize damage to the Soviet Union or to minimize Soviet physical capacity to damage the United States. At the same time McNamara also rejected the notion of strategic nuclear war as a necessarily terminal event. While concerned with the possible cost implications of the No City strategy's open-ended force requirements and apparently never convinced that actual control of nuclear war would be *likely*, McNamara publicly endorsed—as his successors would—the notion that strategic, like theater, nuclear weapons might be used in a limited fashion to coerce the Soviet Union into halting aggression in Europe on terms acceptable or favorable to the United States.[29]

Because avoiding cities and industry logically meant hitting military targets, on first reading the No Cities strategy could be taken for a plan to disarm the Soviet Union, leaving the United States invulnerable.[30] Ultimately, however, the evidence does not support this interpretation. McNamara and his successors consistently distinguished between a strategy aimed at disarming the Soviet Union and one aimed at using U.S. strategic forces in a controlled, flexible, and limited fashion for bargaining purposes.[31] Assistant Secretary of Defense John McNaughton, speaking six months after McNamara's Ann Arbor speech, was explicit on this point:

> there is the assertion that "city-avoidance" must equal "disarming first strike." This is wrong. . . . The "city-avoidance" strategy is no more nor less than an affirmation that, whatever other targets may be available and whoever initiates the use of nuclear weapons, the United States will be in a position to refrain from attacking cities. But it will have in reserve sufficient weapons and it will have the targeting flexibility to destroy enemy cities if the enemy strikes cities first.[32]

The United States would not challenge the reality of MAD. It would not attempt to gain or maintain the measure of nuclear superiority that would allow it to wage all-out nuclear war and yet avoid substantial damage to its society.[33] The United States would, rather, solve the problem of how to use nuclear forces to deter Soviet aggression in Europe by creating a credible threat to wage a nuclear war—even one using strategic nuclear weapons—that was not an all-out nuclear war and which could therefore be fought without ending Western civilization.

Although rhetorical shifts in the mid- and late 1960s led to the popular misconception that the United States based its nuclear deterrence solely on its capacity to inflict "assured destruction," the United States was not to deviate either from the strategy of Flexible Response in Europe or from the strategic targeting plans incorporated in the No Cities strategy. The term "assured destruction" reflected a recognition by Secretary McNamara and his successors that for purposes of keeping defense spending within bounds, this capability was the key one on which to focus public and congressional attention; it did not, however, reflect U.S. thinking on how a nuclear war would actually be fought.[34]

"Countervailing"

The second application of the concept of controlled nuclear response was to the problem of deterring limited nuclear attack on the United States itself. As Bruce Blair has summarized:

Besides being the linchpin for most thinking and analyses related to NATO and the defense of Western Europe, flexible response has been seized upon as an answer to a paradox that has long plagued the general nuclear war strategy of assured destruction. The paradox is that if strategic deterrence based on the threat of unrestrained retaliation fails, then it would not be rational actually to carry out the threat. In the wake of Soviet attack, even large-scale attack, there would be a continuing necessity to influence the opponent's decision process to deter attacks by his residual forces or otherwise coerce restraint while attempts are made to negotiate a truce. In view of this necessity, leaders would have nothing substantial to gain and much bargaining leverage to lose by comprehensive retaliation. Moreover, the mass destruction of Soviet urban and industrial targets would be so disproportionate a response to limited nuclear attack as not to be credible. The threat of comprehensive retaliation thus might not deter low-level threats or attacks confined, for instance, to military facilities located in sparsely populated regions of the country.... National policy requires that nuclear strategy allow for selective attacks on the Warsaw Pact and Soviet target base, whether those attacks would be undertaken in defense of Western Europe or in response to Soviet attack on the United States.[35]

The new application of the ideas of controlled response was prompted by the development of expanded Soviet military capabilities. In the 1960s the Soviets possessed two basic capabilities: to undertake aggression in Europe and to destroy American society. In the 1970s they developed the additional capability to launch a militarily significant, though not disarming, attack on military and key industrial facilities in the United States. If the question of the early 1960s was how to use nuclear weapons to deter Soviet aggression in Europe, the controversial nuclear question of the 1970s—supplementing, but not replacing, that of the 1960s—was how to deter a limited Soviet attack on targets in the United States. Secretary of Defense James Schlesinger faced this issue squarely, and his answer in 1974 explicitly harked back to McNamara's:

During the early 1960s it was stated quite clearly by President Kennedy—and also by a large majority of Americans in both parties—that the United States needed alternatives other than suicide or surrender, that it needed options which did not imply immediate escalation to major nuclear war. If anything, the need for options other than suicide or surrender, and other than escalation to all out nuclear war, is more important for us today than it was in 1960 because of the growth in capabilities possessed by other powers. . . . The Soviet Union now has the capability in its missile forces to undertake selective attacks against targets other than cities. This poses for us an obligation, if we are to ensure the credibility of our deterrent, to be certain that we have a comparable capability in our strategic systems and in our targeting doctrine, and to be certain that the USSR has no misunderstanding on this point.[36]

Schlesinger's formulation triggered the heated and unresolved debate over counterforce. Where McNamara had created options that would give the president several basic choices, such as whether or not to strike Soviet cities, Schlesinger insisted that the president have a much broader and more detailed range of choices, even down to launching single missiles. If the Soviets had the capacity to launch a small "surgical" strike against U.S. military targets, the United States needed to have such a capability for retaliation. Schlesinger's successors have annually reaffirmed this strategy of deterring a limited nuclear attack by threatening precisely tailored, "appropriate" strategic responses; since 1974, U.S. targeting flexibility and options for a wide range of counterforce and countervalue strategic strikes have been maintained and expanded.

To distinguish it from "prevailing"—i.e., war-winning—strategies, this post-1974 official doctrine of matching the Soviet Union in options for limited strategic war was eventually dubbed the "Countervailing" strategy during the Carter administration. Both Countervailing and war-winning strategies conclude that "hard-target kill" capabilities—capabilities for destroying the opponent's strategic missile forces, deployed in "hardened" protective silos—are necessary for U.S. deterrence. The reasons for acquiring hard-target kill capabilities differ dramatically in Countervailing and war-winning strategies, however.

The Countervailing strategy demands acquisition of some "hard-target" capabilities on the grounds that the ability to reply tit for tat to a Soviet attack on U.S. missile forces is the surest way to convince the Soviet Union that the United States would indeed respond and deny it a net military or political advantage from its attack, thereby eliminating Soviet incentives for undertaking such an attack. Though it expands the range of U.S. nuclear options, a Countervailing posture does not require or imply the capacity to disarm the Soviet Union with a preemptive blow. To preserve U.S. cities during a nuclear war, the Countervailing strategy counts on Soviet forebearance, enforced by the fear that the United States might respond by destroying Soviet cities or military and political leadership, rather than on the disarming power of U.S. nuclear strikes. By contrast, war-winning strategies find hard-target kill capabilities attractive precisely because they offer the prospect of a meaningful nuclear superiority, one that would permit the United States to fight an *all-out* nuclear war with the Soviet Union if necessary and emerge with American society largely intact.[37]

In 1985, Secretary of Defense Weinberger emphasized this distinction, stressing the central position of controlled nuclear response in U.S. strategy:

> In 1974, Secretary Schlesinger's nuclear policy modifications were met with concern and misunderstanding. Yet his important step, which increased the flexibility with which a President might respond to an attack (and therefore our ability to deter one), was denounced by some as a move toward "nuclear warfighting." The same thing occurred in 1980 to Secretary Brown. The Reagan Administration has not been spared similar criticism and misrepresentation. The fact remains, however, that deterrence through flexible response continues to be our policy and strategy today.... While we cannot predict how a conflict would escalate should deterrence fail, the credibility of our deterrent forces increases as we demonstrate flexibility in our response options and in our forces. That flexibility offers the possibility of terminating a conflict and reestablishing deterrence at the lowest level of violence possible, avoiding further destruction.[38]

Controlled nuclear response has thus come to be viewed as the panacea for U.S. deterrence problems created by MAD. First in 1961 and then in 1974, the idea of reducing the violence of a nuclear war was employed to try to make nuclear use rational as a response to Soviet provocation. Since 1974, while there have indeed been two significant modifications in U.S. thinking and planning for nuclear deterrence, there have been no changes in the fundamental premise that nuclear deterrence is based on the ability to respond in a controlled, appropriate fashion.[39] As Secretary Brown reaffirmed in 1980:

> we must be able to deter Soviet attacks of less than all-out scale by making it clear to the Kremlin that, after such an attack, we would not be forced to the stark choice of either making no effective military response or totally destroying the Soviet Union. We could instead attack, in a selective and measured way, a range of military, industrial, and political control targets, while retaining an assured destruction capacity in reserve.[40]

The first significant change since 1974 was a shift from threatening, as the ultimate sanction, the destruction of the Soviet recovery economy to threatening the destruction of Soviet political leadership. The second significant change was the devotion of increased attention to procuring command-and-control systems that would survive Soviet attack and permit the United States to execute its controlled response options during a protracted exchange.[41] These modifications were aimed at enhancing U.S. ability to control and deter escalation in a nuclear conflict and in no way represented a departure from the basic ideas of controlled response. As a consequence, they failed to come to grips with the fundamental logical inconsistency in using controlled response to deter aggression in Europe and limited nuclear attacks.

FLAWS AND ALTERNATIVES

What is the problem with relying on controlled response to make nuclear war nonsuicidal, the use of nuclear weapons rational, and threats rationally to choose to use nuclear weapons credible? To the same extent that it appears that a nuclear war cannot be kept limited once the United States undertakes even a controlled use of nuclear weapons, a controlled use is no more rational—that is, no less suicidal and no more "appropriate"—than an all-out nuclear response. Indeed, it may even be less rational, since it does less to blunt the Soviet ability to devastate the United States. As Robert Jervis has cautiously noted:

> Although a limited American response would be less likely to trigger the immediate destruction of American cities than would an all-out strike, the chance of an unacceptably painful Soviet reaction would still be considerable. The credibility of the American threat to retaliate is undermined less by the paucity of the kind of attacks which the United States could stage than by the vulnerability of American cities.[42]

The problem with strategies of limited and flexible nuclear response is that they too lack credibility as rational responses to Soviet aggression. As Jervis has complained after carefully reviewing the official case for the Countervailing strategy: "Although those who argue for flexibility are motivated by the belief that countercity strikes lack sufficient credibility, they ignore the impediments to the credibility of the threat on which they propose to rely."[43] Though his policy preferences differ from Jervis', Colin Gray has voiced the same complaint about controlled response:

No matter how flexible U.S. strategic employment planning may be, if it is not matched by some very significant ability actually to defend North America, it would have to amount, in practice, to suicide on the installment plan. Flexibility, *per se*, carries few advantages. Indeed if the flexibility is very substantial and if the enemy agrees tacitly to a fairly slow pace of competitive escalation, it provides noteworthy time for the self-deterrence process to operate.[44]

The fact that flexibility would not necessarily provide an escape from suicide (or surrender) was evident even to the first authors of the logic of controlled nuclear response. In his seminal work, Schelling observed of mutual exercises in controlled retaliation: "there is no logical reason why two adversaries will not bleed each other to death, drop by drop, each continually feeling that if he can only hold out a little longer, the other is bound to give in."[45]

If options were limited to an all-out U.S. blow almost certain to inspire a massive Soviet response that would kill up to 100 million Americans immediately and a limited U.S. blow that left some chance of terminating hostilities before escalation to city busting occurred, a decision-maker would presumably choose to execute the limited blow. But there exists another option. It is also possible to refrain (or at least to try to refrain) from using nuclear weapons at all in the event that deterrence fails. Capitulation on the political issues in dispute is always an alternative to prolongation or escalation of military hostilities.[46] Even with controlled response options, if a nuclear response is perceived as likely to be ultimately suicidal—or, more broadly, if a nuclear response is perceived as likely to destroy the values being defended, to involve large (albeit probabilistic) costs, or to generate vast uncertainty about final outcomes—then the attractiveness of avoiding the use of nuclear forces will be great.

Since 1961, all-out nuclear war has been viewed as "inappropriate" and incredible as a deterrent threat because it offers no prospect of escalation control. In a MAD world, escalation control is the *sine qua non* of appropriate, rational use of nuclear weapons. If strategies of controlled response cannot offer a satisfactory promise of escalation control then they are logically flawed.

In fact, optimism about the controllability of nuclear war, either tactical or strategic, has not been widespread. Obviously, tactical use of nuclear weapons—that is, use of generally shorter-range weapons to influence the course of events on the battlefield—is less likely to lead inexorably to all-out societal destruction than is a strategic blow employing intercontinental weapons against targets in an adversary's homeland. From the tactical level, escalation has further to go and more possible "firebreaks" must be crossed before destruction becomes total. But even a purely tactical nuclear war would be an extremely dangerous undertaking, threatening to lead to a competition in nuclear escalation and risk-taking, to ill-conceived nuclear retorts, to heightened psychological stress among national political and military leaders, to increasing loss of control over longer-range nuclear forces, or to nuclear actions by third parties.

In sum, the general conclusion has been, as Brown has put it, that "the first use of nuclear weapons, even short-range tactical ones, would entail a high risk of escalation to mutual destruction," and that "any strategic war is likely to end in a massive exchange."[47] Indeed, even at the time when he was endorsing the government's Countervailing strategy, Brown observed about the options the United States had acquired for conducting limited strategic exchanges:

> None of this potential flexibility changes my view that a full-scale thermonuclear exchange would be an unprecedented disaster for the Soviet Union as well as for the United States. Nor is it at all clear that an initial use of nuclear weapons—however selectively they might be targeted—could be kept from escalating to a full-scale thermonuclear exchange, especially if command-control centers were brought under attack. The odds are high, whether the weapons were used against tactical or strategic targets, that control would be lost on both sides and the exchange would become unconstrained. Should such an escalation occur, it is certain that the resulting fatalities would run into the scores of millions.[48]

While it is impossible to know in advance whether a limited nuclear war could be kept under control, analysis as well as intuition tends to support the pessimism of the bulk of the national leadership. A number of factors increase the danger that an American nuclear response would escalate to all-out nuclear war. Among them are the Soviet conception of the nature of warfare and Soviet plans for the use of nuclear weapons; the difficulties of assessing nuclear attacks quickly and accurately; communication problems inherent in a conflict environment; the difficulties of maintaining direct and effective central control over military actions during war; the inflexibility imposed by preplanned options and bureaucratic procedures; cognitive rigidity in leaders' thinking about war; the impact of psychological stress and physical exhaustion; and the possibility of emotional outbursts.[49]

Even putting aside the inherently more speculative problems caused by Soviet doctrine and by psychological pressures, the problems of command and control are overwhelming. In the most thorough unclassified examination of U.S. command-and-control capabilities to date, Blair has considered the potential for using strategic forces in a carefully controlled retaliation. Neither his diagnosis nor his prognosis are cheerful:

> Significant decentralization of operating procedure and information channels cannot be avoided. Significant vulnerability of command centers and communications links cannot be eliminated. Pertinent details of nuclear operations will inevitably escape notice. The exact nature and degree of organizational constraints on executive decisionmaking cannot be fully determined. The consequences of triggering the diffuse organizational reactions associated with mobilization or attack cannot be precisely anticipated. In sum, an irreducible risk of discontinuity between national purpose and military operations will always exist. *The scope for such divergence is sufficiently large that the paradox of assured destruction has not been resolved in practice. Carefully calibrated retaliation and strategic bargaining plans provide more academic than operational answers.* Any large-scale Soviet nuclear attack, even one strictly designed to inflict maximum damage on military forces, would cause sufficient damage to C³I [Command, Control, Communication, and Intelligence] networks to make war uncontrollable, regardless of calculations U.S. political leaders might make and irrespective of retaliatory options created for this very contingency. Soviet nuclear attack would trigger diffuse organizational reactions that, in conjunction with damage to C³I networks, almost guarantee the breakdown of positive and negative control and a quick departure from any preferred course of action.[50]

The implications for use of the U.S. strategic arsenal are clear. As Desmond Ball has concluded in his study of the controllability of strategic nuclear war:

> Given the impossibility of developing capabilities for controlling a nuclear exchange through to favourable termination, or of removing the residual uncertainties relating to controlling the large-scale use of nuclear weapons, *it is likely that decision-makers would be deterred from initiating nuclear strikes no matter how limited or selective the options available to them.* The use of nuclear weapons for controlled escalation is therefore no less difficult to envisage than the use of nuclear weapons for massive retaliation.[51]

Prospects for controlling escalation are, of course, better if nuclear use is limited to tactical operations. However, given problems of maintaining centralized command and control in a complex wartime environment, differences in Soviet and American conceptions of salient limits—i.e., in perceptions of which nuclear actions are equivalent and of the point at which war becomes unlimited or uncontrollable—and the existence of pressures on both sides to escalate if the situation on the ground degenerates, the controllability of even tactical nuclear operations is doubtful.[52] Further, the level of devastation associated with a serious tactical nuclear defense of Western Europe and the possibility that the Soviet Army might nonetheless prove victorious make a strategy of relying on battlefield use of nuclear weapons but eschewing attacks with long-range theater and strategic weapons unlikely to be acceptable to Western Europe. The threat posed by long-range theater nuclear weapons and by strategic nuclear weapons is an essential part of a politically acceptable NATO nuclear strategy.

To be sure, the United States could *bluff* about its willingness rationally to use nuclear weapons. It might *threaten* to choose rationally to use nuclear weapons in response to a limited provocation even though it calculated that such a response would be irrational. The possibility of basing nuclear deterrence on a bluff, however, has been rejected by American decision-makers. The difficulties of bluffing are great. As Secretary Brown argued in dismissing the idea of basing deterrence on a threat of assured destruction: "if we try bluffing, ways can be found by others to test our bluffs without undue risk to them. Moreover, military postures and plans cannot very well be constructed on the basis of pretense."[53]

In sum, official thinking has concluded that effective nuclear deterrence requires that the United States have "appropriate" nuclear options—options that it would be tempted to use. But the vulnerability of American society to a Soviet nuclear riposte makes the use of nuclear forces extraordinarily untempting.

Nuclear Superiority

One possible solution to this problem is to reduce the vulnerability of American society. Conservative critics of official doctrine have argued that the United States needs meaningful nuclear superiority. They complain that without the ability directly to prevent the Soviet Union from destroying American society, use of nuclear weapons will remain something that—in Secretary Weinberger's terms—"the U.S. Government could not, in good conscience, and in prudence, undertake." Without the ability to prevail, rather than simply countervail, the United States will rationally be deterred from using its nuclear forces.[54]

If they are to be willing to carry out nuclear attacks, U.S. decision-makers will need to be convinced not only that the Soviet Union can be shown that aggression does not pay but also that the United States will not be devastated in return. An American president is unlikely to be willing to engage in a cosmic gamble that the Soviets will forebear from harming U.S. cities once nuclear blows are exchanged. As a consequence, as Colin Gray has put it, strategic nuclear threats

> can be credible, and can be invoked prudently, only if their contemplation does not paralyze a US president into indecision. The first duty of the US government is to avoid defeat, not to enforce defeat on the enemy. We should take small consolation from the knowledge that the United States could defeat the Soviet Union, in Soviet terms, if the price tag for that accomplishment is known to lie close to 100 million prompt American deaths. Many in the US defense community today do not appear to recognize that the offense cannot be executed if the country cannot be defended.[55]

Advocates of nuclear superiority therefore argue that mutual societal vulnerability is incompatible with the United States' nuclear deterrence task. While not disputing that, regardless of U.S. actions, the Soviet Union will retain the ability to inflict some substantial damage on the United States, advocates of nuclear superiority argue that threats of controlled response will be effective only if the United States has the military advantage necessary to wage an all-out nuclear war and "survive."[56] In practical terms superiority entails the acquisition of some effective combination of preemptive forces to destroy Soviet weapons before they can be used, active defenses to prevent surviving Soviet weapons from reaching the United States, and passive defenses to reduce casualties and destruction resulting from those Soviet nuclear weapons that do reach the United States.[57]

The nuclear superiority school faces three distinct criticisms. The first is that meaningful nuclear superiority—one that would guarantee U.S. societal survival in an all-out nuclear war—is unattainable. As Brown noted while Secretary of Defense:

> There is no prospect that the Soviet Union, *any more than the United States,* can develop a disarming first strike in the decades ahead—if

the United States reacts to modify its forces appropriately. Similarly, there is no prospect that the Soviet Union, *any more than the United States*, can—over the next 10 years—design a serious damage-limiting capability, if we react. That is simply not in the cards.[58]

Neither side is likely to remain passive while the other undertakes the qualitative and quantitative improvements that render adversaries' military arsenals impotent. Equally important, Soviet (and American) ability to launch nuclear forces on tactical warning of nuclear attack means that a disarming first strike, under any circumstances, would be a risky endeavor, based on the questionable assumption that the enemy would sit still while being attacked with thousands of warheads.

Even with active and passive defenses, it will be impossible to escape MAD in the foreseeable future. As Brown has concluded: "My own judgment is that neither passive nor active defenses would help the United States or the Soviet Union survive an all-out strategic exchange as organized societies in a recognizable form, as long as each side takes the necessary—and quite manageable—steps to ensure that its retaliatory capability is preserved."[59]

Second, even if it *were* possible to develop meaningful nuclear superiority, the attempt to gain such superiority might prove extremely dangerous. Superiority that offered the prospect of giving the ability to "win" a nuclear war would obviously pose a tremendous threat to a rival state or its government, challenging not only its security but perhaps also its political legitimacy.[60] Even if such a situation did not result in preventive war—as one side or the other deliberately launched a war to avoid passing into nuclear inferiority or to take advantage of a temporary superiority—it would be likely to create an unstable international situation fraught with political crises, each with the potential for miscalculation. Crises might result from attempts by the superior power to undermine its rival's interests, from efforts by the inferior power to reassure allies through a show of firmness, or from steps by either superpower to ensure or eliminate superiority. It is perhaps useful to recall that the Soviet decision to place missiles in Cuba, with its threatening consequences for world peace, appears to have been largely motivated by the temporary American superiority in strategic weaponry and by Soviet interest in offsetting the USSR's vulnerability.[61] Desperate situations can provoke desperate actions. At a minimum, superiority does not imply international stability or harmony.

Finally, even if nuclear superiority were achievable and did not provoke preventive war or political and military adventurism, it might not provide the leverage its advocates claim. First, of course, U.S. decision-makers could never be certain that U.S. defenses—preemptive, active, or passive—would work as advertised. Hence, decision-makers would still be likely to perceive constraints on their freedom of nuclear action. Second, and perhaps more important, even if U.S. decision-makers were entirely convinced that U.S. defenses would work and American society would survive a nuclear war, the residual Soviet capacity to harm the United States in response might be sufficient to deter the execution of nuclear threats. The French argument for a *force de frappe* seems relevant here. Like France, the Soviet Union need not be able to threaten to destroy an opponent totally in order to constrain that opponent's military actions: all the Soviet Union needs to be able to do is credibly threaten an unacceptable cost, one disproportionate to the gains at stake. Even if the United States were confident that it could "survive" and "win" a nuclear war, would it be willing to suffer 2 or 20 million casualties simply in order to force the Soviets to withdraw from Western Europe or to punish them for having attacked some U.S. military base? If Soviet aims were clearly limited—say, to the humiliation of a revanchist West German state and the destruction of its growing economic and military capabilities —would the United States really deliberately choose to risk some millions of American lives even if it *knew* that U.S. society would survive?

In the early 1970s, Secretary of Defense Schlesinger sought to demonstrate that American fatalities in a strictly limited strategic exchange might be fairly small, perhaps only in the hundreds of thousands. The preponderance of evidence was against him, however, and his successors were forced to admit that even a strictly strategic duel might produce casualties out of proportion to its benefits.[62] As Secretary of Defense Donald Rumsfeld observed in 1977:

> It must be emphasized ... that the results, even in limited and controlled exchanges, could be appalling. They could involve the potential for millions of fatalities, even though the distinction between 10 million and 100 million fatalities is great and worth preserving. No U.S. decision-maker is likely to be tempted by this prospect, especially in view of the dangers of nuclear escalation.[63]

And yet, for the threat rationally to undertake a limited and controlled exchange to be credible, this prospect must be—or must at least be made to appear—tempting.

Indeed, the available historical evidence seems to suggest that nuclear superiority, even if clearly recognized, does not make nuclear options particularly attractive. During the Berlin crisis in mid-September 1961, for example, the Kennedy administration possessed apparently convincing evidence that it could launch a preemptive counterforce first strike that would destroy all but a few Soviet nuclear weapons. If the Soviets chose to respond with their surviving weapons, U.S. fatalities might have been as low as two million or as high as fifteen. While it was clear that the United States possessed the kind of overwhelming superiority that would permit it to emerge from such a war as a functioning society, the possibility of even these limited (though by historic standards high) casualties made the execution of the preemptive strike unthinkable to national decision-makers.[64] Similarly, during the Cuban missile crisis a year later: "As in the Berlin crisis, despite overwhelming nuclear superiority, nobody was willing to 'send signals' with nuclear weapons, nobody wanted to walk up an 'escalation ladder' supported by limited nuclear strikes, nobody wanted to think much about using nuclear weapons rationally."[65] In sum, nuclear superiority does not necessarily significantly broaden the range of rational nuclear action.

Nuclear or Political Retrenchment

Options other than the pursuit of nuclear superiority have, of course, been suggested as alternatives to present policy, particularly in dealing with the problem of extended deterrence in Europe. Rather than increase its capabilities in some fashion, the United States could attempt to "solve" the logical conundrum of deterrence in a MAD era by reducing the contingencies in which it relies upon nuclear weapons for deterrent power. In the Kennedy era the United States abandoned the attempt to use nuclear weapons to deter events in the Third World; other reductions in reliance on nuclear threats may be possible today. True, at least until that distant time when there exists the technological capacity to construct a strategic defense shield that could render U.S. territory invulnerable to nuclear attack, the U.S. is likely to have, ultimately, to rely on the threat of a nuclear response to deter limited nuclear attacks on American soil.[66] However, the role of nuclear weapons in extended deterrence could conceivably be reduced. Accepting the reasoning of advocates of nuclear superiority that MAD is inconsistent with extended nuclear deterrence, Earl Ravenal has expressed the dilemma as follows:

America's willingness to protect its allies rises or falls with the prospective viability of counterforce and, more generally, with the United States' ability to protect its own society from nuclear attack. If there is any explicit doubt—technical, economic, political—that the United States will achieve invulnerability, then there is implicit doubt that its extensive nuclear commitments, especially to Western Europe, can survive. What emerges from this analysis is that the attempt to implement extended deterrence—to defend, say, Western Europe efficiently and thoroughly by substituting the threat of nuclear weapons for the conventional defense of the theater— requires conditions which, if they can be fulfilled at all, are expensive or dangerous or counterproductive. . . . We are brought back to the stark, primal choice: expensive, exacting regional defense; or a more restricted security perimeter.[67]

Are these, then, the choices which ultimately confront the United States in dealing with extended deterrence in Europe? Is the nuclear coupling of Europe to America impossible? Need the United States, in the end, choose between nuclear and political retrenchment—between, on the one hand, building a conventional alternative to the nuclear threat on which deterrence in Europe has traditionally rested or, on the other hand, abandoning the U.S. commitment to the defense of Europe? Neither choice is particularly attractive. The first promises to be costly and is of uncertain acceptability to the NATO member most directly affected by it, the Federal Republic of Germany. The second represents an even greater step into the political unknown, raising new and potentially catastrophic questions about the stability of Western Europe in the absence of a U.S. guarantee.[68]

The logic developed in the following chapters suggests, however, that nuclear coupling is possible. Even in the absence of nuclear superiority—indeed, even in the absence of a full array of countervailing options for limited nuclear response—the United States can effectively use its nuclear capabilities to deter both Soviet aggression in Europe and limited Soviet nuclear attacks on the United States itself.

IRRATIONALITY-BASED NUCLEAR DETERRENCE

The principal participants in current debates on U.S. nuclear policy have assumed that the credibility of the U.S. threat to employ nuclear weapons depends on the rationality of that use. They have assumed that the only credible threats are ones that the United States would, given Soviet provocation, intelligently conclude it would be better off executing than not. Arguing for improved countervailing capabilities, for example, Secretary of Defense Weinberger has reasoned: "If our threatened response is perceived as. . . contrary to our national interest, it will be judged to be a bluff."[69] In a similar vein, though arguing in favor of a U.S. military superiority that would make a U.S. nuclear victory possible, Colin Gray and Keith Payne have asserted that "if American nuclear power is to support U.S. foreign policy objectives, the United States must possess the ability to wage nuclear war rationally."[70] As a consequence, Gray has argued that "a prudent, responsible US government should develop nuclear war plans which. . . .the United States would have an interest in implementing in the undesired event."[71] At the other end of the debate, advocates of retrenchment have also based their arguments on an assumption about rationality. In arguing for a "No First Use" policy, for example, Bruce Russett has written that: "Nuclear war would likely be an act of national suicide rather than an act of rational policy. . . . The defense of vital interests therefore must be undertaken predominantly by conventional military forces, not nuclear weapons."[72]

Though arriving at different answers, all parties in this defense debate have addressed the same question: "By what means—if any— can the United States make it rational to carry out coercive nuclear threats?" *This is an unsatisfactory formulation, however, of the United States' nuclear deterrence problem.* By focusing exclusively on rational action it misjudges the nature of the problem, as well as an entire class of possible solutions.

There are *two* reasons why the United States might use its nuclear weapons. First, it might use them *because it was rational to do so—* because an intelligent calculation by U.S. decision-makers revealed that the actual use of nuclear weapons would maximize their consistently calculated expected utility. Second, however, the United States might use nuclear weapons *even though it was irrational to do so.*

The United States might perform an irrational act for two reasons. First, it might physically have no choice: machines and automation might make human choice—rational or irrational—impossible. Computers could be programmed to respond automatically to particular stimuli, such as "blips" on NORAD's warning radars. Second, *it might carry out the irrational act because the U.S. decision-making process is not that of a rational unitary actor.* This latter idea provides the central theme for the chapters that follow.

The possibility that U.S. nuclear deterrence is based on the weakness of rationality inherent in the U.S. decision-making process has been overlooked. Discussions of nuclear policy have generally assumed either that the United States will necessarily be inalienably and manifestly rational or that (to the extent that departures from rationality may occur) it ought to be so. One early study of the idea of controlled nuclear response, for example, simply noted: "It is assumed that the requisite degree of rationality and a technically adequate command and control system will apply on the U.S. side."[73]

In actuality, however, the United States is not inalienably rational: actual decisions may diverge from those that would be made by an intelligent, utility-maximizing unitary actor. Further, given the information available to the Soviet Union about the United States and its decision-making process, the probability of irrational U.S. behavior in certain contingencies is likely to be manifest.

Moving from the positive to the normative, there is also no reason to assume that the United States *should* seek to have the capabilities to behave rationally in all situations. Despite the assumption made by some deterrence theorists that "the essential logic of deterrence rests upon the assumption that all players will be 'rational' in assessing expected costs and benefits,"[74] deterrence may not only exist despite irrationality, but may actually result from it.

To be sure, a measure of at least stochastic predictability is necessary for deterrence to function, but irrationality is not synonymous with unpredictability. Though the state being deterred must be able to make some prediction about the future behavior of its would-be deterrer, that behavior need not represent an intelligent attempt by the deterrer to maximize its expected utility. If the deterrer can demonstrate some sufficient probability that in a given contingency it will in fact be unable to act rationally and that its irrational behavior will lead to execution of the deterrent threat, then irrationality is not only predictable but also represents a critical condition for the existence of deterrent power.

Does this mean that irrationality can be beneficial and, in some sense, rational? At any given point in time, of course, it is never rational to behave irrationally *at that point in time*. It may, however, be rational *credibly to deny oneself the ability to act rationally in the future*. The benefits gained from the *expectation* that one will behave irrationally may outweigh the costs of that irrationality. This seeming paradox reflects the difference between what is rational to threaten and commit oneself to do in advance—*ex ante*—and what is rational to do if the threat fails—*ex post*.[75] The *ex ante* self-denial of future rationality may be a means of credibly committing oneself to the execution of deterrent threats that would be irrational *ex post* to carry out.

This insight opens new doors in the search for a satisfactory solution to the U.S. nuclear deterrence problem. It allows us to develop a new answer to our question: "In an era of MAD capabilities, what qualities of the U.S. nuclear force posture make it possible for the United States to use the threat of nuclear response to deter not only massive Soviet nuclear attacks on American cities but also carefully limited Soviet nuclear attacks on U.S. targets and major Soviet nuclear or conventional aggression against close U.S. allies?"

2

RATIONALITY
AND IRRATIONALITY

THIS CHAPTER explores concepts of rationality and irrationality. This exploration provides the necessary foundation for consideration in the following chapters of the implications of irrational behavior for coercion. This is not a book on organizational behavior or the psychology of decision-making, and specialists in these areas may be disappointed by the cursory treatment of the subject. (By contrast, other readers may be somewhat surprised by the extent to which the subject is treated—or dismayed that it is addressed at all.) The aim here is simply to define terminology and establish basic concepts necessary for an effective discussion of coercion.

Four specific topics need to be addressed: the nature of rationality and rational behavior, the failings that would make a decision-making process irrational, the possible causes of such failings, and the notion of irrational—as distinct from inadvertent or accidental—war and escalation.

RATIONALITY

As we shall use the term "rationality," it reflects a decision-making *process*, rather than the substance of a decision or an outcome. An actor is rational if he employs a rational decision-making process; a rational decision-making process is one that uses information intelligently in selecting policies which maximize the decision-maker's consistently evaluated expected utility.

To say that an actor exhibits rationality is to say that his decisions are intelligent ones, aimed at improving his well-being, where well-being is measured by the actor in some consistent fashion.[1] As Klaus Knorr has succinctly put it:

> The actor is rational if he is a value maximizer. He identifies courses of action appropriate to the achievement of his goals, evaluates these courses both in terms of expected costs and gains and in terms of probability of success, and selects the one that indicates the greatest net gain of valued things.[2]

Three points in this definition deserve to be highlighted. First, rationality is defined in terms of a process that seeks to *maximize* utility. Rational decision-making involves an attempt to do the best one can for oneself. This implies that the decision-maker will expend the resources at his disposal in an economic fashion to reach his goals, and will make trade-offs between his goals to maximize his total happiness. Second, for a decision-making process to be rational, it need not produce decisions that *actually* maximize the actor's utility: it need only use information intelligently in making decisions that maximize consistently evaluated *expected* utility. Third, this definition says nothing at all about the values that enter into utility calculations.

Indeed, a variety of values may be included in an actor's utility calculation. These values may be pragmatic or they may be emotional. Glenn Snyder has noted:

> "Rationality" may be defined as choosing to act in the manner which gives the best promise of maximizing one's value position, on the basis of a sober calculation of potential gains and losses, and probabilities of enemy actions. This definition is broad enough to allow the inclusion of such "emotional" values as honor, prestige, and revenge as legitimate ends of policy. It may be perfectly rational, in other words, to be willing to accept some costs solely to satisfy such emotions, but of course if the emotions inhibit a clear-eyed view of the consequences of an act, they may lead to irrational behavior. It would be irrational, however, to satisfy a momentary passion if sober judgment revealed that the satisfaction obtained would not in the long run be worth the cost.[3]

Rationality and Rational Behavior

A possible objection to this definition of rationality is that it is not a practical one for the study of real-world phenomena. We have defined a rational actor as one with a decision-making process that intelligently attempts to maximize a consistently evaluated expected utility. In the real world, however, it is likely to be impossible to delve inside a decision-maker to discover whether the decision-making process being used is in fact rational. We can see what an actor *does*— that is, his actual behavior—but we are much less likely to be able to see how he arrives at his decision to behave in that fashion.[4]

A related objection is that rationality, as we have defined it, is an extraordinarily demanding standard against which to judge decision processes. If rational decision-making is an ideal that real-life decision-makers can never quite reach, is the distinction between "rational" and "irrational" useful?

To deal with these complaints, we must distinguish between rationality and rational behavior. *"Rational behavior" represents behavior that is not inconsistent with that which would have been produced by a rational decision-maker.* Thus while a rational decision-maker will, by definition, exhibit rational behavior, an irrational decision-maker may also *behave* rationally. A man who believes that cars are outer-space creatures that devour people may avoid loitering in busy roadways. Given the actual dangers of standing in the middle of a highway, the man's behavior is rational, at least if he associates positive utility with avoiding grievous bodily injury. The man's behavior in staying out of the path of cars is rational, despite the fact that his decision-making process is irrational, because he stays out of the roadway just as he would have (given his desire to avoid being hurt) had he possessed a rational decision-making process.

Of course, in the absence of empirical evidence about the values held by the actor (e.g., that the man wishes to avoid being struck by traffic) and about the information available to him about options and possible outcomes, it is impossible to prove the existence even of rational behavior, much less of rationality. But if we do know something about the values of our actor—or feel comfortable making some assumptions about them—and if we do know or can estimate the information available to him, then we can talk about rational *behavior* even if we lack intimate empirical knowledge about the rationality of the decision-making process itself.

These denotations of rationality and rational behavior differ in important respects from some of the concepts of rationality and rational behavior in general usage. Recognition of some of these alternative meanings will be useful in avoiding pitfalls later in the discussion of rationality and coercion.

Rational Behavior and Sensible Behavior

In common usage, perhaps particularly in discussions of nuclear deterrence and war, "rationality" is frequently judged in terms of values rather than in terms of the process by which decisions are made. As Stephen Maxwell has noted:

> Many of the arguments about nuclear weapons have centred on such questions as "Could it ever be rational to engage in all-out nuclear war?" and "Is it rational to exterminate an opponent's population when he has already exterminated one's own population?" It frequently emerges that in moral and political debate these questions are to be interpreted as questions about morality. "Rational" is used as a synonym for "moral." The answer one gives will therefore depend on one's standard of moral judgment.[5]

By contrast,

> In deterrence theory. . . . to describe an action as "rational" is to say that it is consistent with the actor's values, whatever those may be. Hence it does not invite debate about whether the values are themselves "rational", in the extended sense of the word in which it is synonymous with "moral."[6]

To use the terms employed by Karl Mannheim, in popular usage rationality involves "substantial rationality" rather than "functional rationality," where "substantial rationality" is defined as "rationality in the choice of ends themselves" and "functional rationality" involves "rationality in the choice of means to an end."[7]

As we have already observed, our definition of rationality says nothing about the decision-maker's values or their sources. The decision-maker's preferences may be rooted in emotions—such as love, hate, honor, or desire for revenge—or in practical economics. Unlike the "rational actor" of popular usage, ours need not be emotionless any more than he need base his actions on values the observer deems "moral."

Further, common parlance sometimes uses "rational" as an antonym for "reckless": a rational decision-maker is, in this usage, necessarily a highly risk-averse one.[8] A decision-maker who values his most-preferred outcome so highly that he is willing to run grave risks of calamity to achieve it would not, in popular conversation, be termed rational. By contrast, just as our definition of rationality makes no judgment about the values held by the decision-maker, it makes none about the decision-maker's willingness to gamble on improved outcomes. Purchasers both of lottery tickets and insurance may be rational. To distinguish between our definition of rationality and the one in popular usage, we will use Patrick Morgan's term, "sensible," to describe decision-making and behavior that is subjectively perceived as substantively rational and risk averse and will continue to use the term "rational" to describe any decision-making process that exhibits functional rationality.[9] Rationality and rational behavior are thus independent of a decision-maker's values, while sensibleness and sensible behavior are not. As Anthony Downs has summarized:

> the term *rational* is never applied to an agent's ends, but only to his means. This follows from the definition of *rational* as efficient, i.e., maximizing output for a given input, or minimizing input for a given output. Thus, whenever economists refer to a "rational man" they are not designating a man whose thought processes consist exclusively of logical propositions, or a man without prejudices, or a man whose emotions are inoperative. In normal usage all of these could be considered rational men. But the economic definition refers solely to a man who moves toward his goals in a way which, to the best of his knowledge, uses the least possible input of scarce resources per unit of valued output.[10]

Since no *a priori* limits are placed on the values a rational actor may hold, even apparently self-destructive behavior may be rational. A rational decision-maker may value collective and "other-regarding" benefits as well as "self-regarding" ones.[11] Self-sacrifice is rational if an actor has an internally consistent value system that ranks some combination of values higher than individual survival. Patriots are often martyrs for their country; religious fanatics—witness Iranian tactics in the war with Iraq—are willing to die as well as kill in service to a holy cause; it is a commonplace that parents will make tremendous sacrifices for their children. Even lingering premodern social norms—such as "women and children first"—may lead to a consistent value system that makes self-sacrifice preferable and self-sacrificial behavior rational. And just as self-sacrifice is not necessarily irrational, sadism, masochism, and risk preference are not in themselves irrational. Individuals who carefully and intelligently consider the social costs, inconvenience, and danger associated with pulling the cat's tail, wearing a hair shirt, or going rock climbing yet still undertake these activities may be making rational decisions.

As all of this suggests, rational behavior does not require behavior consistent with an outside observer's value system, only behavior consistent with the actor's own value system. Given the absence of a universally shared value system, rational behavior may not appear sensible to other actors. For example, I may find the willingness of Soviet dissidents to voice anti-regime views—or the willingness of U.S. Navy pilots to risk death landing F-14 fighters on the rolling deck of an aircraft carrier—crazy given the dangers involved, but this does not mean that such behavior is irrational. The individuals involved may simply possess a utility function that weights various costs and benefits differently than does mine. Similarly, violent action, including resort to force or terrorism, may not appear sensible to the status quo actors against whom it is directed but may be entirely rational for the revolutionary, reformist, or revisionist actors who perpetrate it. The assassination of Israeli officials by PLO terrorists, the destruction of a commercial airliner by Zimbabwean guerrillas, or plans to sink the *Queen Elizabeth* by the Libyan government may not seem sensible to the typical Western observer—i.e., they may appear immoral or reckless—but they may be entirely rational for the parties carrying them out, given their different standards of morality and greater willingness to run risks.

Rationality, Perfect Rationality, and Objective Rationality

As rationality and sensibleness need to be distinguished, so too do rationality, perfect rationality, and objective rationality. Perfect rationality and objective rationality represent special cases of rationality. To understand how the three differ it is necessary to introduce the ideas of decision-making under conditions of *risk* and *uncertainty*. Decision-making under risk means that policies available to a decision-maker may lead to one of several outcomes, each of which has a known probability of occurring. My decision whether to bet on a fair coin toss involves decision-making under risk: if I do bet, there is a 50 percent chance (a known probability) of doubling my money and a 50 percent chance (again a known probability) of losing it. Decision-making under uncertainty means that even the *probability* of the various payoffs that may follow from various policies (e.g., betting on heads, betting on tails, or not betting at all) is not known with certainty. If I am trying to decide whether to bet on an "unfair" coin toss and do not know how the coin is weighted, then I face uncertainty.[12]

Perfect rationality involves rationality in the absence of uncertainty. That is, perfect rationality requires both a rational decision-making process and "perfect information on the probability, costs, and gains of various outcomes."[13] Such a combination is extremely unlikely to occur in the real world, where in general we do not know the precise bias of coins upon which we have an opportunity to bet or the precise payoffs of our gambles. Confusion of rationality with perfect rationality may, then, result in exaggeration of the unlikelihood of finding rational behavior.

In the absence of risk—i.e., if decisions lead to particular outcomes and payoffs with 100% probability—perfectly rational decision-making will necessarily yield an outcome that *actually* maximizes utility. This is what Herbert Simon has described as *"objectively* rational" behavior. Simon has distinguished between rational and objectively rational behavior, inquiring rhetorically:

> Shall we, moreover, call a behavior "rational" when it is in error, but only because the information on which it is based is faulty? When a subjective test is applied, it is rational for an individual to take medicine for a disease if he believes the medicine will cure the disease. When an objective test is applied, the behavior is rational only if the medicine is in fact efficacious.[14]

As we have defined them, rationality and rational behavior imply subjective rather than objective standards: rationality involves maximizing only expected, not actually realized, utility. As Downs has put it:

> Rationality thus defined refers to processes of action, *not to. . . their success at reaching desired ends. It is notorious that rational planning sometimes produces results greatly inferior to those obtained by sheer luck.* In the long run we naturally expect a rational man to outperform an irrational man, *ceteris paribus*, because random factors cancel and efficiency triumphs over inefficiency.[15]

In the short run, however, there is no reason to presume that random factors will cancel out and that rational behavior will lead to optimal, objectively rational outcomes.

Indeed, if risk is present, then even *perfectly* rational decision-making may be objectively irrational: even perfectly rational decision-making may result in an outcome that does not actually maximize utility. Even with perfect knowledge about the coin being tossed and the payoffs associated with possible outcomes, a rational gambler (or casino) may still lose money some evenings.

If information is imperfect—if uncertainty exists about the probability of various outcomes or their payoffs—then behavior is even less likely to be objectively rational. In this world, given that perfect information is generally unobtainable, even if we do our best to maximize our happiness we are unlikely to pick the one policy out of the infinite number available that yields the highest level of utility actually possible.

Complaints have been raised about this approach to the idea of rationality which defines it in terms of a decision-making process that uses the imperfect information available in an intelligent fashion to maximize consistently calculated expected utility. The economics "behavioral theory of the firm" literature has been responsible for two such complaints.

Rationality Under Risk and Uncertainty

First, there is the question of what kind of decision rule is rational when one allows risk or uncertainty in the environment. What is a decision that gives the best promise of maximizing utility when any given decision does not lead with 100 percent certainty to a single identified outcome?

Typically, the literature has suggested that under conditions of risk a rational decision-maker will calculate the expected utility of each policy option by averaging the expected utility of the various possible outcomes associated with that policy, weighted by the conditional probability of their occurrence. He will then select the policy that has the highest expected utility.[16]

If *"surprise aversion"* is allowed, this approach seems satisfactory. While *"risk aversion"*—that is, declining marginal utility of the good valued—is already taken into account in the assignment of utility to various possible outcomes, decision-makers are also likely to have what can be thought of as "surprise aversion." For an everyday illustration, consider the gentleman who is indifferent between attending the opera or a football match and whose wife will meet him after work with tickets to one of these events. A risk situation, with a known 50 percent chance of opera tickets and 50 percent chance of football tickets, is likely to have a lower utility than the certainty of either. Different physical and psychological preparations may be necessary for the two events: the mood necessary to enjoy opera to the fullest may be incompatible with that necessary to enjoy a football game to the maximum. Even if it is not, having to "worry" about what the upcoming evening holds in store may have disutility. Given a choice in the morning, I may rationally prefer the certainty of a dull evening at home over the prospect of a pleasant evening out if the latter entails a day of fretful wonder about the evening's entertainment. The "surprise" in itself may thus have negative utility. Of course, it is possible that a "surprise" may have positive utility: I may, for example, rationally agree to go to dinner with a senior colleague rather than have a more congenial dinner alone precisely because I do not know whether he will steer us to a Chinese restaurant or an Italian one, and this added excitement more than makes up for what otherwise promises to be a boring encounter.[17]

The expected utility of any policy in a situation of risk, then, can be thought of as "the average, weighted by the probabilities of occurrence, of the utilities attached to all possible consequences"[18] *minus* the decision-maker's surprise aversion. Surprise aversion may have a positive, zero, or negative value.

The literature is less decided on what constitutes rational behavior under conditions of uncertainty—conditions where even the *probability* of various outcomes or payoffs, given the policy selected, is not known. James March and Herbert Simon, for example, have suggested a "minimax risk" rule: "consider the worst set of consequences that may follow from each alternative, then select the alternative whose 'worst set of consequences' is preferred to the worst set of consequences attached to the other alternatives."[19] A "minimax risk" strategy, however, maximizes expected utility only for a risk-averse individual and only if no information at all is available—a case that for our purposes we can dismiss.

A more useful approach to defining rationality under conditions of uncertainty, therefore, is to argue that under such conditions a rational decision-maker will assign intelligently calculated subjective probability assessments to the various outcomes.[20] In the real world, after all, decision-makers are not acting in the complete absence of information. They are not playing against a completely capricious or unfamiliar opponent. Some information about an opponent's behavior—regardless of whether that opponent is another person or "nature"—will be available. Some estimate can be formed, albeit with a range of uncertainty, about the opponent's probable behavior.

To repeat, then, we assume that a rational decision-maker in an environment marked by risk will intelligently calculate the expected utility of each strategy, bearing in mind his surprise aversion, and select the strategy with the highest expected utility. A rational decision-maker in an environment marked by uncertainty will rationally estimate expected probabilities for the various outcomes associated with each policy and will use these subjective estimations, along with calculations of expected utility, to select an optimal strategy.

Rationality, Maximizing, and Satisficing

A second complaint raised by the "behavioral theory of the firm" literature about a definition of rationality based on maximization of expected utility is that maximization is an analytically impossible task. Finding the "best" solution is likely to be infinitely time-consuming.[21] A decision-maker after all, is likely to have an infinite or effectively infinite number of possible options, and identifying and evaluating all of them would be an overwhelming task. Analysts of organizational behavior have suggested that decision-makers "satisfice"—that is, select the first option they find that reaches some minimum standard—rather than optimize.

If satisficing standards are set rationally, though, and if the costs to the decision-maker of identifying and evaluating courses of behavior are taken into account, then satisficing is optimizing. We shall develop the ideas of "cost of search" and rational levels of information gathering and processing more fully below. Given the existence of costs associated with collecting and analyzing information, as long as satisficing standards reflect the ease or difficulty of marginal improvement, a satisficing decision rule represents an intelligent attempt to maximize total utility. While concluding that a satisficing approach to describing decision-making is more likely to be "fruitful," March and Simon have made this point explicitly:

> In making choices that meet satisfactory standards, the standards themselves are part of the definition of the situation. Hence, we need not regard these as given—any more than the other elements of the definition of the situation—but may include in the theory the processes through which these standards are set and modified. The standard-setting process may itself meet standards of rationality: for example, an "optimizing" rule would be to set the standard at the level where the marginal improvement in alternatives obtainable by raising it would be just balanced by the marginal cost of searching for alternatives meeting the higher standard. Of course, in practice the "marginal improvement" and "marginal cost" are seldom measured in comparable units, or with much accuracy. Nevertheless, a similar result would be automatically attained if the standards were raised whenever alternatives proved easy to

discover, and lowered whenever they were difficult to discover. Under these circumstances, the alternatives chosen would not be far from the optima, if the cost of search were taken into consideration. Since human standards tend to have this characteristic under many conditions, some theorists have sought to maintain the optimizing model by introducing cost-of-search considerations.[22]

For our purposes, we can legitimately choose to avoid this particular debate: we do not need to know whether real-life "rational" decision-making can best be viewed as satisficing with rationally determined standards or as optimizing with cost of information taken into account. Both represent intelligent attempts to maximize expected utility. A satisficing approach employing rationally set standards constitutes an entirely rational decision rule.

Analytic Paradigms and Cognitive/Cybernetic Paradigms

Perhaps a more important—certainly a more sweeping—criticism of the attempt to use concepts such as rationality to describe decision-making and behavior has been made by John Steinbruner, who has argued against using a "rational-analytic" paradigm at all.[23] As we noted in the Introduction, the criticism this book offers of classical deterrence theory aims principally at that theory's reliance on assumptions of rational behavior. This book, however, continues to work within an analytic paradigm that posits actors who do generally seek to maximize their values. This book presumes that behavior will be rational except when variable but identifiable forces at the individual or organizational level result in significant deviations from rational decision-making.

Under the circumstances, though, why not abandon a rational-actor or analytic paradigm entirely, rather than attempt to recognize that deviations from rationality occur while still assuming a general tendency toward intelligent value-maximizing behavior? Steinbruner has advocated just such an abandonment. He has offered a fundamentally different perspective of decision-making, suggesting that it can best be understood as an action-reaction phenomenon, not a rational-choice one. His cybernetic paradigm rejects the notion that actors aggregate conflicting values, and it models decision-making as a feedback loop, along the lines of a thermostat, in which particular environmental changes elicit particular patterns of behavior:

> The major theme is that the decision process is organized around the problem of controlling inherent uncertainty by means of highly

focused attention and highly programed response. The decision-maker in this view does not engage in alternative outcome calculations or in updated probability assessments.[24]

Steinbruner has complemented this cybernetic approach with a theory of cognition which suggests the existence of

general tendencies to set up decision problems conceptualized in terms of a single value, to associate but a single outcome with the available alternatives, and to restrict information utilized to a relatively limited number of variables. Thus, the propositions of the analytic paradigm—the idea of value integration; the conceptualization of a range of outcomes; the broad sensitivity to information —are all doubted by the core principles of cognitive theory. The central idea of the cybernetic paradigm—uncertainty control—is also adjusted by the more general picture of the mental operations which emerges from cognitive theory. To the cognitive theorist, the mind actively but subjectively resolves uncertainty because of its universal tendency to generalize. It does so, however, without confronting the full thrust of variety inherent in any complex problem. In sketching the way in which subjective uncertainty resolution occurs—that is, by resort to sources of belief strength independent of evidence from the empirical world—the principles of cognitive theory explain how problem structures are set up within which cybernetic mechanisms can operate.[25]

In presenting his cognitive/cybernetic paradigm, Steinbruner broke from the traditional approach—the approach we continue to pursue in this book—of trying to explain the occurrence of irrationality *within* an analytic paradigm which assumes a general tendency toward rationality. Rather than deal with anomalies by recognizing the existence of forces in the individual and environment that may constrain the ideal rational process and then including these constraints and variable contrary pressures in his model, Steinbruner deliberately and explicitly formulated a new paradigm to compete with the old.[26]

Applying a cognitive/cybernetic paradigm to the problem of deterrence, Steinbruner has been able to conclude that "under cybernetic assumptions the great problem of deterrence is that an attempt to use strategic forces in any active way runs a grave risk of initiating an uncontrollable process leading to an imperfect implementation of an established plan."[27] More precisely, the policy implication derived from employing a cognitive/cybernetic approach in the study of the problems of nuclear deterrence is that:

Unless a clearly defined and widely acknowledged secondary
threshold can be established at a very low level. . . limited counterforce does not appear to be a very workable doctrine under cybernetic assumptions. It seems more likely to provoke the enemy than
to control him—like sticking needles in an enraged bull.[28]

Similarly, drawing on Steinbruner's cognitive/cybernetic model and
examining the Cuban missile crisis, Jack Snyder has been able to
conclude that "compellence strategies—generally viewed as rather
reckless even by conventional analysts—appear even more troublesome in this light"[29] and that "while strategic stability has been
recognized as important by strategists working in the rational-analytic framework, it becomes doubly important when viewed in the
light of cognitive theory."[30]

But though such insights are important, there is no indication that
it is necessary to abandon the analytic paradigm to gain them. Schelling, for example, observed the importance of clear thresholds and of
strategic stability.[31] Likewise, notions such as the "fog of battle" and
awareness of limits on decision-making resources substantially pre-
date the cognitive/cybernetic paradigm. Realization of the limits of
rationality can be comfortably incorporated into the dominant paradigm. Indeed, it is difficult to imagine that research based on cogni-
tive/cybernetic assumptions about the fundamental nature of decision-making will yield any significant insight that cannot be readily
incorporated into an analytic paradigm, much as the insight of bureaucratic politics has been.

But why *prefer* the analytic paradigm to a cognitive/cybernetic one?
The difficulty with applying—or attempting to apply—a cognitive/
cybernetic paradigm to policy problems is that unless we can model
the particular cybernetic feedback loop and unless we know the specific influences that are shaping cognitive conceptualization we can
predict nothing.[32] By contrast, as Klaus Knorr has argued after reviewing the sources of irrationality in the real world:

These various limitations on the explanatory power of the model of
rational decision-making do not make it useless. Whatever the constraints that push man to deviate from rational behavior, he remains a persistent value-maximizer. He will try, as much as operating conditions and various idiosyncrasies permit, to do better for
himself rather than worse. To that extent, admittedly variable, he
behaves rationally. Provided we are alert to the factors that limit
rationality, the rational-choice model will have more explanatory

power than alternative models for most foreign policy decisions that are not routine.[33]

Thus, the challenge is to take advantage of the greater explanatory power of the rational-choice model while remaining sensitive to the potential irrationality of the actors—that is, while remaining sensitive to the types of insight afforded by a cognitive/cybernetic interpretation or derived from a careful look at the world. Only the rational-choice model has provided an adequate framework for analyzing conflict among states, yet it threatens to yield misleading results if deviations from rationality are not recognized as possible. As Mancur Olson has observed:

> I may be exaggerating what has been achieved by basing thinking on the notion that human beings are purposeful, calculating and generally sane creatures. Yet a comparison between systems of theory, like game theory and economic theory, that are built on this premise, and the stalled efforts to build theories on opposing assumptions makes it hard to come to any other conclusion. . . . In constructing our visions or theories of the way the world works and deciding how we can make it better, we must begin with some sense of the purposeful and rational elements of human nature yet also take account of the slowness, weakness and inconstancy of this rationality.[34]

TYPES OF IRRATIONALITY

What does it mean to suggest, as Olson does, that the rationality of decision processes may suffer from slowness, weakness, or inconstancy? In order to understand the possibilities of credibly threatening an irrational escalation in the use of nuclear weapons, we need a fairly thorough conception of irrationality. It is necessary, therefore, to briefly develop a typology of irrationality.

Irrationality—the existence of an irrational decision-making process—means that one of three things has occurred. The decision-maker may have failed to calculate intelligently the various options available and their costs and benefits; the decision-maker may have failed to evaluate the expected utility of these costs and benefits in a consistent fashion; or the decision-maker may have failed to select policies that maximize this expected utility. Each of these possible failings—*nonintelligent calculation, inconsistent evaluation,* and *unreasoned choice*—deserves examination.

Nonintelligent Calculation

Nonintelligent calculation of possible courses of action and their costs and benefits involves a failure to gather and analyze—to "process"—available information intelligently. Information processing includes several distinguishable tasks involved in the "search" and "evaluation" stages of decision-making. It includes the collection and analysis of available information necessary for the identification of possible courses of action and estimation of the probable outcomes associated with them.

The intelligent calculation requirement for rationality does *not* mean that to be rational a decision-maker needs to, or will, seek to gather and analyze with infinite precision all possible information relevant to identifying and assessing courses of action. In other words, a rational decision-maker will generally not maximize his knowledge about his options and their expected consequences.

This reflects the fact that a rational actor seeks to maximize his net utility, not the gross benefits accruing from a particular decision. These ends differ because information processing involves costs in terms of time and other physical and psychological resources. There is an opportunity cost associated with information processing. The rational decision-maker therefore makes a trade-off. As Downs has explained:

> The information-seeker continues to invest resources in procuring data until the marginal return from information equals its marginal cost. At that point, assuming decreasing marginal returns or increasing marginal costs or both, he has enough information and makes his decision.[35]

It is typically assumed that a "rational" chess player would attempt to calculate all possible sequences of moves, an impossibly difficult task.[36] Clearly, however, our rational player would not behave in this fashion: he would not ponder a move for as long as it takes him to analyze all possible sequences. First, even if such behavior were permitted or feasible, the player's interest in winning this particular game is limited: there may be other things he wants eventually to do before he dies of old age. Second, if time constraints are imposed on the game, use of excessive amounts of time on any given move will jeopardize the player's ability to win even this particular game: the value of a single better move must be traded off against the shadow price of the decision-making resource (in this case, clock time) expended.

How much information a rational decision-maker actually gathers and analyzes will depend on several factors. Downs has suggested that:

> Three factors determine the size of his planned investment [in information]. The first is the value to him of making the correct decision as opposed to an incorrect one, i.e., the variation in utility incomes associated with the possible outcomes of his decision. The second is the relevance of the information to whatever decision is being made. Is acquisition of this particular bit of knowledge likely to influence the decision one way or another? If so, how likely? To answer these questions, a probability estimate must be made of the chances that any given bit of information will alter his decision. This probability is then applied to the value of making the right choice. . . . From this emerges the return from the bit of information being considered, i.e., the marginal return from investment in data on this particular margin. The third factor is the cost of data. The marginal cost of any bit of information consists of the returns foregone in obtaining it.[37]

But how can a decision-maker rationally decide whether he has collected and analyzed enough information? He will process information until marginal expected cost of processing information equals marginal expected benefit, but this calculation of expected cost and expected benefit itself involves information. How much of *this* information should rationally be processed? Plainly, there is the danger of an infinite regression here: to conclude that the marginal cost of information equals marginal benefit and that he has enough information to select a policy, a rational decision-maker must also gather information on the marginal cost and benefit of additional information until the marginal cost of this second-order information (information on information) equals marginal benefit, and so on, *ad infinitum*. Clearly, for our rational decision-maker to function he must be allowed to make an initial assignment of probabilities about the cost and benefit of additional information, an assignment which is then adjusted by later evidence. In other words, our decision-maker must be allowed to use a Bayesian probability calculation. This is not so unreasonable an allowance. As Downs has noted, there exists a previous stream of free information which permits the initial estimation of marginal cost and benefit functions.[38]

What then would it mean to fail to use information intelligently and why might this occur? Intelligence is the ability to learn and to deal effectively with a changing environment. Intelligent calculation of options, costs, and benefits involves the application of one's existing knowledge in obtaining and applying new information in order to solve new problems effectively.[39] Glenn Snyder has noted that failure to process information intelligently "may stem from such sources as commitment to a dogma or theory which is inapplicable to the situation or which shuts out relevant data; education, training, and experience which prevents attainment of the 'whole view'; or limited or distorted perspectives resulting from bureaucratic parochialism."[40]

In his discussion of rationality under conditions of uncertainty, Anatol Rapoport has suggested that a decision-maker need only be rational *relative to his own system of beliefs about reality.*[41] Rationality, in this view, does not impose any standards on the decision-maker's assumptions about how the world works—it does not speak to the realism of his cognitive "road maps" and "rules of thumb" about other actors, causal relationships, and his own capabilities. It says only that, given these cognitive models, the decision-maker strives to maximize his utility. This standard seems insufficient for our purposes, however. As Downs has pungently noted: "Even hopeless psychotics often behave with perfect rationality, given their warped perception of reality."[42] As a consequence, our requirement for the intelligent use of information is more burdensome: *the cognitive belief system itself must meet standards of rationality.* In order for the use of information in identifying options and calculating costs and benefits to be intelligent, the cognitive framework within which a decision-maker processes information must itself be intelligently derived. To return to an earlier example, staying away from cars may be a smart thing to do if one believes that cars are extraterrestrials that eat people, but if one has no credible evidence that cars come from outer space and do in fact eat people—and has much evidence that this is not the case—then such a belief system itself is nonintelligent and irrational. Regardless of how effectively one uses information to identify options that allow one to avoid cars, such calculation is not intelligent and such decision-making not rational.

Inconsistent Evaluation

The second type of irrationality involves failure by the decision-maker to aggregate values and order preferences in a consistent fashion. Not only must a decision-maker use information intelligently to identify possible policies and assess the costs and benefits of their probable outcomes, *he must evaluate the utility of these costs and benefits in a consistent fashion.* As Alexander George and Richard Smoke have noted: "Decision theory presumes within the concept of rationality that the actor's value hierarchy is itself internally consistent."[43] Since a rational decision-maker must possess a single, consistent utility function, the second possible reason why decision-making may be irrational can be described as "inconsistent evaluation."

In general, inconsistent evaluation may arise in two dimensions. First, it may occur across issue areas. For example, the values on which I implicitly order my policy preferences regarding career questions may differ from those on which I implicitly order my choices regarding life style. In making career decisions I may rank success highly and personal goals as unimportant; in making life-style decisions, by contrast, I may rank family happiness as a major goal and power and fame as minor ones. Like so many people who engage in this sort of inconsistent evaluation, I will probably end up making mutually incompatible time commitments and will achieve neither my career goals nor my personal ones. This inconsistency in my evaluation of what I value—of the net utility yielded by the costs and benefits of various policies—makes my decision-making process irrational. Analogously, the United States may base domestic energy production policy on one weighting of values and ordering of preferences while basing policy preferences regarding the use of force in Southwest Asia on another. (A more notorious example deals with tobacco: as part of its farm policy the United States subsidizes the production of tobacco, while as part of its health policy the United States attempts to minimize its consumption.)

Second, inconsistent evaluation may occur temporally. I may prefer A to B today and B to A tomorrow. Temporal consistency does not in any sense require permanence of preference orderings. Rather, rationality requires consistent evaluation only within the relevant time period. If I am faced with the choice of attending either the symphony or the opera, it is necessary only that my preferences—my ordering of how much I value the net benefits of each of the alternative outcomes—remain consistent from the time I buy the tickets to the time I use them. For my purchase of opera tickets to be rational behavior I need not still prefer Wagner to Beethoven after the performance, nor need I have preferred Wagner to Beethoven before purchasing the tickets. In many cases, however, the relevant time period extends well into the future. A drunk driver, for example, may temporarily value excitement more and safety less. Even if his inebriated state does not prevent him from intelligently calculating the consequences of driving intoxicated, his drunken decision to drive recklessly is irrational: in the morning—when he sobers up and the weighting of values in his utility function reverts to that of a model citizen—he will still have to pay the costs incurred the night before (e.g., fines, a jail sentence, a revoked driver's license, social condemnation, and psychic guilt), and in an evaluation made in the morning's harsh light these costs outweigh the thrill.

Inconsistent evaluation may arise in two ways. First, a *unitary* decision-maker may lack a single, consistent value system. An individual may be psychologically unable to reconcile inconsistent objectives, either across issue areas or time. This does not appear to be an uncommon human difficulty.[44]

Second, and more importantly, inconsistent evaluation of the costs and benefits of particular outcomes may arise *because the decision-maker is not a unitary actor.* Decisions—such as whether to wage nuclear war—are not made by single individuals acting in isolation but by organizations. As we will note below, organizations are likely to find ordering values consistently across issue areas and time difficult.

Unreasoned Choice

The final possible failing in decision-making is *a failure to act in accordance with evaluations of expected utility.* In this case, where selection of policy is unrelated to estimates of utility, "unreasoned choice" is occurring. Unreasoned choice is random choice, or choice that is not goal-oriented, whatever the nature of the actor's goals. ("Masochistic" choice—deliberate selection of policies that impose pain on oneself—is not unreasoned choice; it merely suggests the existence of a utility function that associates positive rather than negative utility with the sensation of pain.) Daydreamers and sleepwalkers, or extraordinarily hot-tempered individuals, are obvious practitioners of unreasoned choice.

Summary

As Schelling has put it, rationality implies the existence "not just of intelligent behavior, but of behavior motivated by a conscious calculation of advantages, a calculation that in turn is based on an explicit and internally consistent value system."[45] These requirements imply the three types of irrationality we have identified: non-intelligent calculation, unreasoned choice, and inconsistent evaluation.

Nonintelligent calculation can be understood as an inability to use available information to its full marginal value in developing an unbiased estimate of the costs and benefits of the possible policy options. Inconsistent evaluation reflects an inability to form a single consistent evaluation of the utility of predicted costs and benefits. Unreasoned choice is choice inconsistent with utility evaluations.

CAUSES OF IRRATIONALITY

If we assume that, were they able to do so, decision-makers would generally prefer to maximize their values, whatever these may be,[46] then there must be some reason for the irrationality and irrational behavior sometimes exhibited by real-world decision-makers. There must be some reason for failures to calculate options and payoffs intelligently, to evaluate the utility of these payoffs consistently, or to be guided by this evaluation in making policy choices.

Indeed, four sorts of reasons can be identified. Failure of rationality may be caused by *personality disorder, cognitive failure, situational stress,* or *organizational dysfunction.*[47] The first three causes suggest failure at the individual level of decision-making; the last, failure at a collective level. Of the causes of failure at the individual level, personality disorder suggests a flaw in the individual himself. Cognitive failure and situational stress involve difficulties arising not because of pathological abnormalities in the psychological makeup of the individual but because of the situation in which he is placed and "normal" human decision processes. Situational stress is sometimes described as a problem of "hot" cognitive process—that is, of the interaction of cognitive process and unusual pressure. By contrast, what we refer to as "cognitive failure" involves pathologies of normal "cold" cognitive processes.

Each of these causes of irrationality, alone or in combination with each other, may lead to one or more of the three types of failures of rationality (nonintelligent calculation, inconsistent evaluation, and unreasoned choice). Some causes of irrationality, however, are more likely to generate particular types of irrationality. Cognitive failure, for example, frequently results in nonintelligent calculation, while organizational dysfunction is an obvious source of inconsistent evaluation.

In the real world, of course, it may prove difficult to distinguish with any certainty the causes of one bit of irrational behavior or another. It is difficult to say with any conviction that one irrational act was caused by stress, not a personality disorder, or that another irrational act was a consequence of cognitive failure, not organizational dysfunction. Indeed, because there may be several contributing causes, such a statement is likely to be meaningless.

Nonetheless, because an increase in the probability of any of these four causal factors will mean an increase in the probability of irrationality, our focus on them is warranted. Voluminous tomes have been written on each of these topics; the discussion here is not meant to be definitive but to outline those points that are essential explicitly to add to an intuitive understanding in order to evaluate the role of irrational behavior in nuclear coercion.

Personality Disorder

By personality disorder we mean the existence of what Jack Snyder has summed up as "ideosyncratic psychopathologies that may prevent value optimization."[48] There may be some abnormality in the psychological makeup of key individuals which prevents them from adopting or implementing policies which would be effective in reaching their goals. Decision-makers may destructively undercut their own efforts to do better for themselves.

A certain tension inheres in such a definition, however. After all, is it not possible that psychopathological behavior, because it relieves or assuages internal psychological stresses, maximizes the psychological utility of the individual? If an individual is uncomfortable or feels guilty when he gets what he wants, might it not be rational for him to act counterproductively, so as to prevent the attainment of his stated goals? Is it possible that, in Downs' words, "behavior which is irrational according to our definition is highly rational in the psychic economy of the individual's personality"?[49] That is, is it possible that psychopathological behavior is rational, though not sensible?

We could try to solve this problem by accepting Downs' approach:

Neurotic behavior is often a necessary means of relieving tensions which spring from conflicts buried deep within the unconscious. But we are studying rational political behavior, not psychology or the psychology of political behavior. Therefore if a man exhibits political behavior which does not help him attain his political goals efficiently, we feel justified in labeling him politically irrational, no matter how necessary to his psychic adjustment this behavior may be.[50]

But how are we to discriminate legitimate "political" values from other values? After all, we have permitted our decision-maker to hold whatever values he happens to possess—emotional and pragmatic; self-regarding, collective, and other-regarding; national, organizational, and personal.

The solution proposed to this logical problem by Sidney Verba seems most satisfactory. Verba has argued that rational decision-making excludes what he has termed "non-logical influences," where "a non-logical influence is any influence acting upon the decision-maker of which he is unaware and which he would not consider a legitimate influence upon his decision if he were aware of it."[51] In other words, "if the individual chooses an alternative that does not maximize the goals that he consciously considers to be pertinent in the situation, the decision cannot be called rational even though it maximizes others of his values which he did not consider."[52] Thus if I know that throwing bricks at my neighbor's window will release pent-up aggressive instincts, and if a release of such instincts is something which I factor into my utility calculations, then my drive to throw bricks does not suggest a psychopathological personality but simply manifests one of the many values that must be considered when calculating the utility of various courses of behavior. If, however, I am unaware of my aggressive instinct and need for its release, or if I consider this an inappropriate value to factor into my utility calculations, then any decision to throw bricks which is driven by my aggressive instincts will be irrational.

Cognitive Failure

Because of the limitations of the human mind, individuals must rely on simplifications in dealing with information and making decisions. We cannot return to first principles every time we need to make a decision. Even if it were physically possible, the marginal cost of such an effort would usually far exceed the marginal gain from eliminating reliance on a belief system—a simplified cognitive heuristic framework or shorthand view of the world. Cognitive processes involving reliance on belief systems may be rational.[53] Indeed in some cases even reliance on patently incorrect belief systems may be rational: the physical and psychological effort of learning may be quite large in comparison to the costs of the errors caused by these cognitive models.

But if the costs of failing to learn promise to exceed the costs of learning, for cognitive processes to be rational, belief systems need to be altered as the decision-maker's environment changes and to be refined as his need for precision increases.[54] *Cognitive failure* reflects adherence by a decision-maker to an outdated or inappropriate system of beliefs—one which does not intelligently reflect or which inadequately summarizes the realities of interactions in the world. Old ideas—old systems of belief—die hard. There may be friction in the cognitive system: changes in the world (or changes in the world of the individual decision-maker, such as might occur when he moves into new postions or settings) may not be reflected in the decision-maker's simplified heuristic model in a timely fashion. As Knorr has put it, rationality

> may be hemmed in by ideological beliefs about the outside world. Such beliefs are, at their inception, rooted in human experience, and, at that state, they often represent realistic responses to a specific set of historical circumstances. They then permit simplifying assumptions of great value in forming and implementing foreign policy. However, their fit with reality is bound to diminish as circumstances change. Because these doctrines are deeply ingrained, they tend to resist ready adaptation or burial when the tests of reality indicate that their validity is vanishing, and they often end in a sterile reign of jargon that, nevertheless, traps people in postures too rigid to permit new perceptions and innovative action.[55]

Because a system of beliefs provides the framework for interpreting and employing new information—that is, for viewing oneself and the world—failure to adapt one's system of beliefs intelligently to reflect changing conditions or changing knowledge about conditions may lead to misperception about both one's own and others' intentions and capabilities. For example, failure to adapt beliefs about the utility of nuclear escalation to reflect the development of invulnerable nuclear arsenals or to take into account new evidence on the climatic effects of limited nuclear war is likely to result in a distorted view of costs, benefits, and probabilities. Because the human mind attempts to fit incoming information into existing cognitive frameworks and tends to distort or ignore discrepant information, the resistance of cognitive frameworks to change has the potential to cause an unmotivated bias in perception. Decision-makers see what their rigid cognitive belief systems lead them to expect.

Not all misperceptions, however, result from cognitive failures. Indeed, not all misperceptions involve irrationality at all. Though leading to objectively irrational behavior, misperceptions may occur in rational decision-making. In the absence of perfect information, even intelligent use of information may result in perceptions that are objectively incorrect.[56]

Situational Stress

Decisional stress is a common experience, one with which we are all familiar from our daily lives. Stress is associated with situations in which important values are perceived as being at stake and in which there is need for a decision.[57] The range of the potential effects of stress on decision-making is worth highlighting.

Stress may, for example, lead to nonintelligent calculation. Irving Janis and Leon Mann have found that stress—or, in their terminology, "severe decisional conflict"—can lead to two distinct decision-making pathologies. The first of these, "defensive avoidance," occurs in high stress situations in which the decision-maker has lost hope of finding an attractive solution. In such a case, the decision-maker is likely avoid recognizing threat cues: "Defensive avoidance is manifested by lack of vigilant search, selective inattention, selective forgetting, distortion of the meaning of warning messages, and construction of wishful rationalizations that minimize negative consequences."[58]

By contrast, situational stress may also lead to a pathology termed "hypervigilance." If a decision-maker in a high stress situation perceives threat cues as salient and sees options rapidly being foreclosed, he tends to experience cognitive constriction and disruption of his thought processes. In its most extreme form hypervigilance produces panic. As Janis and Mann have clinically noted:

> The person's immediate memory span is reduced and his thinking becomes more simplistic in that he cannot deal conceptually with as many categories as when he is in a less aroused state. Disaster studies indicate that panic is most likely to occur when people believe that the danger is great and the only available escape routes will soon be closed. Expecting that he will be helpless to avoid being victimized unless he acts quickly, the person in a state of hypervigilance fails to recognize all the alternatives open to him and fails to use whatever remaining time is available to evaluate adequately those alternatives of which he is aware. He is likely to search frantically for a solution, persevere in his thinking about a limited

number of alternatives, and then latch onto a hastily contrived solution that seems to promise immediate relief, often at the cost of considerable post-decisional regret.[59]

It is not difficult to imagine the occurrence of defensive avoidance —with its associated tactics of procrastinating, shifting responsibility, and "bolstering" of least objectionable options—during prolonged periods of international tension. Decision-makers are likely to avoid confronting pressing decisions, to delude themselves that they have no options (and that, by contrast, the opponent self-evidently has many), and to persuade themselves that whatever actions they do take are cost-free. Nor is it difficult to imagine the occurrence of hypervigilance in an international crisis—when, for example, pressures mount for a rapid decision to use nuclear weapons before the opponent launches a massive first blow. Under such conditions, decision-makers are likely to seize on the most obvious "solution" or "way out" of their predicament without considering the costs or other possible courses of action.[60]

In addition to nonintelligent calculation, however, situational stress may also result in inconsistent evaluation. Alexander George and Robert Keohane have noted the occurrence of what they describe as "value-extension" in times of crisis, when personal and personal-political values grow in importance and can come to overshadow "national" values.[61] In general, one would intuitively expect to see a transient increase in the importance of emotional values during periods of stress.

Both of these points about the possible impact of stress on decision-making—the potential for nonintelligent calculation (either as a result of defensive avoidance or of hypervigilance) and for inconsistent evaluation—are particularly relevant in thinking about nuclear war. Psychiatry professor Lester Grinspoon has summarized the possible effects of stress quite succinctly:

> Picture the situation of a national leader faced with what appears to be a massive nuclear attack which has come after a period of rising international tension. The chief decision-maker is overloaded with responsibility, probably tired and deprived of sleep, losing alertness, possibly aging or ill. He has about a half-hour to make a decision on which the fate of humanity may depend. . . . At the same time, fear brings feelings down to a primitive level and distorts perception. . . . His instinct will be to strike back in revenge, especially against an enemy who has been presented as the embodiment of evil. The desire to destroy the enemy may become greater than

the desire to stay alive, and it will be hard to stay calm and wait. There will be a strong desire for action to relieve the tension and punish the foe.[62]

While stress may exist and result in decision-making pathologies at times other than the outbreak of hostilities, decision-makers seem highly likely to suffer the effects of stress when there exists a clear possibility of war—i.e., during crisis—or when war actually begins or threatens to escalate. Lebow, for example, has noted the occurrence of emotional collapse—an extreme example of the effects of stress— of key decision-makers when war actually breaks out. He has commented on the incapacitation of the Kaiser as Germany stumbled into World War I; of Stalin when Hitler invaded the Soviet Union; and of Nasser in 1967 when the Israelis launched their preemptive blow.[63]

Stress may be a problem not only for the national leader but for the other participants in the decision-making process as well. Individuals around the president will be subject to much the same pressure that he is. This shared situational stress may exacerbate the detrimental effects on decision-making. Defensive avoidance, for example, seems particularly likely to occur in some types of small-group settings: Janis has documented and described the phenomenon of "groupthink" in closed, homogenous small groups.[64]

More importantly, however, events such as war may generate significant situational stress for some individuals involved in decision-making even when they do not generate significant amounts of stress at the center of the process. A limited conventional war in Europe, for example, may be extremely stressful for commanders of nuclear weapons in Europe even if it is much less so for individuals removed from the battlefield, in the relative safety of the White House, Pentagon, or airborne command post; this imposes difficult organizational requirements for sharing of information, aggregation of values, and control of subordinates. Clearly, therefore, the physical organization of the decision-making process—with its impact on who makes decisions, where, and under what circumstances—may be critical in determining whether stress will have a significant impact on a state's behavior.

Organizational Dysfunction

Personality disorder, cognitive failure, and situational stress all reflect problems that may affect the ability of individuals to engage in rational decision-making. These problems, of course, may be exacerbated by the setting in which individuals interact, but they all involve *human* failings. Even if individuals succeed in acting intelligently to maximize their consistently calculated expected utility, however, irrationality may still occur. As Daniel Frei has observed in considering how nuclear war might come about: "Even if men act in a rational way, Governments may not necessarily do so."[65]

The term "organizational dysfunction" covers a wide range of possible sins. For example, decision-makers may be organized in such an inefficient or inappropriate fashion that, either routinely or during periods of tension, information is not used to its full marginal value. The president and other central decision-makers charged with determining how the United States will use its nuclear forces may not be informed of the destination of incoming Soviet missiles, even though this information is "in the system." Perhaps more importantly for our purposes, though, organizational dysfunction may result in failure by the decision-maker to possess a single consistent ordering of preferences.

The whole notion of organizational dysfunction—the notion that decision-makers may suffer not only human failings (albeit perhaps made critical by group settings, as in "groupthink") but organizational ones as well—forces us to confront the fact that states are not individuals. It thus compels us to face the definitional question we have avoided to this point but which we must now resolve if we are to discuss rationality and coercion effectively: who or what is a state decision-maker? How can we visualize a decision-maker that is not simply a single individual?

The traditional approach to examining coercion, grounded in the realist school of intellectual analysis,[66] has been to assume a unitary actor *whose incentives reflect the national interest.* In noting the dangers of this approach, George and Smoke have argued that,

> In fact, of course, this simplification does great violence to the reality—in many cases sufficient violence that a national decision will seem either incomprehensible or "irrational" if viewed through the spectacles of this model. Almost any interesting decision taken by a modern state is the product of tugs-of-war among institutions within its society or bureaucracy, and of the personal and self-interested maneuverings of many top decision-makers. All these players have their own interpretation of the "national interest" in a given situation and, of course, also have their own purposes, which are not necessarily the same as "the national" purpose. . . . With respect specifically to deterrence theory, it is vital to keep con-

stantly and clearly in mind the fact that one must deter not an opponent "nation" or "player" but a majority of the relevant individuals, groups, and/or institutions in decision-making circles within that nation.[67]

A more useful approach, therefore, is to define "decision-maker" as a collection of those individuals, groups, and organizations with significant input into the decision-making process. The composition of the decision-maker is likely to change not only as the structure of the process changes over (long or extremely short) periods of time but also as the definition of the decision problem changes.[68]

This definition of a decision-maker offers the possibility of recognizing and summing all relevant levels of analysis in describing the state actor's utility function. Any state decision-maker will be sensitive to a number of interests—individual (personal and personal-political), bureaucratic and organizational, state, and special (e.g., class) interests—in addition to the national one.

Among the definition's less obvious implications is that maximization of the decision-maker's expected utility must take into account not only the external effects of various policies—that is, their effect on the decision-maker's position vis-à-vis other states and its own domestic audience—but also their internal effects as well. Accomplishment of a state's international and domestic goals must be weighed against negative internal effects that may affect ability to achieve future ends. A rational state decision-maker looking at the total stream of costs and benefits will examine the probable consequences not only in the international and domestic environment but in its own internal operational environment. A policy that promises to generate dissent within the decision-maker—expressed in the form of either psychological stress or organizational conflict—may not be rational even if it improves the decision-maker's international and domestic position. This, by the way, obviously has implications for the problem of determining the optimal amount of information processing: if gathering and analyzing information has costs in terms of internal cohesion, then the amount of information processing rationally undertaken will be less than would otherwise have been the case.[69]

For our purposes, two types of nonunitary decision-making need to be distinguished. First, the decision-maker may have a *collective* decision center: although the actor can be modeled as a single decision center, power within that center is shared by a collection of individuals or groups.

Shared power in policy choice is exemplified by decision-making in a democratic forum (where choice is by majority action) and in a collegial forum (where choice is by consensus). But the sharing of power may occur in policy formulation or implementation as well as in policy choice. On the one hand, even when a single individual (such as the president) is charged with policy choice, he is likely to rely on other individuals for gathering and analyzing information on options, costs, and benefits. He is, in other words, likely to share power with advisers and the bureaucracies that control access to information and specialized knowledge. On the other hand, a unitary actor such as the president is likely also to have to rely on colleagues and bureaucracies for implementation of the policy chosen. If the chosen policy cannot be implemented unilaterally—by, say, simply pressing a button—the central decision-maker shares power with those subordinates who must interpret his instructions, translating commands that may or may not be ambiguous into actual policies in the field. As a consequence of this advice and interpretation, even if single individuals control policy choice, the decision-maker is more accurately modeled as a nonunitary actor.

Shared decision-making power raises the problem of determining what is in fact *collectively* rational:

> A serious difficulty arises for theories of utility maximization whenever a decision is to be made not by an individual, but by a group of persons. If the decision is to maximize utility not for an individual, but for the group, then the utilities of the individual must somehow be combined to provide a group utility (or expected utility) for each alternative. If the utility functions for one member of the group were identical with those of each of the other members of the group, then, of course, this problem would be trivial. But if, as is highly probable, utility functions do vary from one member to another, then the question of how utilities are combined in arriving at a group decision is an unsolved problem.[70]

Real-life nonunitary decision-makers do, of course, succeed in implicitly aggregating utility functions, weighting the individual utility functions by the power of the individual. The problem, however, is that nonunitary decision-makers are unlikely to aggregate utility functions in a consistent fashion across issue areas or time.[71] In practice, the way utilities are combined in coming to a group decision reflects the relative power of group members, but the relative power of group members—indeed, as we noted above, even the identity of group members—is likely to change both from issue to issue and from time period to time period. As a consequence, decisions in foreign policy areas heavily influenced by, say, the Agriculture Department (e.g., decisions to sell grain to the USSR) may be inconsistent with those in areas heavily influenced by the State or Defense Departments (e.g., decisions to block the sale of pipeline equipment to the USSR). The weight accorded various values (e.g., a prosperous farm sector, good relations with allies, military security) in calculating the collective good is likely to vary. Since both the identity and relative power of participants in the decision process are likely to vary with issue area and time, to the extent that participants do not share precisely the same set of values, the decision-maker's utility function (and therefore preference ordering) will be inconsistent.[72]

Second, though, in addition to having collective decision-making in which power is shared, a decision-maker may have *multiple* decision centers, each wielding *independent* power. Decision centers are independent when none possesses credible sanctions that would cause other centers to bend to its will. Sanctions might be either positive or negative and involve either physical or psychological inducements. For example, to say that the officers of a nuclear missile submarine do not constitute a decision center independent of the National Command Authorities is to say that those officers will obey orders from the National Command Authorities. They will launch their missiles as commanded—even if they prefer not to and have the physical capability to disobey—because (for example) they fear for their careers or (given that their careers are likely to be short in any case) simply because they feel it is wrong to disobey.

Short of complete independence, decision centers may enjoy conditional independence, negative independence, or both. Conditional independence suggests that some set of circumstances will trigger independence. Destruction of communication links between the National Command Authorities and the submarine officers, for example, may result in the latter's independence. Negative independence suggests that each decision center has a veto power over the actions of the other. An independently minded B-52 crew and the National Command Authorities, for example, may be negatively independent: neither can arm the aircraft's nuclear payload without the coooperation of the other.[73]

Multiple decision centers pose the problem of *differences* between collective and individual rationality:

> in terms of what objectives, whose values, shall rationality be judged?
> Is behavior of an individual in an organization rational when it serves his personal objectives or when it serves the organizational

objectives? Two soldiers sit in a trench opposite a machine-gun nest. One of them stays under cover. The other, at the cost of his life, destroys the machine-gun nest with a grenade. Which is rational?[74]

The commander of a naval battle group, faced with destruction of his force and the deaths of the sailors under his command unless he authorizes use of nuclear anti-aircraft or anti-submarine weapons, will possess a very different utility function than does the state decision-maker as a whole. The commander of a nuclear missile battery in Europe who knows that his immediate family, close comrades, and friends have already perished in Soviet attacks on NATO installations in West Germany and that he himself faces imminent death regardless of whether he fires the missiles under his control or allows them to be destroyed, provides a similar, though perhaps more dramatic, example. Thus, in the absence of perfect centralized control, individual rationality can be expected to have some likelihood of leading to collective irrationality.

IRRATIONAL, INADVERTENT, AND ACCIDENTAL WAR

Given this understanding of rationality and irrationality in the real world, it seems useful finally to turn to the question of rationality and irrationality during war. Since we are interested in examining the utility of threats irrationally to wage nuclear war, it behooves us to be explicit in defining what we mean by terms such as "irrational war" and "irrational escalation."

"Irrational war" could mean a number of different things. By "irrational war" we mean one the entry into which represents irrational behavior: had the actor possessed a rational decision-making process he would not have entered the war. Similarly, any escalatory step that the actor, if rational, would not have chosen to carry out can be described as "irrational escalation."

Irrational actions can be distinguished from "inadvertent" and "accidental" ones. An understanding of the logical distinction between irrational, inadvertent, and accidental actions not only serves to refine our notions of irrational war and escalation, but to provide a foundation for understanding various logically distinct threats to use nuclear weapons.

Inadvertent War

Earlier in this chapter we noted that an objectively irrational pattern of behavior might result from rational decision-making. Because of the existence of risk and uncertainty in the world, bad outcomes may follow from rational decisions. Thus, rationality is not a sure-fire prescription for avoiding disaster. As Secretary of Defense Robert McNamara pointed out—although about possible Communist behavior—in his famous Ann Arbor address of 1962:

> the mere fact that no nation could rationally take steps leading to a nuclear war does not guarantee that a nuclear war cannot take place. Not only do nations sometimes act in ways that are hard to explain on a rational basis, *but even when acting in a "rational" way they sometimes, indeed disturbingly often, act on the basis of misunderstandings of the true facts of the situation. They misjudge the way others will react, and the way others will interpret what they are doing.*[75]

The ultimate consequences of policies are not always—indeed, are seldom—clear in advance. Even if they are, the counterfactual—what will happen if we do not act—is unlikely to be clear. Thus, even if we act intelligently on the basis of all the evidence worth collecting and in a fashion intended to maximize our consistently evaluated expected utility, our actions may fail to maximize actual utility. In other words, rational behavior may have *inadvertent* consequences.

What does it mean to say that a war is inadvertent?

> To the extent that all war is to be avoided, any war is "inadvertent." We must, however, distinguish between those initiated at some point in history "in cold blood" and with full knowledge of the relevant factors, and those which would be judged "after the fact" as "unnecessary"—that is, those initiated due to a miscalculation based on inadequate information *at the time.*[76]

What, then, does it mean to say that the decision to use nuclear weapons or to escalate an ongoing conflict might be inadvertent? Is such a thing plausible? Klaus Knorr has observed that

> Any limited conflict—for instance, a conventional war—between nuclear powers carries the risk of escalating to the strategic level at which, as long as the mutual balance of terror prevails, the payoffs are hugely negative for both contestants. The risk of *deliberate* escalation may be small, if not infinitesimal, under these conditions; the risk of *inadvertent* escalation may be greater. . . .
> The inadvertent precipitation of nuclear war remains a substan-

tial risk. One crisis or even several crises, well managed do not insure that every crisis will subside or be terminated without a fatal mis-step. Governments *are* capable of blunder; and, after all, Khrushchev evidently acted on a serious miscalculation of the United States reaction when he authorized Soviet missiles to be emplaced in Cuba. Risks are hard to calculate.[77]

This point lends insight into how the United States might logically claim that it could behave rationally and yet ultimately engage in a strategic nuclear war—and at the same time hold that a strategic nuclear war would be disastrous for all concerned.

After all, if information is imperfect or if risk exists, any series of decisions, *each one rational*, may lead to an increasingly nonoptimal outcome. For example, consider a typical defense strategist's nightmare: political instability in the Persian Gulf threatens important U.S. interests. Acting under both risk and uncertainty, but intelligently calculating that the likelihood of Soviet response is low, the United States might rationally undertake military action. Conflict with the Soviet Union might thus begin inadvertently: had the United States known that war with the Soviet Union would result, it would not have pursued the policy it did. U.S. policy may be judged after the fact to have unnecessarily brought on conflict with the Soviet Union. The possibilities for inadvertence do not end here, however. Despite the fact that the United States did not seek war with the Soviet Union and would have given much to avoid it, once war has begun it may be rational for the United States to escalate its involvement—perhaps by attacking Soviet staging bases or forces at sea—in the hope of terminating the war on terms favorable to the West. If the United States is lucky and its intelligent calculations are correct, then this rational escalation will prove (given that the United States had inadvertently gotten itself into this situation) to be objectively rational; if the United States has again misjudged the Soviet response, then this escalation will in itself have inadvertent consequences. Many small unlucky (but rational) guesses may compound over time to yield horrible outcomes.

Misjudgment thus does not necessarily imply irrationality. It does, however, imply decision by human actors. It implies the existence of an objectively irrational choice by decision-makers at one or more points in the stream of decisions leading to or through war. As Stephen Maxwell has noted:

> Inadvertent war is one in which mechanical failure plays no part. The failure is one of political judgment. For example, a statesman

might under-estimate the value of a disputed objective to an opponent and escalate the conflict to a level which the opponent considered to be beyond the point of no return. Alternatively, a contestant who would have judged a particular objective to be not worth nuclear war might deliberately initiate nuclear war over the objective, following repeated declarations of commitment which increased not the value of the objective, but the penalty of failing to honour the commitment.[78]

Accidental War

Of course, the term "inadvertent" is sometimes used less precisely. Schelling, for example, has spoken of war initiated inadvertently as war initiated "through some kind of accident, false alarm, or mechanical failure; through somebody's panic, madness, or mischief; through a misapprehension of enemy intentions or a correct apprehension of the enemy's misapprehension of ours."[79] The third of these three sets of causes is what we have described as inadvertence; the second approximates what we have described as irrationality; only the first is what we shall term "accidental."

Accidental war is war that arises without choice, either rational or irrational, or that follows rationally from an act that was undertaken without choice. Thinking about possible paths to nuclear war, Maxwell has suggested that:

> To describe a nuclear war as accidental could mean two different things. For it is just conceivable that a full strategic exchange between two states could be caused *exclusively* by mechanical failure, without the intervention of human decision. It is a question for philosophers whether a nuclear exchange, from which intention was absent, could properly be called a war at all. More commonly, "accidental" has been applied to intentional nuclear exchanges which have been caused partly by an initial mechanical failure. A popular scenario for this sort of war begins with the malfunctioning of a "fail-safe" device and develops, *via* mutual fear of preemptive attack, into a full strategic exchange.[80]

Why distinguish between events resulting from irrationality, inadvertence, and accident? For our purposes, these distinctions are important because they have different implications for credibility. A threat irrationally to use nuclear weapons is different from one inadvertently to use them, which is different still from a threat accidently to use them. Very different factors are involved in making each threat credible. We will have reason to recall these distinctions when, in chapter 4, we consider modes of commitment. To threaten an *inadvertent* nuclear response to provocation is to claim that one is committed to using nuclear weapons because a rational, though mistaken, decision to use nuclear weapons will be made; in the terms we will develop in chapter 4, such a threat involves a putative "commitment-through-rationality." To threaten an *accidental* nuclear response to provocation is to claim that one is committed to using nuclear weapons because one has denied oneself mechanical control over one's own actions; we will call this "commitment-through-denial-of-choice." Finally, to threaten an *irrational* nuclear response to provocation is to claim that one is committed to using nuclear weapons because one will lack the capacity for rational decision-making; this can be described as a "commitment-through-irrationality."

Having at least superficially explored the notions of rationality and irrationality and considered why irrational behavior might occur and what "irrational war" might mean, it is now possible to examine in theoretical terms how irrationality may be used in deterrence. To this end, we now turn our attention to the logic of coercion.

3

COERCIVE POWER AND
COERCIVE STRATEGIES

SUCCESSFUL DETERRENCE requires coercive power. To understand what aspects of U.S. nuclear force posture are logically associated with successful deterrence and the role that irrationality might play, we must thus step back and examine the phenomenon of power—the ability to achieve a desired outcome in a situation involving some disharmony of interests.

Four questions arise. First, what is coercive power and what are the necessary and sufficient conditions for its existence? Second—a question prompted by the answer to the first—what does it mean to suggest that an opponent is coercible? Third, what are the logically possible modes of nuclear coercion? Fourth, what are the demands on rational action associated with each of these modes of coercion?

COERCIVE POWER

Power represents the ability to achieved a desired outcome.

Coercive power represents the ability to achieve a desired outcome *by influencing another actor's behavior.* More precisely, as Klaus Knorr has suggested:

> When power is used coercively, an actor (B) is influenced if he adapts his behavior in compliance with, or in anticipation of, another actor's (A) demands, wishes, or proposals. B's conduct is then affected by something A does, or by something he expects A to do. In consequence, B will modify his behavior (if he would not have done so otherwise), or he will not change his behavior (if he would have altered it in the absence of external influence).[1]

In other words, coercion of B by A involves A's structuring of his own threatened actions in such a way that B adapts his behavior and chooses the course of action that A prefers. B is, thus, either *"compelled"* to do something A wishes be done (that is, B chooses to initiate some action desired by A) or is *deterred* from doing something that A wishes not be done.[2] From B's perspective, B is faced with the *threat* of some pain if he does not yield, the *promise* of some reward if he does yield, or both. As a consequence, B alters his behavior.

Coercion thus involves altering the relative attractiveness of the various courses of action open to an opponent. Whether this alteration involves increasing the pain (or decreasing the pleasure) associated with the policy the coercer seeks to discourage, reducing the pain (or adding to the pleasure) associated with the policy the coercer wishes to encourage, or both, at least implicitly coercion involves *both* a negative sanction (for noncompliance) and a positive sanction or "assurance" (for compliance).

Because we are interested in the problem of *nuclear* coercion, our discussion will tend to focus fairly exclusively on threats and ignore promises. Clearly, though, the positive sanction or "assurance" a coercer must offer his opponent about the consequences of yielding to a nuclear threat may involve a promise of some positive reward, rather than a commitment to maintain the status quo or to impose less pain if the opponent complies than if he does not. That is, when I threaten my neighbor with a beating if he does not do as I demand, the positive sanction I offer for his compliance may be a reward of ten dollars, rather than simply a commitment not to beat him or to beat him only halfheartedly. Our focus on the negative sanction involved in nuclear coercion should not obscure the fact that coercion—either deterrence or compellence—involves giving the opponent a choice. It involves giving him a choice, but also giving him a reason to prefer to behave as the coercer wishes him to. Thus the character of the positive sanction may be as important as that of the negative sanction; deterrence and compellence may fail because the assurance is not sufficiently clear or certain, or because the positive sanction fails to include a sufficiently large reward.[3]

Coercive power is only one of two types of power. Coercion is only one of two ways of using power resources to achieve a desired end. Power resources (i.e., military, economic, and political-penetrative assets) may also be wielded in a *direct* fashion. Direct power involves the application of power resources "to modify or preserve a status quo between actors *without any attempt to secure compliance.*"[4] While coercive power represents the ability to gain one's end by altering an opponent's behavior, direct power represents the ability to gain one's end despite or irrespective of an opponent's behavior. A bank robber may use a stick of dynamite to relieve a banker of his treasure by blowing the safe open himself or by coercing the banker into opening the safe by threatening to blow him up.

Though the same power resources can be used directly or coercively, direct power may exist when coercive power does not. In the early 1980s, for example, the Israelis lacked the coercive power to make the Iraqis halt their development of an Osirak nuclear reactor facility but had the power resources to stop it directly. There also may be some objectives that an actor could win through coercion but *prefers* to gain directly. Obviously this might be the case if costly "promises" are involved in coercion—that is, if some expensive reward must be given for compliance—but it also may be the case if no rewards are offered. A new police officer on a beat may prefer to bring in a lawbreaker forcibly rather than peacefully because of the reputation it gives him among his new colleagues and among the criminal class.[5]

Conversely, though, coercive power may exist when direct power does not. In 1915, the United States could not prevent German submarines from waging unrestricted war but could, by threatening involvement in the European conflict, coerce Germany into temporarily altering its submarine activities. Indeed, there are some objectives that, if a conflict of interest exists, can be achieved only through coercion. Typically, making peace is one such objective: one cannot directly force an opponent to end hostilities (though one may be able to destroy his ability to wage war effectively); one may, however, be able to convince him to do so. Similarly, today, the United States cannot directly prevent the Soviets from destroying American cities, U.S. military facilities, or the cities and military facilities of U.S. allies; the United States may, however, be able to deter the Soviets from doing these things.[6]

Conditions for the Existence of Coercive Power

Empirical work has suggested a long string of variables that are likely to be related to successful coercion.[7] By moving from an empirical to an analytical framework, however, it is possible to be rather precise about the exact requirements for coercive power. There are exactly two necessary conditions for the existence of coercive power;

taken together, these two also represent the sufficient conditions for the existence of coercive power.

First, the opponent must be coercible. There must be some coercive strategy available to the coercer which would lead his opponent to choose to yield.[8] In other words, for A to be able to coerce B, *B must have a contingent strategy.* B's behavior *must depend on* the strategy chosen by A. If B would choose the policy A prefers regardless of the strategy A pursues, then B is not being coerced. If B would never choose the policy A prefers (or would choose it only in response to conditions over which A has no control), then B cannot be coerced by A. If B's behavior is contingent on the coercive strategy chosen by A, we will say that B is "coercible," or that the coercer possesses "an effective coercive strategy."

Second, for coercive power to exist the coercer must have the capacity credibly to commit himself to the effective coercive strategy. The coercer must be able to convince his opponent that he will actually carry out the strategy that would lead the opponent to yield. The mere existence of an ability to inflict or withhold tremendous pain is logically not sufficient to result in coercive power: the idea of "existential" nuclear deterrence—the notion that simply because nuclear weapons exist, they deter—is logically false. For nuclear deterrence to operate, the opponent must also believe that the coercer is committed to a strategy that has some unacceptable probability of resulting in nuclear war if deterrence fails.

These two conditions for coercive power—the existence of a coercible opponent (an opponent with a contingent strategy) and the ability credibly to commit oneself to an effective coercive strategy—deserve further attention. In this chapter we will proceed by examining the concept of coercibility and the problem of ensuring that the opponent has a contingent strategy. In the following chapter we will consider our second requirement, credible commitment, in greater detail.

COERCIBILITY

States faced with demands from powerful neighbors—demands either to change the status quo or to refrain from changing it—are not always coercible. They do not always have contingent strategies. There are two reasons why this may be so.

First, the target of coercive pressure may in fact rationally find that suffering the comparative unpleasantness imposed by the coercer is preferable to yielding. The would-be coercer may not possess a negative sanction dreadful enough or a positive sanction sweet enough to induce a rational opponent to alter his behavior (although it is possible that the same sanctions might induce an irrational opponent to alter his behavior).[9]

Second, the target of coercive pressure may be unable to act in accord with a rational preference to yield: he may either suffer from some form of irrationality that causes him to be insensitive to threatened sanctions or he may have somehow already irrevocably surrendered control over his policies. Thus the coercibility of an opponent depends not only on the coercer's ability to inflict pain or provide pleasure but on the opponent's ability to modify his behavior in response to these incentives. Ironically, as a consequence, if increases in the size of the coercer's threat reduce an opponent's ability to respond rationally to these threats, greater and greater threats may make the opponent less and less coercible. More generally, a coercive strategy that leads to cognitive failure, situational stress, or organizational dysfunction in the opponent's decision-making runs a significant risk of being ineffective. Obviously, since these causes of decision-making failings do not always result in irrationality, since irrationality does not always result in irrational behavior, and since irrational behavior may involve passive yielding as well as rigid unyielding, a coercive strategy that creates these problems for an opponent's decision-maker is not necessarily doomed to ineffectiveness. But in designing a coercive strategy it is imperative to take into account the strategy's likely impact on the opponent's capacity for rational action. As we shall observe in greater detail in chapter 8, one of the great failings of the U.S. Countervailing nuclear strategy and one of the serious dangers associated with continuing to pursue present policies is that, because of its emphasis on the acquisition of nuclear capabilities for threats that rationally could be executed, the current U.S. coercive strategy makes it hard for Soviet decision-makers to act upon a rational preference to yield.

Rational Preferences to Yield

But a coercive strategy may also fail because it does not result in a rational preference to yield. As a consequence, it is necessary to explore when a rational preference to yield will exist. What conditions will lead an opponent rationally to prefer to yield?

It was suggested in the preceding chapter that "decision-makers" in problems of international coercion need to be understood as aggregations of those individuals and organizations within the state with significant ability to affect the state's behavior. We noted that this implied that a decision-maker will have a number of interests besides the "national" one. The decision-maker's utility function will reflect some weighted summation of preferences at all relevant levels of analysis (e.g., personal, small-group, organizational, national).

If the state decision-maker subject to coercive pressure is rational, whether or not it has a contingent strategy will depend on six factors. In a situation in which a state is being pressured to eschew launching an offensive war, the first of these factors is the potentially aggressive state's valuation of its war objectives—the value accruing to the potential aggressor from the control of a piece of territory and its population and from the destruction of military, economic, and political assets belonging to other states. The second factor is the probability that the aggressive state will achieve its objectives, given the coercer's various possible responses. The third is the cost the aggressive state expects to have to bear, again given the coercer's various possible responses. The fourth is the potential aggressor's estimate of the probability of each of these various possible responses by the coercer.[10] The fifth factor is the potential aggressor's surprise aversion —that is, the disutility he associates with the existence of lack of certainty about the outcomes he may experience if he is not deterred. There may be some disutility associated simply with not knowing what is going to happen; lack of certainty by itself may impose physical or psychological costs. A rational actor may prefer policies whose outcomes have a high degree of certainty over those whose outcomes are less certain.[11] These five factors can be combined to give a measure of the expected utility associated with being undeterred.

The sixth factor is the expected utility associated with being deterred. There is no reason to expect that the costs or benefits of being deterred will equal zero. "Being deterred" need not have the same costs and benefits as "not having had the intention and not being dissuaded." Indeed, it is conceivable that a decision-maker may find net utility in selecting a goal and being deterred from attempting it by a coercer's pressure. First, in order to deter, the coercer may promise and dispense rewards for compliance. Second, even if no rewards are involved, the existence of external threats may provide important benefits for the actor being coerced. As the target of coercive pressure, I may gain sympathy and support from concerned neighbors. As a national leader, I may find it possible to carry out unpopular measures because an outside power has imposed costs on my preferred course of behavior. I may, for example, be able to gain support for an unpopular armament program or for an austerity budget because a coercer has forced my state to alter its agenda; I may even gain generalized political support as part of a rally-around-the-leader reaction, support that will allow me personally to remain in power or to achieve domestic objectives.

More typically, however, yielding to coercive pressure would be expected to have net costs rather than net benefits, both in the external and internal environments. While the costs of yielding to coercive pressure are logically likely to be lower in deterrence situations than in compellence ones (both because yielding to deterrent threats is less likely to involve giving something up and because it is less likely to require conspicuous and embarrassing compliance),[12] being deterred may still leave an actor worse off than he was before. Being deterred involves a loss of face, even though the audience may be small— indeed may be limited to oneself. It is ironic but true that the boy given a new airgun but told that his father will whip him if he uses it is likely to be unhappier than the boy without an airgun.

As our definition of rationality suggests, a rational decision-maker will have a contingent strategy if the intelligently calculated and consistently evaluated expected utility of yielding is greater than that of not yielding. If the state decision-maker being coerced is not rational, however, it may still have a contingent strategy. Indeed, irrationality may result in oversensitivity to sanctions: an irrational decision-making process may cause a state to yield to coercive pressure which it would not have yielded to rationally. Before World War II, for example, the British failed to use intelligently the information available to them to calculate rationally the true effects of German bombing. As a result the British greatly overestimated the likely damage and were more cautious in opposing Germany than they might otherwise have been.[13]

Coercive Strategies

What types of strategy could a coercer adopt that might result in his opponent's having a rational preference to yield? That is, what sorts of coercive threats would result in coercibility for a rational or oversensitive opponent?

Obviously, any coercive strategy may be pure or mixed. A coercive strategy may involve imposing pain (given noncompliance) with 100 percent probability or with some probability less than 100 percent. That is, a strategy may threaten the *certainty* of pain in the event of noncompliance or it may threaten some *risk* of pain in the event of noncompliance. Similarly, a strategy may threaten the certainty of some reward (whether it be an improvement over the status quo, the maintenance of the status quo, or simply a smaller penalty) in the event of compliance or the probabilistic chance of it.[14] I may, for example, be committed to shoot you if you trespass in my garden—a contingent but pure strategy. (That is, my shooting you is *contingent* on your trespass; *given* that you are in my garden I will shoot you with 100 percent probability.) Or I may be committed to shoot *at* you if you trespass, but with a pistol with only half the chambers loaded or from a distance that statistically gives me only a 50 percent chance of hitting you—a contingent mixed strategy.[15]

Coercive strategies that are probabilistic in their imposition of pain are generally said to involve "threats that leave something to chance."[16] A threat that leaves something to chance has two fundamental characteristics. First, given that the threat is executed, whether pain is inflicted or not lies outside the control of the threatener. If, although only half my bullets will hit their target, I can *decide* which half, then I am no longer making a threat that leaves something to chance. Second, until deterrence or compellence fails and the threatener executes the threat, he does not know if pain will be inflicted. If I *know* that the particular chamber of my revolver is empty (or full), then I no longer am making a threat that leaves something to chance. If either condition—absence of control and absence of knowledge—does not hold, then the decision to pull the trigger will not represent a decision to inflict pain probabilistically on an opponent.

Most real-world threats can best be understood as threats that leave something to chance. Even if I claim that my strategy is a pure one, it probably is in fact mixed. I may say that I will shoot you if you trespass in my garden. But what I really mean is that I will *try* to shoot you if you trespass, and my ability to do so successfully will depend on such factors as whether the bullets in my gun work and I am a good shot. In this simple case the coercive strategy is that you will not be shot if you do not go into my garden (that is, if you comply with my demands), but there is some probability, x, that you will be shot if you do trespass.

Of course, any assurance I make about my behavior if my opponent yields may also involve probabilistic, rather than certain, consequences. I can make assurances or promises that leave something to chance just as I can make threats that leave something to chance. There may be a probabilistic difficulty in avoiding shooting you even if you yield and stay out of my garden. My eyesight may be so bad that I may be unable to tell with certainty whether you are in my garden or not. Or I may have such a hair-trigger on my gun that it has a tendency to go off by mischance. In this case my coercive strategy is that I will shoot you with some probability y if you do not trespass and with (presumably larger) probability x if you do. Ignoring for the moment the impact of surprise aversion and assuming there are no costs or benefits associated with being deterred, if the product of the difference between probability x and probability y and the disutility threatened is enough to outweigh the net value gained by trespassing, then this threat will be sufficient to render a rational opponent coercible.[17]

Most threats to do small things *also* generally involve some mixed threat of doing something larger. As Schelling noted long ago, a threat to wage conventional war in Europe might be frightening partly because it carries with it some risk that things would get out of hand.[18] There is some risk that the waging of a conventional war would result in a loss of control over one's actions and in the precipitation of a nuclear blow against the aggressor—just as there is some risk that shooting a trespasser will result not simply in the superficial injury intended but in a mortal wound. How big the chance is that a conventional conflict in Europe would result in the use of U.S. nuclear forces depends on how fragile U.S. ability to refrain from escalation is—just as how big the chance is that I will unintentionally kill a trespasser depends on how unreliable my gun, aim, and nerves are as I attempt only to graze him.

But what sorts of things might a coercer threaten to do (either with certainty or in a threat that leaves something to chance) that might cause an opponent to have a contingent strategy? What ways of inflicting pain can be logically distinguished?

MODES OF COERCION

There exist three possible *modes of coercion* or types of coercive strategies relevant to nuclear deterrence. In other words, there are three basic types of nuclear deterrent threats that may result in an effective coercive strategy. These are *denial, retaliation,* and *punishment.* Each of these represents a different mode of imposing pain on an opponent if he fails to yield, and each imposes different requirements for weapons *and for decision-making.* Real-life threats may combine more than one of these three modes, but they are analytically distinct.

Denial

The simplest mode of coercion involves threats by the coercer directly related to the end sought by his opponent. Logically, one can deter by denying the prospect of success. An opponent may be deterred from undertaking some action because of the coercer's credible commitment directly to prevent him from achieving, without unacceptable difficulty, the goal that motivated that particular action.[19] For example, if my neighbor wishes to enjoy the pleasures of my garden and I wish to deter him from trespassing, I may threaten to take up my cudgel and drive him out if he enters. In a denial situation, a rational opponent will possess a contingent strategy if the coercer possesses the minimum capabilities that the opponent believes are necessary to prevent him from accomplishing his goal, raise the difficulty of accomplishing it to levels unacceptable given the value of the objective, or reduce the final value of the object so that it is no longer worth the effort. To deter by denial I could, for example, erect an unclimbable fence around my garden, buy a pack of attack dogs, or prepare to burn down my garden if my neighbor enters it.

The opponent's "goal" and "objective" in this context must refer to political goals and objectives rather than to (purely instrumental) military ones. National values, as well as internal or domestic political ones, may be enhanced even if military operations are unsuccessful. The values of the Nicaraguan state decision-maker might, for example, be enhanced by Nicaraguan provision of military support to Salvadoran rebels even if the Salvadoran government is certain to prove militarily successful. The Nicaraguans may feel better about themselves for having made a sacrifice and tried to defend or liberate their neighbors; they may have damaged their international opponents' ability to fight in the future; they may have impressed their opponents with their willingness to fight against the odds; they may have impressed third parties with their willingness to fight; and they may have used the intervention to eliminate domestic political problems or opposition.[20] If any of these factors are critical in Nicaraguan decision-making, the Nicaraguan state would not be denied its "objective" in giving aid even if the Salvadoran rebels lose (indeed, some of these objectives may even be enhanced by a military defeat for the rebels); hence it will not have a contingent strategy based on the Salvadoran government's ability to prevent the rebels' victory and will not be deterred from giving aid because the Salvadoran government and its U.S. backers can credibly commit themselves to the defeat of the rebels.[21]

This gets to the difference between *defense* and *denial.* Defense is a direct exercise of power, denial an effort to use power coercively. Defense is directed against an opponent's hostile actions; denial addresses an opponent's aims—his motivation in undertaking the action. Defense seeks to *prevent harm to self*—no more, no less. Denial seeks to *prevent gain to the opponent*—no more, no less. While the two will frequently be similar, because relationships are not zero-sum they need not be synonymous.

I can, for example, defend myself against my neighbor's loud music by closing my windows. If his aim in playing the loud music is to force me to listen to his abysmal taste in music, then closing my windows is an act of denial, and my ability and commitment to do so may deter him from playing his loud music. If, however, my neighbor's aim is to provide accompaniment for a dance or to entertain his deaf wife, then my defense abilities, however good, are unlikely to deter, even if my threat to defend is credible.

If I can defend myself, why should I be concerned that my defense would not also serve to deny my opponent his object? There may be costs, even to successful defense. In the absence of loud music, I may prefer to have my windows open. There is a cost to me associated with closing them. To draw an international security analogy, consider that with sufficient preparation the United States might be able to defend the territory of the Federal Republic of Germany from Soviet occupation; the defense itself, however, is likely to prove costly, both in terms of the military and economic resources expended and in terms of the destruction of the nation being defended. If my ability and commitment to defend does not also serve to deny, and I am therefore unable to deter, then I will have to pay these costs. By contrast, if my ability and commitment to defend does promise to deny and serve to deter, then I will escape paying these costs.

This logical distinction between defense and denial is not a moot one in international politics. For example, the Israeli ability to defend against the Egyptian offensive in 1973 was expected, and yet because the object of Egyptian policy was not to defeat Israel or reconquer the Sinai, but rather to relieve domestic pressure and demonstrate to the United States and the world that Israeli military superiority did not guarantee peace in the region, the Israelis lacked an effective denial capability and were in fact unable to deter Egyptian attack.[22]

Deterrence scenarios that envision Soviet adventurism in Western Europe to shore up a crumbling position in Eastern Europe encounter this distinction between defense and denial, although generally without realizing it. Imagine that the aim of a limited Soviet attack on the Federal Republic were, for example, to justify Soviet presence in the Democratic Republic and to use wartime nationalist sentiments to undercut popular discontent with economic and social conditions. In that case, would conventional NATO defense capabilities be sufficient to deter Soviet attack—even if they were sufficient to stop a Warsaw Pact drive short of the Rhine and eventually drive Pact forces back to the intra-German border?

But just as the deterrer's ability to defend successfully may not be enough to result in an effective coercive strategy, it may also represent more than is necessary. A coercer may have the ability to deny even if he does not have the ability to defend. For example, even if I do not have the ability successfully to defend my garden against my neighbor's trespass—that is, even if he is bigger than I am and can beat off my attempts to protect my property—I may be able to deny him his objective of *enjoying* his trespass. Similarly, even if the United States cannot successfully defend the Federal Republic, U.S. actions may serve to deny the Soviets the objective for which they undertook aggression. A long war in Germany—even if certain ultimately to prove militarily successful for the Soviets—might, for example, weaken rather than strengthen the Soviet position in Eastern Europe.

Equally interesting, even if they do not threaten to deny completely an opponent his aims, threats to defend may deter by denial because they alter the final value of the objective or the required effort, making one not worth the other. After all, for a coercer's denial ability to yield an effective coercive strategy against a rational opponent all that is necessary is that the coercer have the ability to deny his opponent his objective *at an effort acceptable to him.* The coercer can deter by denial if he has the ability to make the achievement of the object sufficiently difficult or to so reduce the value of the object that the offensive action no longer promises a net positive utility for the aggressor. My attempts to defend my garden—even if they are entirely ineffectual in keeping my neighbor out—may force him to carry a heavy cudgel of his own (a nuisance from his touristic point of view) or may result in the destruction of the flowers he came to enjoy. Similarly, the Soviets might conclude that though they could strengthen their crumbling position in Eastern Europe by attacking, the price would be unacceptably high in terms of Soviet military materiel[23] and the devastation of Europe, East and West, would render their dominant position a liability rather than an asset.

The power resources required for denial, while limited to those necessary to deny the opponent the achievement of his objective at an effort acceptable to him, are likely to be highly specialized. The cudgel I use to deny my neighbor entry into my garden will be of little use—at least for denial purposes—in deterring him from playing loud music. The capabilities for denial useful in deterring Soviet military aggression in Europe are likely to be quite different from those useful in deterring Soviet sponsorship of wars of national liberation in the Third World. This is inherent in denial as a mode of deterrence and is unique to it.

Retaliation

The pain threatened by a coercive strategy need not be one caused by denial, however. The coercer may threaten something other than denial of the pleasure sought by the opponent: the negative sanction may involve some *unrelated* hurt that the coercer can impose. An opponent may have a contingent strategy not because the coercer can deny him the accomplishment of his objective at an acceptable price, but because the coercer can do something else, something else that hurts more than the objective is worth. This is the idea of retribution, and it gives rise to the twin notions of *retaliation* and *punishment,* our second and third modes of coercion.

Typically, the terms "retaliation" and "punishment" are used interchangeably. This, however, glosses over fundamentally important differences between types of retribution, differences that critically influence both whether an effective coercive strategy is possible and whether a credible commitment can be established.

The threat of retaliation is the threat systematically to inflict an unrelated pain *until the opponent ceases his noncompliance.* It is the threat to carry out a carefully *controlled* retribution. To use our illustration of the homeowner who wishes to deter his neighbor from trespassing in his garden, an example of retaliation would be for the homeowner to respond to the neighbor's intrusion by breaking windows on the neighbor's house until the neighbor leaves the garden. The longer the neighbor remains in the garden, the more windows will be broken. *The administration of pain is part of an ongoing bargaining process.*[24]

Deterrence by retaliation requires, first, that the opponent be sensitive to pain and have a contingent strategy based on the pain the coercer might inflict and, second, that the coercer can credibly commit himself both to inflict pain systematically until the action to be deterred is halted or reversed and to execute the positive sanction thereafter. Retaliation is a *continuing* carrot-and-stick process involving tacit or explicit communication: "if you do not refrain or desist from doing whatever it is I find objectionable, I will do something *unrelated* but painful to you *until you comply with my demands;* if or when you refrain or desist, I will refrain or desist." Execution of retaliation *itself* represents a coercive process and therefore encompasses both a threat and an assurance.

In deterrence by retaliation, as in deterrence by denial, there is a blurring of the distinction between deterrence and compellence. The deterrent threat is of an ongoing nature, giving its wielder an intra-conflict compellent ability: retaliation gives the deterrer some prospect of convincing his opponent to *return* to the status quo ante. Once "deterrence fails" and the opponent begins his attempt to achieve his goals, the deterrer's ability to use coercion to achieve *his* desired outcome is not gone.

Why would an opponent ever be compelled by retaliation to yield when he was not deterred by the threat of retaliation in the first place? Or, from the other point of view, why might a coercer believe that the execution of a threat might be effective in compelling a return to the status quo ante even if the issuance of the threat did not deter? There are three possible reasons. First, this situation may arise because the opponent is behaving irrationally—either before or after the aggression and retaliation. My neighbor might invade my garden while he was sleepwalking and the crash of breaking windows might bring him to his senses; or he might have rationally trespassed in my garden (and rationally be willing to pay the price, measured in broken windows, of continuing to occupy it) but may fly into an irrational rage or a confused panic when he sees his windows being broken.

Second, such a situation may occur because the opponent's estimate of the benefits of aggression or of the pain he will have to suffer as a result of the coercer's response changes because of new information associated with actually carrying out the aggression and experiencing the coercer's response. The opponent, after all, does not have perfect information. He may have rationally misestimated the value

of aggression, the coercer's probable response, or the pain that response would actually cause. My neighbor may have thought my
garden was more attractive than it actually is, or he may not have
believed that I actually had a stockpile of bricks and the guts to throw
them, or he may have underestimated the psychological pain associated with watching his windows be broken. As a consequence, he may
beat a hasty withdrawal when he becomes better informed on these
matters. (It should be clear that the impact of surprise aversion would
tend to cut the other direction: the actual commencement of the
retaliation would reduce the neighbor's uncertainty about my response. Hence, if he is a surprise-averse individual, staying in my
garden involves less disutility than entering it in the first place.)

Third, even if the opponent is rational and his estimates of the pain
inflicted and the benefits gained remain unchanged, he may choose
first not to yield and then to yield if the marginal benefits from
aggression decline over time or the marginal costs of continued retaliation increase over time. My neighbor, for example, might ultimately
withdraw because though he has enough spare window glass and time
to fix four or five windows, fixing a dozen would exceed his resources.[25] More significantly, he might rationally invade my garden
and then rationally withdraw in response to my retaliation if the
initial trespass allowed him to examine the flowers he wanted to see
(or allowed him to demonstrate to his wife how brave he was and how
little he cared about my threats) and if continued presence in my
garden yielded declining returns in terms of enjoying flowers (or
demonstrating machismo).

Obviously, badly designed retaliation might have the reverse impact: because of its compellent quality and the possible reputational
costs associated with conspicuous compliance to a compellent demand, the initiation of retaliation might *increase* the net marginal
benefits from continued aggression. Indeed, my neighbor may find
that the reputational costs of retiring from my garden are so increased
by my attempt to compel him to leave that he rationally chooses to
stay, even though my flowers now bore him and he would rather
enjoy the pleasures of his own home. In this case the overall impact
of the retaliatory action is to increase, rather than decrease the net
marginal utility of occupying the garden. The cost of broken windows
is more than offset by the reputational challenge.

When would a rational opponent have a contingent strategy as a
result of a threat of retaliation? That is, when would an opponent be
deterred by a coercer's credible commitment to retaliate? At any given

point in time a rational opponent will have a contingent strategy if, standing at that point in time and looking to the future, he can see no time period, beginning at the present and running any distance into the future, for which the positive expected utility of committing aggression exceeds the negative expected utility of the retaliation.[26]

Punishment

The third mode of coercion involves threats of simple punishment for noncompliance. Punishment involves no intraconflict compellent threat: it involves threats unlinked to any tacit or explicit negotiation aimed at achieving compliance once noncompliance has occurred. In contrast to retaliation, punishment does not involve ongoing bargaining. In our homeowner illustration, an example of a punitive threat would be a threat to burn down the neighbor's house if he trespasses. In the event of his noncompliance, the neighbor is punished for his trespass, but he is given no incentive to withdraw from the garden. The execution of a threatened punishment does not involve a coercive process: it represents a negative sanction without a positive assurance promised in the event of future compliance.

The distinction being drawn here between the two types of retribution, punishment and retaliation, is worth highlighting. Retaliation is an ongoing process, designed to pressure the opponent into eventual compliance: it involves the imposition of continuing pain that can consciously be stopped or reversed. Punishment is either a single, irreversible action or an ongoing action undertaken with the expectation that it cannot be stopped by the initiator as a result of later concessions by the opponent or that it physically cannot or will not lead to a restoration of the status quo ante.

States sometimes sentence convicted murderers to death. To the extent that the death penalty represents an attempt to coerce rather than an application of direct power (that is, to the extent to which the sentence is a response to the convict's past misdeeds, rather than a defense against the future crimes he is expected to commit if allowed to live), this sentence is a punishment. There is no expectation that the homicide victim can be restored to life or even that the murderer will reform as a result of the state's act of retribution. On the other hand, jailed criminals may be offered the possibility of parole if they show signs of having given up their evil ways; in this case, continued incarceration involves an element of retaliation—the possibility of parole (like the possibility that I may stop breaking my neighbor's windows) offers an incentive for the criminal to change his behavior *even after the coercer has begun administering pain.*

The most striking example of a punitive threat in the present era is the threat of massive retaliation or assured nuclear destruction in response to an all-out nuclear attack. This one case should not obscure the fact that punishment need not be completely devastating or even massive. As the French argued when designing their *force de frappe*, the size of the coercive threat need only be scaled to the size of the potential gain the opponent expects from noncompliance. In other words, an effective coercive punishment does not necessarily require the potential for massive destruction. Further, in addition to being less than massive, punishment may also be limited—that is, less than the total that could be inflicted—and still yield a contingent coercee strategy.

For a rational opponent to have a contingent strategy, he must value his object less than the expected net disutility of the threatened punishment. That is, a rational opponent faced with threats of punishment will have a contingent strategy if the disutility of the threatened punishment (which may, of course, involve a probabilistic threat) is greater than the net utility associated with achieving the objective.

Denial, Retaliation, and Punishment in U.S. Strategy

Before going further, it is important to recognize explicitly that this typology of three logically possible types of threats—denial, retaliation, and punishment—is not an irrelevant academic construct devoid of identifiable applications in real-world thinking or security strategy. Quite to the contrary, this typology provides a necessary basic framework for understanding the defense community's thinking on nuclear weapons and the evolution of official U.S. nuclear deterrence strategy. Without identifying how the three distinct, but not always distinguished, ideas of denial, retaliation, and punishment are employed, it becomes impossible to analyze and evaluate different positive and normative explanations of nuclear deterrence.

Interestingly, denial, as we have described it, has never been central in the U.S. official explanation of how nuclear deterrence worked. Before 1954, nuclear weapons were primarily thought about in terms of defense rather than deterrence—that is, they were considered tools for direct power rather than coercive power. They were a means for imposing military defeat on the Soviet Union, destroying its military infrastructure and military-industrial capacity so that a conventional military victory—like the one scored by the Allies over the Axis powers—could be achieved. Nuclear weapons simply provided an easy means of bleeding the Soviet Union into exhaustion so that the country could be occupied or credibly threatened with occupation, and thereby forced to surrender.

In 1954, of course, Secretary of State John Foster Dulles enunciated the doctrine of Massive Retaliation, a punitive strategy. Soviet transgressions, Dulles warned, risked provoking a massive strike on the Soviet Union that would destroy its military, political, and economic power. Such a strike was explictly not aimed at denying the Soviets the political advantage in the periphery that had inspired their aggression. Nor did the Massive Retaliation strategy involve a carefully controlled application of force aimed at coercing the Soviet Union into halting or reversing its aggression out of fear of repeated or escalating nuclear attack. Rather, Massive Retaliation threatened the Soviet Union with a single, overwhelming attack, designed to maximize military and industrial damage, thereby reducing the Soviet Union to military and political impotence.

For a short time during the late 1950s, the Eisenhower administration did flirt with the idea of using nuclear weapons for denial in Europe. The development and introduction of tactical nuclear weapons created a fleeting hope that nuclear weapons might be effective and acceptable as a means of halting Communist aggression on the battlefield. The collateral damage of large-scale tactical use and the possibility of use by the aggressor as well as the defender doomed this idea, however.

When the Kennedy administration did accommodate U.S. official strategy to the new reality of mutual societal vulnerability, therefore, it did so by attempting to abandon nuclear punishment not in favor of nuclear denial but in favor of nuclear retaliation. The idea of Flexible Response and the No Cities strategy was, if deterrence failed, to use nuclear weapons gradually to increase the costs to the Soviet Union, first in a probabilistic fashion and then in controlled real terms. Nuclear use was expressly seen not as a means of gaining victory directly, denying victory to the Soviets, or punishing the Soviets for their aggression, but as a means of compelling the Soviets to seek peace. Despite the misleading public monicker of "Assured Destruction," U.S. official strategy throughout the 1960s continued to be based on this understanding of how nuclear weapons would be employed for coercion.

Similarly, the ideas of strategic countervailing, adopted by Secretary of Defense James Schlesinger and his successors as a means of deterring limited Soviet attack on the United States itself, were also based on the concept of retaliation. While some observers have attempted to explain the Countervailing strategy as an exercise in denial,[27] such a characterization does fundamental injustice to the official strategy's logic. The logical foundation of the Countervailing strategy is not that the United States will deny the Soviet Union the ability to conduct the sorts of limited attacks on the United States which might cripple its war-making industry or inflict substantial damage on its military capabilities while leaving U.S. society intact. Nor—at least to date—has the United States seriously attempted to make it unacceptably difficult for the Soviet Union to conduct such an attack.[28] The logic of Countervailing has been that if the Soviet Union commenced limited attacks on the United States, the United States would respond in a flexible and controlled fashion, inflicting such pain on the Soviet Union that the Soviet leadership would be convinced that the costs of continuing the exchange exceeded the benefits and that any continuation of the conflict promised only increasing disutility. As Secretary of Defense Caspar Weinberger has phrased it, Countervailing's formula is that "flexibility offers the possibility of terminating a conflict and reestablishing deterrence at the lowest level of violence possible, avoiding further destruction."[29] As long as the Soviets continued to trespass by attacking targets in the United States, the United States would retaliate by throwing nuclear bricks back; as soon as the Soviets ceased to transgress, the United States would halt its retaliatory strikes and reestablish deterrence, hopefully before destruction had been too great.[30]

COERCIVE STRATEGIES AND INCENTIVES FOR EXECUTION

As we noted at the beginning of this chapter, for a coercive strategy to result in coercive power not only must it result in the opponent having a contingent strategy but it must also be a strategy to which the coercer can credibly commit himself. In judging modes of coercion and selecting coercive strategies, therefore, a decision-maker must bear in mind the difficulties of establishing credible commitment. Thus, a question that arises in the case of each mode of coercion is not only whether it will yield a contingent coercee strategy but whether the coercer would *want* to carry out the threat in the event the opponent failed to yield.

The Rationality of Denial

While the difficulty inherent in establishing credible commitment is recognized in discussions of compellence[31] and is generally noted in considerations of modes of deterrence other than denial, in discussions of deterrence by denial credible commitment is often assumed to be an automatic or inevitable product of rational self-interest. There is, however, no reason to believe that this is the case.

As we have noted, there may be a difference between denial and defense. Denial, with its emphasis on preventing gain to the opponent rather than preventing hurt to oneself, may involve prohibitive costs. A scorched-earth policy, for example, may in some cases be effective for denial even if it is ineffective for defense; it also, however, destroys what was valuable to the coercer as well as to the aggressor. Moreover, even to the extent that denial is synonymous with defense, a state decision-maker may prefer to yield rather than to defend itself or its interests. Certainly this is true when only peripheral interests are involved, but it may also be the case when fundamental interests are engaged, when the defense of national territory is involved, and even when the survival of the state is at stake. The surrender of the Sudetenland by Czechoslovakia in October 1938 and the dissolution of the Czechoslovak state and establishment of the Bohemian protectorate in March 1939 provide examples of this. Eduard Beneš, the president of Czechoslovakia who acquiesced in the surrender of the Sudetenland rather than defend his country after diplomacy and allies had failed, was to comment about the Czech capitol of Prague following World War II: "Is it not beautiful? The only central European city not destroyed. And all my doing."[32] As we had an opportunity to note in the preceding chapter, even self-destructive behavior may be rational under our definition. Czech decision-makers apparently reasoned that the preservation of the Czech nation was more important than the survival of the Czechoslovak state.[33] Though the Czechs may have had the means to protect their independent state, the cost would have been a war fought on Czech soil and waged with Czech blood.

Thus, we would take strong exception to the historic argument suggested by Richard Rosecrance, who, looking back to the period before long-range airpower and nuclear weapons made societies vulnerable even when the armies defending those societies had not been defeated, has claimed that

> In previous ages, when there was no distinction between deterrence and defense, there was also no difference between *ex ante* and *ex post* incentives. If one was attacked, he would defend against the attack. Resistance to attack was then his best alternative (the one providing the greatest utility under the circumstances). If a national leader decided not to resist, he opened his population to harm by the invading power and subjected himself to control by a foreign head of state.[34]

A logical distinction between deterrence and defense always exists, even in situations in which deterrence based on retribution is not possible. Further, decisions to defend oneself are neither automatic nor inevitable.

In general, then, there is no automatic commitment to threats to deny. A coercer may possess the troops and weapons necessary for an effective coercive strategy of denial; if the coercer maintains rational control over his actions, however, he will employ these resources only if he intelligently calculates that the benefits will exceed the costs. I may possess the cudgel and strong arm that will permit me to defend my garden from—and deny it to—trespassers, but if that effort to defend and deny promises to leave my garden trampled and destroyed, I may prefer to allow the trespass to take place. I may value the preservation of the garden so highly that I would prefer to see it under my neighbor's control than to see it destroyed, and it may therefore be rational to acquiesce in his illegal trespass.

Rationality of Retaliation

Obviously, actors are not automatically committed to the execution of threats of retaliation or punishment either. A decision-maker will, *ex post*, rationally choose to carry out retaliation or punishment only if the expected benefits of inflicting this retribution exceed the expected costs, given that the opponent has already failed to yield. Of course, the chance that threats to retaliate will be *ex post* rational to execute is enhanced because the execution of retaliation threats increases the likelihood of eventual compliance: because of the compellent element of retaliation, execution of retaliation threats offers some chance of eventually coercing one's opponent into complying with one's wishes.

But there are a number of factors that may result in a rational preference, *ex post*, not to carry out retaliation. First, of course, it is possible that the event to be deterred—for example, a limited nuclear attack on the United States—could be carried out quickly and irreversibly. (Indeed, a limited attack on the United States would probably have to be carried out quickly if it were to avoid the launch, alert, or dispersal of the most probable potential targets.) In our homeowner analogy, if the wayward neighbor is interested only in dodging in quickly and cutting a few flowers, it is unclear what room there is for retaliation: the flowers have been cut and cannot be restored. Thus, there might be little for the retaliation to coerce the opponent into halting or reversing and therefore little rational incentive to carry out the retaliatory threat.

Second, even if the above does not apply, retaliation runs the risk of provoking a rational counterresponse by the opponent. In response to my window-breaking campaign, my trespassing neighbor might break my arm, break my windows, or burn down my house. That is, he might engage in denial (denying me the ability to inflict the limited pain I have threatened), in retaliation of his own (aimed at stopping the ongoing retaliation I have threatened), or in punishment (punishing me for having commenced the retaliation). Analogously, U.S. retaliation with strategic forces in response to Soviet aggression in Europe might prompt a Soviet counterattack on U.S. strategic forces aimed at eliminating U.S. ability to carry out controlled retaliation; it might prompt limited Soviet retaliation as part of a competition in inflicting pain; or it might prompt an all-out attack on American cities, society, military infrastructure, and other war-making resources.

Third, the execution of retaliation would risk interfering with the opponent's rational decision-making process and triggering an irrational response. My normally cool-headed and calculating neighbor might fly into a rage or panic when he hears the tinkle of broken glass coming from his home. Even if the Soviets would not rationally choose to respond to U.S. retaliation, retaliation might provoke irrational Soviet behavior—because it created situational stress or organizational dysfunction, or because it revealed hitherto hidden cognitive failure—and the Soviets might irrationally inflict pain on the United States.

Fourth, the opponent might *already* be irrational and might therefore be unable to act on a rational preference to yield associated with retaliation. If my neighbor is sleepwalking or drunk, there may be little point to breaking his windows. If the United States concluded that Soviet decision-making was in fact irrational—that, for example, organizational dysfunction had resulted in a cessation of central control over military actors or cognitive failure meant that decision-makers were entirely insensitive to information suggesting that the United States did not in fact seek the total destruction of the Soviet Union—it would not be *ex post* rational to execute any retaliation that in order to be rational required Soviet rationality.

Finally, communication and information systems necessary for explicit and tacit negotiations may be—indeed are quite likely to be—critically strained by aggression and retaliation. From my back garden my neighbor may be unable to hear me breaking his front windows; from his front steps I may be unable to see if he has vacated my garden. Worse, even if my neighbor could normally hear me vandalizing his home he may be able to arrange to be unable to do so—he may, for example, wear ear plugs so that he will be unable to detect my retaliation and therefore will be unswayed by it. The possibility that communication and information-gathering may be disrupted, either unintentionally or deliberately, reduces the likelihood that retaliation will indeed compel, and it therefore reduces the likelihood that retaliation will be rational to execute.

Rationality of Punishment

Because they do not hold out the prospect of compelling the opponent eventually to comply, threats of punishment are even less likely than threats of retaliation to be *ex post* rational to carry out. Nonetheless, they still may be rational to execute. There are three sorts of contributory reasons why the execution of the punishment may maximize expected utility given that the opponent has not been deterred.[35]

First, particularly given that my opponent was not deterred, my utility function may be negatively dependent on his: I may be better off *because* he is worse off. We may be in a zero-sum or worse-than-zero-sum game. Because I hate my neighbor, I may enjoy watching him suffer even if I do not derive any material benefit from his suffering. I may feel pleasure simply *because* he feels pain: I may sleep happier knowing that my neighbor must sleep in the street because I burned down his house.

Second, even if my welfare is not negatively dependent on my neighbor's, carrying out the punishment may provide some direct benefit to me: even if I regret my neighbor's suffering, I may, for example, derive warmth or pleasure from observing houses burn.

More to the point, in burning his house down I may change my capacity to defend myself, to exact retribution, and to deny my neighbor his aggressive objectives. I may destroy his supply of incendiary, counterincendiary, and trespassing materials in the blaze. Infliction of punishment may be of value to me because it destroys some of my neighbor's ability to inflict pain on me: my actions may enhance my prospects for defense or damage limitation. My punishment of my neighbor may also improve or preserve my ability to exact retribution from him—and thereby my ability to coerce him—in the future. In the absence of the punitive action, I may slowly or catastrophically lose my ability to respond to my opponent's provocations, or my opponent may gradually or suddenly develop an ability to protect himself against my blows. If, for example, the United States does not respond to a Soviet attack on U.S. ICBM silos, bomber bases, and SSBN ports, it may find its ability to punish the Soviet Union in the event of a massive Soviet attack on the full range of American targets in the future declining: problems of maintaining an alert force will increase without any corresponding decrease in the Soviet threat. Finally, in addition to imposing pain on my opponent for his past misdeeds, improving my capacity for self-defense, and improving my capacity for exacting further retribution, punishment may improve or protect my ability to deny my opponent his aggressive objectives in the future. Nuclear retribution against the Soviet Union, for example, may increase U.S. ability to block Soviet attempts to occupy Western Europe.[36]

Third, execution of the threatened punishment may enhance my reputation and increase the likelihood that my opponent or others will be deterred in the future. If I do burn down my neighbor's house this time, he will believe me the next time I threaten him. Indeed, more generally, if I do burn down my neighbor's house, everyone will be more likely to believe everything I threaten.

But, again, there are factors that tend to make it less likely that punitive threats will be rational to execute. First, the rational execution of a threat to inflict punishment could itself be deterred by a rational threat of counterpunishment. The execution of my threat rationally to burn down my neighbor's home may be deterred by his counterthreat to respond by burning down mine—a threat he might rationally execute since he would have little left to lose at this point. The execution of my threat is likely to be irrational if after my arson my neighbor will still possess a goodly stock of incendiary material as well as a rational interest in burning down my home. Even if punishment and counterpunishment are clearly limited in magnitude, this logic may work. I may threaten to punish my neighbor for his trespass by shooting his dog, but if I believe his counterthreat to punish this murder by poisoning my cat, I may find it irrational to actually carry out my threat. Similarly, the execution of a U.S. threat to punish the Soviets for an attack on Europe by destroying a given number of Soviet cities[37] may be irrational if the Soviets can credibly counterthreaten to respond by destroying a similar number of U.S. cities.

Second, punishment may strain the opponent's decision-making process. If I punish my neighbor for his trespass by shooting his dog he may temporarily lose his clear-headedness in his rage. Similarly, just as a limited Soviet attack on the United States would strain the rationality of the U.S. decision-making process, any U.S. punitive response would strain the Soviet one, and this strain has some probability of resulting in irrational behavior. And any action which is perceived as having an unacceptably high likelihood of provoking an (irrational but) unacceptable response is itself irrational and can be executed only by an irrational actor.

In all three modes of coercion we have looked at—denial, retaliation, and punishment—creating a credible commitment thus looms as a potential difficulty. Given this background, it seems finally time to turn explicitly to the subject of commitment and to examine what a credible commitment is and how it may be established. This is the task of the following chapter.

4

CREDIBLE COMMITMENT AND
MODES OF COMMITMENT

THE HEART of the problem of nuclear deterrence in a MAD environment is the difficulty of establishing a credible commitment to an effective coercive strategy. This chapter proceeds first by exploring the logical elements of credible commitment, then by considering the three logically distinct possible modes of commitment—commitment-through-rationality, commitment-through-denial-of-choice, and commitment-through-irrationality—and finally by examining the relationship between credible commitment and actual commitment.

CREDIBLE COMMITMENT

Even if an opponent does have a contingent strategy—that is, even if an opponent is coercible—coercive power will not exist unless the coercer credibly commits himself to an effective coercive strategy. My neighbor will not be deterred from trespassing in my garden—even if he has a contingent strategy based on my ability to harass him, break his windows, or burn down his house—unless I am credibly committed to do one or more of these things. My neighbor must estimate that I will execute some effective coercive strategy.

The concept of credible commitment thus involves two parts. First, there is the notion of commitment. Second, there is the notion of credibility.

Commitment to a strategy suggests that the committed actor has arranged that, for whatever reason, he will actually carry out the strategy *ex post*, after the opponent yields or fails to yield. Credible

108

commitment to a strategy implies the perception by the opponent of a commitment by the coercer.

Pure and Mixed Strategies

In discussions of commitment and strategies, it should be clear that the strategy to which one is committed may be either pure or mixed. That is, either the threat or the assurance, or both, may involve some risk, rather than the certainty that pain or pleasure will be inflicted. For example, it makes perfect sense to speak of a coercer being committed to a strategy of shooting his neighbor with a 50 percent probability if the neighbor trespasses and with only a 1 percent probability if he does not.[1]

Similarly, the coercive strategy to which my opponent *calculates* I am committed may also be probabilistic rather than certain. Indeed, the strategy my opponent perceives me as committed to may be probabilistic even if there is no risk about what I will do, but only uncertainty in the opponent's mind. For example, if I am committed to a nonprobabilistic strategy but my neighbor is faced with complete uncertainty about my decision, he may estimate that there is a 50 percent probability that I will react to his trespass by burning down his house. In other words, my neighbor estimates a 50 percent chance that I am committed to burning down his house if he trespasses and a 50 percent chance that I am committed to not burning down his house if he trespasses. In this case we shall say that I am credibly committed to a coercive strategy of burning down my neighbor's house with a 50 percent probability.

Given that the concepts of actual commitment and credible commitment, though clearly related in both logical and practical terms, are analytically distinct, it is easiest to proceed by considering them separately. We shall, therefore, first examine the problem of commitment and then, at the conclusion of this chapter, turn to the issue of credible commitment.

Modes of Commitment

One of the principal interests of deterrence theorists has been the study of ways in which actors may actually commit themselves to strategies—may arrange things so that they will carry out their threats or promises. Establishing a commitment may involve a variety of steps. Most obviously, it may involve staking one's reputation, establishing a costly legal obligation, or eliminating other options—for example, burning bridges behind oneself.[2] Lists of practical commitment methods like this suggest a number of ways in which an actor can commit himself to an act that would otherwise be too costly or unpleasant to carry out. Once again, though, it seems more useful to begin by taking a more rigorously analytical approach.

There are *three reasons* why one may, *ex post*, carry out a coercive strategy. First, of course, *one may be rational and it may be in one's rationally calculated best interest to carry out the strategy*. Second, *one may no longer have power of choice: ex post* execution may be automatic, beyond one's control. Third, *one may be irrational and make the* ex post *irrational choice to execute a strategy even though it is not in one's best interest to do so*. In the game of Chicken, for example, an actor may be committed to a strategy of not swerving because: (1) he is rational, and prefers death to humiliation; (2) he threw the steering wheel out the window and has no ability to swerve, even though he may rationally wish to swerve if the other player does not; or (3) although he prefers humiliation to death and still grasps the steering wheel, his mind does not work consistently or effectively enough to ensure that he will swerve at the last minute.

Thus, *ex ante*, there are three possible modes of commitment— three possible ways of committing oneself to carry out an action *ex post*. First, one may act *ex ante* to arrange future costs and benefits so that it will be rational to carry out the coercive strategy *ex post:* I can, for example, make boasts and bets prior to playing Chicken which make death preferable to dishonor. Second, one may act *ex ante* to deny oneself the physical capability to avoid executing the coercive strategy: I can remove the steering wheel from my car prior to the start of the game. Or, third, one may act *ex ante* to ensure some probability of irrational behavior in certain contingencies and thereby commit oneself to the execution of the coercive strategy: I can consume excessive quantities of alcohol prior to the contest, making rational decision-making problematic. Each of these approaches to establishing an actual commitment deserves to be examined in detail.

COMMITMENT-THROUGH-RATIONALITY

The most obvious mode of commitment is commitment-through-rationality. An actor may structure his incentives *ex ante* so that it will be rational to carry out the threatened coercive strategy *ex post*.

If the decision-maker has the ability to behave rationally *ex post*, then he will actually carry out the threatened strategy.

But what exactly would commitment-through-rationality to an effective coercive strategy mean? In what situations does it exist?

Perhaps the easiest way to conceptualize commitment-through-rationality is to think about it in terms of a match between actual rational *ex post* preferences and threatened behavior. Threats like those to use nuclear weapons—in denial, retaliation, or punishment —involve a strategy of *contingent* behavior by the coercer. They represent a linkage between the behavior of the coercer and that of his opponent: the coercer promises a positive sanction (e.g., the nonuse of nuclear weapons) in the event the opponent yields and threatens a negative sanction (e.g., the use of nuclear weapons) in the event the opponent fails to yield.[3]

It may be that the coercer would rationally choose to carry out both the positive sanction in the event of compliance and the negative sanction in the event of noncompliance. As a homeowner I may conclude that shooting, beating, smashing, or burning make sense if and only if my neighbor trespasses. This represents, however, only one of four possible true states for the coercer's rational *ex post* policy preferences.

The second possibility is that, *ex post*, the coercer would rationally prefer to carry out the positive sanction but not the negative sanction. I may, for example, find that though it is rational to avoid harming my neighbor and his possessions in the event that he stays out of my garden, it would not be in my best interest to carry out the threatened negative sanction even if he does trespass. The social or legal penalties for shooting or beating him, or for breaking his windows or burning down his house, may make the costs of executing the negative sanction prohibitively high. If I am *ex post* rational, then the coercive threat in this case represents a bluff rather than an actual commitment.

The coercer can, of course, take steps to change his *ex post* rational policy preferences to make the negative sanction one that he would rationally execute. I may, for example, plant more expensive flowers or bet my wife $100 that I will shoot, thus increasing the costs of failing to carry out the negative sanction. Or I may find a way of shooting my neighbor secretly or become friendly with the local justice of the peace, thereby reducing the costs of carrying out the negative sanction. I may thus be able to alter my preferences to those described in the first case.

The coercer may also choose to threaten a lesser negative sanction, one that, while perhaps less painful to the opponent, will still suffice to result in a contingent coercee strategy but will be rational for the coercer to execute. I may threaten to beat my neighbor rather than shoot him; or I may threaten to shoot, but with a gun loaded with five blanks and only one live cartridge. Even so, for this lesser threat not to represent a bluff for an *ex post* rational actor, it still must be rational to beat my neighbor or to run a one-in-six chance of actually shooting him.

A third possibility is that, *ex post*, the coercer may rationally prefer to carry out the negative sanction in the event of noncompliance but not to carry out the positive sanction in the event of compliance. I may detest my neighbor so much that I rationally conclude that I would be happiest shooting him, beating him with a cudgel, breaking his windows, or burning down his house even if he does not cross my property line. Again, if the coercer is *ex post* rational, then the threatened coercive strategy represents a bluff rather than an actual commitment: the opponent cannot escape the negative sanction regardless of what he does.

Logically, there also exists a fourth possible true state of rational policy preferences. The coercer may, *ex post*, find it in his best interest to carry out neither the positive sanction in the event of compliance nor the negative sanction in the event of noncompliance. Perhaps I hate my neighbor enough to desire to harm him even if he does not trespass, but am afraid to harm him if and only if he *does* trespass. This unusual situation might arise because I know that only if my neighbor trespasses will the police realize I am the culprit, or because only then, since I have lost the element of surprise, will my neighbor put up effective resistance.

A commitment-through-rationality to a coercive strategy exists only in the first of our four possible cases. Thus if we assume rationality, as classical deterrence theory generally does, only in this first case does an actual commitment exist. Of course, if rationality is alienable then preferences of any of the other three types may also conceivably yield actual commitments; moreover, in the absence of perfect information, a coercer may be able to bluff successfully and convince an opponent that an actual commitment exists when in fact it does not (although, as we shall note below, bluffing is quite difficult, particularly about nuclear threats). If, however, the coercer can rationally act on his preferences and if the opponent has perfect information about the coercer's preferences and rationality, then coercion will be successful if and only if, *ex post*, the coercer actually prefers to carry out both sanctions.

The discussion in chapter 1 suggested that the problem encountered in a MAD world is that rational *ex post* preferences are likely to be those of our second case, not our first case. The United States is likely to find that its threatened coercive strategy is in fact *contingently irrational* to carry out: in the event of Soviet noncompliance, a rational preference to execute the negative sanction and use nuclear weapons is unlikely to exist.

Rational Preferences and Types of Values

Under what circumstances *would* a rational preference to carry out a negative sanction exist? That is, under what circumstances would it be rational behavior, *ex post*, to carry out a threat? What factors are involved in rational calculations regarding the execution of threats?

As we noted in chapter 2, rational behavior involves behavior consistent with intelligent calculation of costs and benefits, consistent evaluation of the utility of various costs and benefits, and reasoned choice of optimal policy. For example, Glenn Snyder has suggested that in deterring territorial aggression,

> If the deterrer is rational, his response to aggression will be determined (within the limits, of course, of the military forces he disposes) largely by four factors: (1) his valuation of the territorial objective and of the other intangible gains (e.g., moral satisfaction) which he associates with a given response; (2) the estimated costs of fighting; (3) the probability of successfully holding the territorial objective and other values at stake; and (4) the change in the probability of future enemy attacks on other objectives which would follow from various responses.[4]

If one also adds a fifth factor, surprise aversion, this seems a satisfactory formulation.[5]

The major thrust of the deductive deterrence theory literature has been the consideration of ways of manipulating factors (1) and (4) *ex ante*—that is, consideration of ways of increasing the *values* at stake so that execution of threats becomes rational. An understanding of the possibilities of achieving commitment-through-rationality thus requires an understanding of the nature of values. Two points need to be developed.

First, the total value of an outcome is the sum of the intrinsic and power values associated with that outcome.[6] Intrinsic values are *end* values: for states, these might include preservation of territorial sovereignty, political freedom, material prosperity, sociocultural way of life, and the physical safety of individual citizens. An untrammeled flower garden is a thing of beauty and as such may have utility in itself. Similarly, the preservation of U.S. cities, industry, and social structure from nuclear attack is of intrinsic value. (By contrast, the preservation of missile silos is not, unless one attributes to them some aesthetic beauty unremarked by the normal eye.) To employ a recent example, if the American students on Grenada were indeed in danger from the Grenada government, then the U.S. military operation against Grenada enhanced U.S. utility because of the intrinsic value (that is, the value of the students' well-being) at stake.

By contrast, power values have no utility in themselves, but are *instrumental* to the achievement of intrinsic values. In international relations, three sorts of power values can be distinguished: strategic values, deterrent values, and political values.[7] The strategic value of an outcome is the outcome's impact on the balance of power resources —for example, its impact on one's own military capabilities and those of one's foes. Driving out my trespassing neighbor may have utility because the bruises and broken bones I inflict on him will reduce his physical ability to invade my garden in the future.[8] Similarly, protecting an ally that possesses industrial potential, technology, trained manpower, or forward bases would have strategic value quite apart from any intrinsic value associated with protecting friends. Or, to return to the Grenada example, if one accepts the claim that the airport on Grenada and that island's position astride sea routes to Panama represented significant military resources, then the removal of these assets from potentially hostile hands was strategically valuable.

Deterrent and political values are reputational values. The deterrent value of an outcome is the value associated with influencing the perceptions of adversaries and potential adversaries. My success in effecting the removal of my neighbor may have value because it alters his expectations (or the expectations of other potentially troublesome neighbors, or of my own rebellious son) of the outcome of future encounters. The U.S. invasion of Grenada might have had value because it convinced the Cubans and Soviets that the United States would react forcefully to meddling in the Caribbean.

Finally, the political value of an outcome is the value associated with influencing the perceptions of neutral or friendly third parties.

My gardener may think more of me for having acted firmly. The Grenada operation might have had value because it convinced friendly governments in the region that a positive attitude toward the United States ensured their security or that they need not make concessions to potentially aggressive Marxist neighbors or domestic movements.

The amount of intrinsic or power value at stake in any situation can be manipulated *ex ante*. For example, the United States keeps the intrinsic value of a free Western Europe high through the maintenance of close cultural contacts. Similarly, a decision-maker can alter the strategic value at stake by rearranging military or economic assets: Chiang Kai-shek, for example, made the defense of the offshore islands rational by leaving the best elements of the Chinese Nationalist army there; perhaps unintentionally, the United States raised the value of the Philippines before World War II by maintaining an army there. The United States enhanced the deterrent value of Berlin by stationing troops there and guaranteeing the defense of the city with solemn oaths: if the United States reneged on that pledge, what would keep the Soviets from assuming the United States would renege on lesser guarantees around the world? In the same way, the political value of a successful outcome in Vietnam rose dramatically as the United States made it clear to its allies and the rest of the world that it supported the independence of South Vietnam.

The second point to be made about the nature of values is that the value of an outcome to a decision-maker is the weighted sum of values at all significant levels of analysis. An outcome may have value to a decision-maker because it benefits the nation, the state, key bureaucracies, important interest groups, or particular individuals.

As a result of the realist tradition underlying deterrence theory, discussion has tended to focus on *national* intrinsic values and *national* power values. National values are not the only relevant ones, however. There is nothing inherently more "rational" about action to defend national values than about action to defend other values the decision-maker holds dear (provided that, as we argued in chapter 2, the decision-maker evaluates costs and benefits in a consistent fashion). Driving my neighbor out of my garden may benefit my household because it protects my flowers; it may also benefit me personally by strengthening my position as head of the household. The outcome of the Grenada operation may have had political value (using the term as we have just outlined it) either because it altered the perceptions of regional allies or because it rallied domestic political support for the Reagan administration by demonstrating that the United States would "stand tall" and pursue an active role in the region. This suggests that the value of an outcome may also be manipulated, *ex ante*, through domestic political policies that do not alter the national interest. Changes in one's own domestic political position, in domestic expectations, or in bureaucratic involvements, for example, might substantially alter the instrumental value of an outcome. Intentionally or unintentionally, a decision-maker may succeed in staking his reputation or legitimacy with his own domestic audience (or— particularly if the decision-maker is a group rather than an individual —even in staking its own internal cohesiveness and ability to function effectively in the future). The Cuban missile crisis apparently provides an example of the importance of domestic politics in (unintentionally) establishing an *ex ante* commitment: the Kennedy administration found it necessary to undertake some sort of a forceful response to Soviet missile deployments in Cuba at least partially because of the proximity of the congressional elections and Kennedy's pledges during the campaign not to tolerate offensive missiles. Particularly given these campaign promises, acquiescence in Soviet missile deployment raised the specter of political disaster for the Democratic party.[9] The Cuban missile crisis may also illustrate how the cohesiveness and effectiveness of the state decision-maker may be at stake: the ability of the Kennedy administration to carry out decision-making tasks in the future would have been endangered by a passive response, a fact that must have increased the rational *ex post* attractiveness of forceful action. As Graham Allison has argued,

> For this President of the United States, nothing short of a forceful response would suffice: the missiles must be removed. To fail to act forcibly would (1) undermine the confidence of the members of his administration, especially those who had so firmly defended his policy toward Cuba; (2) convince his permanent government that this administration had no leader and cultivate their willingness to challenge all of his policies... (8) feed doubts in his own mind about himself.[10]

Values, Probabilities, and Costs

The values at stake, however, represent only one part of the equation a coercer faces when deciding whether execution of the threatened negative sanction is rational. Marginal increases in the values at stake may prove unimportant unless: (1) the *likelihood* can be kept high that the various values engaged can successfully be preserved by executing the threat; (2) the *costs* associated with executing the threat can be kept low; and (3) the *uncertainty* about outcomes associated with execution of the threat can be kept small.

One could, for example, increase the strategic value of the land-based ICBM force to the United States by reducing other U.S. military capabilities. But would the missiles' added value be preserved by executing the U.S. threat to respond to an attack on them by using the surviving missiles to attack Soviet military targets? To be sure, a response might demonstrate that the United States was not a "paper tiger" and that such attacks could not be carried out with impunity. But the bulk of the ICBM force would already have been destroyed and any U.S. response would use up yet more of the state's ultimate punitive capability. Further, if the vulnerability of American cities or the probability of uncontrolled escalation cannot be kept to accept-able levels, then the costs would still be prohibitively high by compar-ison with the values at stake and the probability they might be pre-served by a nuclear response. Particularly if the U.S. decision-maker was also surprise averse—that is, disliked the heightened uncertainty about ultimate outcomes that would accompany a nuclear response —then execution of the threatened negative sanction would remain irrational.

Similarly, in the case of using the threat of a nuclear response to deter Soviet aggression in Europe, the United States could marginally increase the intrinsic value at stake through greater economic and cultural integration, increase the strategic value at stake through greater reliance on European military resources, and increase the de-terrent and political values at stake through reaffirmation of pledges of support. But much of the intrinsic and strategic value of the half-continent would be destroyed in an initial Soviet invasion and most of what remained would be devastated by a U.S. nuclear response.[11] In other words, the execution of the threatened nuclear negative sanc-tion would be unlikely to preserve much of the intrinsic and strategic value at stake. What would be left of Europe that would have been worth fighting for? Further, the instrumental value of Western Europe —strategic, deterrent, and political—to the United States would be greatly reduced by any response that left the United States exhausted and patently less able to defend itself and its interests in the future. Would a United States that had just undertaken even limited nuclear war really be better positioned to deter or defend against future aggression than one that had not engaged in nuclear war in the defense of Europe? Equally to the point, given the costs a nuclear response would entail—including some significant risk that the Soviet Union might escalate and strike targets in the United States itself —and the increased lack of certainty about outcomes, would marginal increases in the values at stake in Europe really be likely to alter the rationality of nuclear use?

To some degree, of course, the probability of successful preservation of the values at stake, the costs of executing threats, and the lack of certainty about outcomes can, like the values at stake, be manipulated *ex ante*. For example, states have traditionally sought to acquire defensive military capabilities large enough to limit the damage an opponent might impose and thereby make victory *at low cost* likely. The key question, then, is whether the probability of the successful preservation of the values at stake has been—or can be—sufficiently increased and the costs of war and lack of certainty about final outcomes sufficiently decreased to make the execution of nuclear threats *ex post* rational.

As a practical matter, even if ways could be found, on the one hand, to increase the likelihood that use of nuclear weapons could effectively preserve the values at stake and, on the other hand, to reduce uncertainty about outcomes or the surprise aversion of U.S. decisionmakers, our inability to reduce the costs of carrying out nuclear threats is likely to remain a critical obstacle to achieving a commitment-through-rationality. As will be examined in the following chapter, with the decline of absolute defense capabilities in the nuclear age, cost reduction is directly related to the potential for conflict limitation. We observed in chapter 1 that the decline of self-defense capabilities has not been reversed and does not appear reversible; as a consequence, the lack of a sufficient guarantee that conflict can be kept limited once the United States crosses the nuclear threshold means and will continue to mean that U.S. use of nuclear weapons is unacceptably costly.

Inadvertent Behavior

But what about inadvertence? Since the notion of inadvertent behavior, as we developed it in chapter 2, implies that under conditions of risk or uncertainty a rational actor might take objectively irrational steps, is not the door left open for commitment-through-rationality to nuclear threats despite the extraordinary costs of executing such threats? Even if the use of nuclear weapons by the United States in response to limited Soviet aggression is an objectively irrational outcome, is it not possible to find some rational path that will lead to it? Is there not some strategy that the United States might rationally pursue which would inadvertently lead to the use of nuclear weapons in response to limited Soviet aggression?

In general, inadvertent execution of a threat might take two forms. First, it might simply involve a single, objectively irrational step or action. That is, inadvertent imposition of pain on an opponent may involve a single rational, but—because of the absence of perfect information or the existence of risk—objectively irrational, decision. The coercer may carry out the threatened negative sanction in the rational but mistaken belief that its benefits will exceed its costs. Obviously, for our case, this is not a particularly relevant possibility: as we have noted, even limited uses of nuclear weapons are likely to appear irrational, given the information that *is* available.[12]

Second and more intriguingly, however, inadvertence might result in the objectively irrational imposition of pain through a two- or multi-step process. A coercer might undertake some limited military action in the rational, but false, belief that his opponent will not respond. Given the opponent's unexpected (either rational or irrational) response, military actions that would not originally have been rational for the coercer to undertake may now be rational to execute —that is, pain that it would not originally have been rational for the coercer to inflict may now be rational. It may now be rational because the first step or the opponent's response to it increased the values at stake, increased the probability of preserving them, decreased the coercer's surprise aversion or lack of certainty, or (most likely) reduced the marginal cost of taking the second step without similarly reducing the marginal benefit. In other words, after the first step is taken, the expected marginal benefit of the second step outweighs its expected marginal cost, even though the total cost of the two steps together outweighs their total benefit. Consider my problem of deterring my neighbor: I may begin to beat my neighbor with a stick when I find him trespassing; if he responds by counterattacking with a switchblade, I may find it rational to draw and use my revolver. If I could have seen what the future held, I would never have started down this road; once I have started, however, I rationally calculate that it is better to continue, and indeed at this point it may be objectively rational to do so.

This notion of inadvertently getting into a situation in which the imposition of pain becomes rational recalls our notion that "things may get out of hand" even without the existence of irrationality. And, in general, an opponent's fear that objectively irrational infliction of pain can occur even in the absence of irrationality ought to promise to yield coercive power.

It does not, however, appear to help with our particular problem of nuclear threats in a MAD world. Our second step—the imposition of pain through the use of nuclear weapons—appears to be irrational even once the first step has been taken and even once the opponent has responded negatively. Our problem is that U.S. use of nuclear weapons as a second step—following anything short of an unlimited attack on the United States—appears nearly as likely to be irrational as such use in a first step. The United States might rationally undertake a conventional defense of Europe; if this defense proved unsuccessful or if the Soviets began using nuclear weapons in a limited fashion, the argument developed in chapter 1 strongly suggests that it would *still* not be rational for the United States to use its nuclear weapons, despite the additional values placed at stake by the commitment of U.S. conventional forces. Despite the existence of a war, and even given limited use of nuclear weapons by the Soviet Union, the increased danger of uncontrolled escalation associated with a U.S. nuclear response appears to more than outweigh the potential benefit of such a response. The expected marginal cost still exceeds the expected marginal benefit.

COMMITMENT-THROUGH-DENIAL-OF-CHOICE

Classical deterrence theory literature and U.S. policymakers have focused nearly exclusively on the concept of commitment-through-rationality. If—even bearing in mind the theoretical potential for rational, but inadvertent, behavior—an actual commitment-through-rationality to the execution of nuclear threats appears improbable, then we must look elsewhere to understand existing U.S. commitments.

The second of the three possible modes of commitment involves the *ex ante* denial of *ex post* choice. In this case, the coercive strategy is carried out automatically, without *ex post* action by the coercer—indeed, despite any possible *ex post* action by him. The coercer cannot avoid executing his threatened strategy.

In a case of denial of choice, there are two possible states of rational *ex post* policy preferences. On the one hand, the coercive strategy that one has denied oneself the ability to avoid executing may be *ex post* rational to carry out. This first case is not particularly interesting: denial of choice does not result in *ex post* behavior different from that which would have been exhibited had the actor retained rational control over his actions. On the other hand, though, the coercive strategy to which one is committed through denial of choice may be *ex post* irrational, either in whole or in part.[13] This second case, by contrast, is clearly interesting. Here denial of choice results in an actual change of *ex post* behavior.

Because, in this second case, *ex ante* denial of choice may force an opponent to yield when he would otherwise not have (consider the example of throwing the steering wheel out the car window in the game of Chicken), it may offer a higher expected utility than retaining freedom of choice. By definition, therefore, *ex ante* denial of choice may be rational.

This notion that an actor can physically deny himself freedom to avoid executing a particular *ex post* irrational strategy, and indeed *may rationally do so*, has been known in the literature as "the rationality of the irrational": it

> can be described as a strategy by which a state irrevocably commits itself to taking a course of action in certain circumstances, which it would not choose deliberately in the event of those circumstances occurring, *if it retained its freedom of choice*. The fact that the action would not be chosen deliberately if freedom of choice was retained constitutes the irrational element of the strategy. The rational element consists of the commitment itself, specifically of the calculation that after all the risks have been taken into account, the commitment serves some national end, perhaps by deterring a hostile move against a highly valued interest.[14]

Both elements of the strategy—the automatic irrational execution *ex post* and the rational *ex ante* decision to deny oneself future choice in order to establish an irrevocable commitment—are critical.

The first requirement, that *ex post* irrational execution of the (pure or mixed) threat follow *automatically*, is a difficult one. In the real world it may prove hard to establish a mechanism that succeeds in denying control. Forward stationing of troops, as in Berlin, has often been advertised as a "trip wire" for nuclear war, yet in the sense of automatically triggering a nuclear response without human decision, it is not one. There is no mechanism in place to deny the United States choice whether or not to use nuclear weapons in the event of a Soviet attack. It is theoretically conceivable (though implausible) that the United States might *choose* to carry out the coercive nuclear threat because, given the presence of troops in Berlin and the existence of long-standing U.S. verbal guarantees, the cost of yielding exceeds that of carrying out the threat: if such a situation existed, however, it would represent a commitment-through-rationality. In haste or passing anger or confusion the U.S. might *choose* to respond to a Soviet attack on Berlin despite the fact that the cost of responding exceeds that of yielding; this situation, however, would represent a commitment-through-irrationality. A true nuclear trip wire would involve handing control over one's own nuclear decisions to a computer or other machine, with all the dangers this entails.

The requirement that commitment must be *ex ante* rational also poses some problems for the practice of the rationality of the irrational. Given the risk that the denial of choice may fail to appear credible or may fail to coerce because the opponent lacks a contingent strategy, the range of coercive aims for which it would be rational to establish an irrevocable commitment may turn out to be very small. After all, as Stephen Maxwell has noted:

> any device advertised as ensuring commitment, analogous to throwing the steering wheel out of the window in the "chicken" game, would be examined sceptically by an opponent in the light of his estimate of the value of the disputed objective to the contestant declaring the commitment. The commitment might, of course, be so unambiguous technically that all doubts were satisfied. In the real world, however, commitments cannot be signalled as unambiguously as the "bridge-burning", and other analogies suggest. This fact would be sufficient to deter any state contemplating an irrevocable commitment, even if it was confident that it enjoyed the effective first move.[15]

If perfect information about the coercer's preferences were available to his opponent and if there were no unambiguous mode of irrevocable commitment, the only coercive aims for which it would be rational for the coercer to deny himself choice would be those for which it would be *ex post rational* to carry out the threat. After all, given perfect information about the coercer's interests and given the possibility of bluffing about the existence of irrevocable denial of choice, the opponent would rationally assume that any other claimed irrevocable commitment was in fact a bluff. Thus, for there to be a "rationality of the irrational" in a game against a rational opponent, one of two conditions must hold. Either the coercer must be able to bluff about his rational policy preferences (and therefore about what he would rationally do), or else the denial of choice must be unambiguous—that is, it must be impossible to bluff about the denial of choice.[16]

The first condition is not an easy one to satisfy. It is likely to be quite difficult, for reasons we will spell out below, for a decision-maker in an open, democratic setting deliberately to bluff about what he would rationally do. Further, to the extent that he *can* bluff about what he would rationally do, he can credibly (though not actually) commit himself rationally to choose to execute the threat and gains nothing from denial of choice.

The second condition, an unambiguous denial of choice, is also difficult to meet. Even if the machine that would automatically trigger nuclear use actually works, how does one demonstrate this fact to one's opponent? Given that the coercer has every incentive to lie—to have secretly built a machine with some flaw in design or construction, so as to escape the chance that the machine might go off—how could the coercer demonstrate that the machine will actually work as advertised? And how could he demonstrate that it was tamper-proof and would continue to work as advertised? And how could the coercer prove these facts to his opponent without revealing details about the machine that might allow the opponent to make it break down, to circumvent the trip wire, or to avoid the "bullet" triggered by the trip wire?

COMMITMENT-THROUGH-IRRATIONALITY

Arranging a commitment by denying oneself choice thus encounters a number of fairly fundamental practical difficulties. Equally important, even on cursory consideration it appears unsatisfactory as an explanation of any current U.S. commitment to use nuclear weapons: the United States has not handed over its nuclear decision-making power to a preprogramed machine. Understanding the U.S. commitment to respond with nuclear weapons to limited Soviet provocations thus requires a consideration of the third logically possible mode of commitment, commitment-through-irrationality.

This third mode of commitment recognizes that, *ex post*, one may *choose* to carry out a strategy even though to do so would be against one's rationally determined best interest. Only an *ex post* irrational decision-maker would behave in this fashion: if an actor has the *ex post* capability to act rationally, by definition he will not choose to carry out an *ex post* irrational act. Commitment-through-irrationality, therefore, involves ensuring *ex ante* a probability of irrationality *ex post*.

Of course, a rational actor may do seemingly irrational things in order to mislead an observer into believing that he is irrational. He may feign irrationality by carrying out apparently counterproductive actions. He will, however, only do so if such behavior is actually *ex post* rational—that is, if such behavior is expected to yield him net benefits. Feigned irrationality may permit bluffing, and the benefits of bluffing may exceed the costs of feigning irrationality. I may fly into mock rages and disregard police officers, or beat my own children for no apparent reason, or insult or assault my neighbor without provocation—even though I find such antisocial behavior embarrassing—if I think that these actions will convince my neighbor that I am irrational and really may burn down his house, break his windows, or shoot or beat him, and if I value this reputational benefit more than I do the costs of my aberrant behavior. In this case, however, I do these aberrant things because I have intelligently calculated that it is *rational* for me to do them, not because I am in fact irrational. Indeed, in this case it would represent irrational behavior for me to eschew these aberrant acts.

I do not need to be able to pose the certainty of irrational behavior in order to achieve commitment-through-irrationality to a mixed coercive strategy. In thinking about commitment-through-irrationality, it is useful to think in probabilistic terms. Assume, for example, that a strategy of shooting my neighbor with a 50 percent probability if he trespasses and with a 1 percent probability if he does not trespass represents an effective coercive strategy. That is, faced with such a strategy my neighbor is coercible. If I can credibly commit myself to the execution of this strategy, my opponent will be deterred from trespassing. Now, for the sake of simplicity, assume that if I shoot at my opponent I have a 100 percent probability of hitting him; that because of the legal ramifications I would never *rationally* shoot my neighbor; and that if I am behaving irrationally I will certainly shoot him. In this situation, what is necessary to establish a commitment-through-irrationality to the effective coercive strategy? If I can arrange my decision-making process so that if my neighbor invades I have a 50 percent probability of irrational behavior and if he stays at home I have only a 1 percent probability of irrational behavior, then I have succeeded in establishing a commitment-through-irrationality to the effective probabilistic coercive strategy. Commitment to an *ex post* irrational mixed strategy thus will result from the existence of a decision-making process that has some *risk* of producing irrational behavior. In other words, actually to commit myself to an *ex post* irrational mixed strategy I need not take actions that make it certain that I will not have the ability to behave rationally—I need only take actions that create some risk that I will be unable to behave rationally.[17]

Within limits, the probability that I will be unable to behave rationally *ex post* is likely to be adjustable *ex ante*. Just as a potential coercer may manipulate his values or his ability to choose freely, he may manipulate the structure of his decision-making process to increase or decrease the likelihood of particular types of irrationality in particular situations. He may do so by changing who makes the decisions, on the basis of what information, in what time frame, and under what transient pressures and stress.

Rationality of Commitment-Through-Irrationality

Just as it may be *ex ante* rational to adjust the values one has at stake (or the probability of successfully preserving them, the cost of attempting to do so, or the uncertainty one faces) so that one will prefer *ex post* to execute a strategy, and just as it may be *ex ante* rational under some conditions physically to deny oneself the ability (if one can in fact convincingly do so) to avoid executing an *ex post* irrational strategy, it may be *ex ante* rational in certain situations to limit one's ability to behave rationally *ex post*. Two possible criticisms of this line of reasoning deserve attention, however.

The first challenges whether a decision-maker would ever *rationally* choose *ex ante* to deny himself the *ex post* ability rationally to choose not to execute a threat unless that threat would in fact be *ex post* rational to carry out anyway. The (correct) argument is that commitment-through-irrationality encounters the same difficulties as commitment-through-denial-of-choice: the *ex ante* rationality of commitment requires either the possibility of bluffing about values or the impossibility of bluffing about the existence of an actual commitment. An opponent is no more likely to be credulous about a claim that the coercer has denied himself the ability to behave rationally than to be credulous about the claim that the coercer has denied himself the ability to make any choice at all.

The difference between the two commitment problems is that it is more likely to be possible to make the denial of rationality technically unambiguous than it would be to make the denial of choice technically unambiguous. Even in situations where it is impossible to demonstrate that the ability to make a choice will no longer exist, it may be possible to demonstrate that the ability to make a rational choice will no longer exist.

Why is the probability of irrational behavior open to technically unambiguous demonstration? As we noted in chapter 2, the occurrence of irrational decision-making is related to personality disorder, situational stress, cognitive failure, and organizational dysfunction. The occurrence of at least some of these, in turn, is likely to depend on the existence of particular physical conditions, the presence or absence of which can be monitored by an opponent. For example, irrational decision-making and behavior may result because command, control, and communications are vulnerable to a breakdown that would create independent decision centers; the vulnerability of U.S. command, control, and communications and the political independence of decision centers is known to Soviet leadership. Similarly, irrational decision-making and behavior may result as a consequence of the tremendous situational stress under which American decision-makers find themselves; this stress is a function of the values at stake and the existence of significant time pressure for a decision—both of which can be predicted by the Soviets. As a consequence, the kind of stress under which U.S. decisions on the use of nuclear weapons will be made will be unambiguous to Soviet leaders.

The second possible challenge queries whether commitment-through-irrationality is compatible with the existence of an effective coercive strategy—that is, whether the opponent will ever be coercible if the coercer relies on the threat of irrational behavior to achieve a commitment to action. After all, an effective coercive strategy may fail to exist not only if the opponent lacks a rational preference to yield but also if he is unable to act on that preference. What is to prevent an opponent from mimicking the coercer and taking steps to ensure that he, too, will be unable to make rational decisions? Might not a coercer end up "exporting" irrationality? And if so, might not the result be a mutually disadvantageous—even disasterous—outcome, in which both sides engaged in irrational destruction, rather than one in which the opponent rationally yielded to the coercer?

It should be clear, though, that the potential for mutually incompatible commitments by the coercer and opponent exists with *any* mode of commitment. If I make side bets which make it rational for me to shoot at my neighbor if he trespasses and if my neighbor has made side bets which make it rational for him to trespass even though I will shoot at him, a mutually disadvantageous (and possibly objectively irrational) outcome will result just as surely as it would had I taken the steps necessary to ensure that I would be *ex post* irrational and had he taken the steps necessary to ensure that he could not respond rationally to the costs I was committed to impose. The same forces operate to keep actors from making mutually incompatible commitments-through-irrationality as operate to keep them from making mutually incompatible commitments-through-rationality or commitments-through-denial-of-choice. An *ex ante* rational decision-maker will not increase the costs to himself of failing to carry out his threats, deny himself the ability to choose not to carry out the threats, or reduce the likelihood of his own rational behavior in certain contingencies unless he calculates that by doing so he will be better off— that is, unless there is a sufficient likelihood that the strategy to which he is committing himself is in fact an effective coercive one and that his opponent will recognize the existence of his commitment.

This rational calculation may be wrong, of course. As we noted in our discussion of rationality, intelligent attempts to maximize utility do not in fact always succeed. In the game of Chicken, both drivers may rationally calculate that the other will swerve and both may be wrong. But it matters little whether each committed himself by making such boasts to the adoring crowd that death was thereafter preferable to dishonor, by throwing the steering wheel out the car window, or by drinking vast quantities of gin as he climbed into the car. The problem is not one of commitment-through-irrationality but of commitment in general. Commitment is never cost-free; by its nature, and regardless of the mode by which it is achieved, commitment involves arranging that one will select some policy besides the one that would otherwise have been preferred.

Both as a logical and as a practical matter, however, it should be clear that an attempt to create a commitment-through-rationality is at least as likely as an attempt to create a commitment-through-irrationality to encourage the opponent to deny himself the capacity for rational behavior. We shall develop this observation more thoroughly in chapter 8, but it should be clear (given the understanding of rationality and of the pressures leading to irrationality developed in chapter 2) that policies designed to make the use of nuclear weapons rational are more likely to provoke irrational action by an opponent than are policies that simply leave open the possibility of irrational execution of nuclear threats. Policies aimed at making nuclear use rational—that is, policies aimed at creating a commitment-through-rationality—are likely to encourage cognitive failure in the opponent (by strengthening obsolete cognitive beliefs about the winnability, controllability, or inevitability of conflict); they are likely to increase the situational stress under which the opponent's decision-makers are forced to operate during crises; and they are likely to encourage administrative steps such as the decentralization and pre-delegation of military authority which increase the dangers of organizational dysfunction. This second criticism of the rationality of commitment-through-irrationality thus seems to have the story backwards: it is the attempt to create a commitment-through-rationality, not the attempt to create a commitment-through-irrationality, which is likely to result in the opponent losing his capacity to act on a rational preference to yield, and hence possibly losing his coercibility.

In sum, then, a decision-maker may rationally choose to tolerate some risk of losing, in certain future contingencies, the potential for rational action. He may actually commit himself to *ex post* probabilistically irrational actions by living with a decision-making process that threatens some risk of succumbing to the effects of personality disorder, cognitive failure, situational stress, and organizational dysfunction.

ACTUAL COMMITMENTS, CREDIBLE COMMITMENTS, AND BLUFFS

To this point, our discussion has dealt with the establishment of actual commitments. As we noted at the outset of this chapter, however, the notion of *credible* commitment differs from that of *actual* commitment. A credible commitment is a perceived commitment. Credible commitment to a strategy implies the perception by the opponent of a commitment by the coercer. It involves the opponent's estimate of the coercer's future behavior—something that is not and cannot be known with certainty.

Credible commitment thus involves communication. The coercer must communicate to his opponent both the threat and the assurance; he must let his opponent know that he has both the capability and intent (rational or otherwise) to carry out a coercive strategy. The coercer must convey to his opponent what his strategy is—what he will do (either with certainty or probabilistically) in what situations.

Communication may involve verbal expression of interests or plans (directed to either external or domestic audiences), visible actions, or both. I may tell my neighbor (or tell my wife in my neighbor's presence) that if he trespasses in my garden I will burn down his house, or I may conspicuously buy gallons of kerosene and a book on how to commit arson, or I may do both. The United States may publicly pledge to use nuclear weapons if NATO is attacked, or it may stockpile tactical nuclear weapons in Europe and train its soldiers to use them in defensive operations, or it may do both.

Communication, though, may also be entirely implicit. An opponent may deduce the coercer's future behavior from knowledge of the coercer's interests and capabilities. Such knowledge may be derived from study of the coercer's past behavior and programs. From my past behavior my neighbor may know that I am the sort of person who values the privacy of his garden or who is likely to respond to trespass by burning down houses. I may not have to make an explicit threat at all. In the international arena, coercion sometimes results from "the anticipation or anxiety of other states that the nation involved may resort to its military strength if a serious conflict of interest arises."[18] In such a case communication is not absent: it is derived implicitly from historic communication.

Clearly, the sending of a communication represents only half the problem. The message sent must also be believed.[19] It may not be enough to tell my neighbor that I will burn down his house if he trespasses, to practice my arson technique, or to have a history of such unlawful action. My neighbor may also see contrary evidence, or he may reason that I am bluffing; indeed, he may even *rationally* reason that I am bluffing. Or he may *irrationally* overlook or downgrade my communications—exhibiting, for example, the sort of motivated bias in information processing that frequently occurs under stress.

Actual Commitment and Credible Commitment

Thus, there may be a difference between a coercer's actual commitment—what he has *actually* arranged he will do in particular contingencies—and his credible commitment—what the opponent *believes* he will do. Even if the opponent is rational and uses the available information wisely, he may misperceive actual commitments if he lacks perfect information and therefore faces uncertainty about the coercer's interests, capabilities, and rationality.

And although actors in international relations possess a great deal of information, they never have perfect information. As Glenn Snyder has noted, in deterrence situations a potential aggressor

> does have some evidence, of course—chiefly, the record of the deterrer's past reactions to aggression, the existing size, composition, and deployment of his military establishment, and his policy declarations, including expressions of articulate public opinion in the deterring country and its allies. Supplementing these sources, the aggressor could turn to what evidence is available concerning the "national character" or "psychology" of the deterrer as it pertains to foreign and military policy. For example, in judging the probability of American nuclear retaliation after an attack in Western Europe, the Soviets would be wise to take note of certain American attitudes: our deep emotional involvement with Western Europe, and our strong sense of honor, which might lead us to fulfill a commitment at whatever cost.

However,

> After making use of all these sources of evidence, the potential aggressor would still have only a set of very general inferences about the deterrer's probable behavior—not certain predictions, or even statements of precise probability. The hypothetical stimulus— i.e., the contemplated aggression—is likely to be unique in many important respects; therefore there is not likely to be any similar situation in the deterrer's action record.[20]

This lack of certainty about the coercer's future behavior reflects uncertainty in three calculations an opponent must undertake. First, what are the coercer's values? Second, what costs and benefits does the coercer rationally calculate are associated with his various possible strategies? Together these first two questions yield an uncertainty about what constitutes rational behavior for the coercer. Third, though, an opponent will also face uncertainty regarding whether the coercer's *ex post* behavior will be rational.[21]

As we noted in chapter 2, uncertainty about what constitutes rational behavior for the coercer and about whether the coercer will behave rationally does not make rational decision-making by the opponent impossible. Acting in the absence of "certain predictions, or even statements of precise probability," a rational opponent will use the available information intelligently to form some probability estimate of the coercer's future behavior. Taking into account his own surprise aversion, he will then calculate the expected utility of yielding and of not yielding.

Clearly, however, a coercer may play upon uncertainty to create situations in which a rational opponent chooses to yield, though if that opponent had certain knowledge he would not have done so. This may be accomplished in two ways.

First, a coercer may attempt to heighten his opponent's uncertainty. Since the opponent may suffer from surprise aversion—that is, he may dislike strategies that are estimated not to have a high degree of certainty of leading to particular outcomes—a coercer may deliberately act to make him less certain about what the coercer will do if the opponent fails to yield. Coercers may conceal their interests, capabilities, and knowledge of enemy capabilities. Indeed, such behavior may occur without a deliberate effort: it may be a by-product of bluffing, or result from internal political processes or from conflictual relationships with third parties, or simply reflect the need for secrecy to assure military success in the event of conflict.

Bluffing and Actual Commitments

Second, and more importantly, a coercer may alter his opponent's estimate of what the coercer will do in various situations, rather than simply increase the opponent's uncertainty about the behavioral probability distribution. That is, a coercer may bluff. He may act to mislead his opponent about the probability of various responses. He may try to convince his opponent that he is committed to an effective coercive strategy when in fact this is not the case.[22]

Bluffs may be unintentional as well as intentional. I may believe myself when I tell my neighbor that I intend to shoot him if he trespasses—even though, in actuality, it is not what I will do. A state may think that an actual commitment on its part exists and only later discover that it does not. U.S. leaders may, for example, assume that a rational commitment to use nuclear weapons in the defense of NATO exists even if it does not. They may simply not have thought carefully about their interests, or the strategy's costs and benefits may have changed since they last considered them.

There are a wide range of possible deliberate bluffs.[23] In general, however, deliberate bluffs may be either about what the coercer would *rationally* choose to do or about whether the coercer will be *able* to make rational decisions. As I brandish my revolver in an effort to deter my neighbor from entering my garden, I may bluff that the penalties imposed on me for shooting him will be small—or that I have intelligently calculated that they will be—or I may bluff that I have totally taken leave of my senses. The United States may bluff about the likelihood that it will use nuclear weapons in response to a Soviet attack on NATO by trying to convince the Soviet Union either that a nuclear war could be controlled and won by NATO or that authority to use nuclear weapons has been predelegated to battlefield commanders (assuming that this is not in fact the case).

The Importance of Actual Commitments

Despite the possibility of bluffing, some positive correlation between actual commitment and credible commitment should be expected.[24] The more information available to an opponent, the less ability the coercer has to bluff. If the opponent has perfect information about the coercer's values, information, and decision-making process—that is, about the choices that the coercer would rationally make and about his ability to behave rationally—a commitment will be credible if and only if it actually exists.

As we have noted, situations of perfect information do not occur in the real world. However, enough historic and current information is likely to be available—particularly about a coercer like the United States, with an open society and decision-making process—to make bluffing extremely difficult about matters as important and as widely discussed as the use of nuclear weapons. The openness of the American political process means that substantial knowledge exists about the values held by the decision-maker (e.g., how much our cities are valued), about the information available to the decision-maker regarding costs and benefits (e.g., what is known about nuclear war and its consequences), and about the ability of the decision-maker to behave rationally.

Democratic political processes, moreover, create an additional problem for deliberate bluffing, even beyond that of the openness of information. If the government succeeds in fooling its domestic audience as well as its foreign one about what it would rationally choose to do, it is likely to be removed from power, at least if the issue is important to the domestic audience, as the use of nuclear weapons is likely to be. And if the society is open as well as democratic, fooling the domestic audience is likely to be necessary if one is successfully to fool one's opponent. Thus, deliberate bluffs about what a decision-maker like the United States would rationally do with its nuclear weapons are unlikely to be credible and difficult to make so.

But deliberate bluffs about the existence of rationality may also be difficult to make credible. As Glenn Snyder has mused:

> is it possible for a government to *appear* irrational and *be* rational? This would mean appearing to be willing to act contrary to one's payoffs, or appearing to have miscalculated them, when in fact one has calculated, and intends to act, rationally. A democratic government may not be able to practice credibly this kind of sophisticated deceit. In the United States it is difficult enough to achieve a consensus about what is rational; to attempt to go further and practice "calculated lunacy," while secretly intending to act sanely, may be infeasible if only because of the risk of being found out in the pretense. Perhaps the only way a democratic government can appear irrational is actually to *be* irrational.[25]

The amount of evidence available to the Soviet Union regarding U.S. ability to behave rationally under various conditions is substantial. The Soviets are aware of the organization of the U.S. government and its standard operating procedures, of the degree of centralized control over nuclear weapons, and of the relevant communication technology and its vulnerability. The Soviets also know the conditions and time pressures under which nuclear decisions will need to be made and can make reasonable assessments about the kind of situational stress decision-makers at various levels will experience. Soviet officials meet their U.S. counterparts and are able to note the presence or absence of personality disorders; or if they do not have the opportunity to make firsthand observation, they receive extensive secondhand information from the American press. As for cognitive failure, in a democracy such as the United States there is an abundance of evidence available to the public and to foreign observers about existing cognitive assumptions and rigidities.

This evidence is, to be sure, filtered through the opponent's own cognitive lenses. An opponent may irrationally misestimate one's capacity for rational action. But it does not seem substantially easier for an open, democratic state to bluff about its ability to behave rationally than to bluff about what it would rationally choose to do. And when dealing with the threat to use nuclear weapons, it seems difficult deliberately to bluff about either. As U.S. secretaries of defense have routinely observed in their annual posture statements, U.S. ability to engage in nuclear bluffing is limited; if bluffs are attempted, the Soviet Union can devise ways to expose them at acceptable risk and cost.

Coercion and Commitment

Where does this leave us in our attempt to understand the sources of coercive power? Our discussion of the conditions for the existence of coercive power has identified a logical connection between coercive power, credible commitment, and actual commitment. Before going further in developing our line of reasoning or applying it to the problem of nuclear deterrence, it is useful to see how the logic of the last two chapters fits together. In chapter 3, we began by defining coercive power as the ability to gain a desired outcome by influencing the behavior of an opponent. We noted that there were two necessary, and together sufficient, conditions for the existence of coercive power: the opponent must be coercible (have a contingent strategy) and the coercer must be able credibly to commit himself to an effective coercive strategy. An opponent might not be coercible either if the coercer did not have adequate positive and negative sanctions to create a rational preference to yield or if the opponent were unable to act upon a rational preference to yield. We examined three modes of coercion —or three types of strategies for the coercive employment of nuclear weapons—which might be effective in creating a rational preference to yield: denial, retaliation, and punishment.

We then turned our attention to the problem of credible commitment. Credibility requires that the threatened coercive strategy be communicated, either explicitly or implicitly, and that the communicated threat be believed. In the absence of perfect information, there exists a possibility for bluffing, either about what a decision-maker would rationally do or about his ability to act on his rational preferences. But enough information is available to international actors, particularly about open and democratic states, to make bluffing difficult on major matters such as willingness to undertake nuclear war. One would expect, therefore, to find a strong positive correlation between credible commitments and actual commitments.

There are three possible ways to achieve actual commitments. A decision-maker may, *ex ante*, structure his incentives to make execution *ex post* rational. Or he may, *ex ante*, deny himself choice and make execution *ex post* physically unavoidable. Or he may, *ex ante*, structure his decision-making process in such a way that his *ex post* behavior will be probabilistically irrational.

CREDIBLE COMMITMENT AND MODES OF COMMITMENT

This analysis has avoided focusing on features that might be unique to *nuclear* coercion. Nuclear weapons do, however, have some important implications for the practice of deterrence. In the next chapter, therefore, we continue our exploration into the sources of nuclear coercive power by considering the impact of nuclear weapons.

5

NUCLEAR WEAPONS AND CONFLICT LIMITATION

I N THE Introduction, in reviewing recent work on deterrence theory, we observed that the direct application of insights from empirical study of conventional deterrence might provide misleading answers about behavior in situations of nuclear deterrence. It is necessary and appropriate, therefore, carefully to consider the novel characteristics of nuclear weapons and their implication for the general logic developed in the preceding chapters. Such a consideration in turn will force us to examine the concept of conflict limitation.

NUCLEAR WEAPONS

What changes in the nature and practice of coercion have occurred as a result of the development of nuclear weapons and of invulnerable nuclear arsenals? What is it about nuclear war that makes it different from conventional war—and what does this imply about threats of using nuclear weapons?

The Impact of Nuclear Weapons

It should be apparent that these questions cannot be answered on the basis of empirical examination. The necessary evidence does not exist. Nonetheless, one can reason deductively that nuclear weapons logically do make a difference—that nuclear weapons have greatly decreased the difficulty of imposing negative sanctions. It is not that the nature of pain has qualitatively changed or that a physical possibility for inflicting pain has been created that was not already present in some situations. As Thomas Schelling has noted:

It is not true that for the first time in history man has the capability to destroy a large fraction, even the major part of the human race. ... With a combination of bombing and blockade, eventually invasion, and if necessary the deliberate spread of disease, the United States could probably have exterminated the population of the Japanese islands without nuclear weapons. It would have been a gruesome, expensive, and mortifying campaign; it would have taken time and demanded persistence. But we had the economic and technical capacity to do it; and, together with the Russians or without them, we could have done the same in many populous parts of the world. Against defenseless people there is not much that nuclear weapons can do that cannot be done with an ice pick. And it would not have strained our Gross National Product to do it with ice picks. . . .
War has often been "total war" for the loser. With deadly monotony the Persians, Greeks, or Romans "put to death all men of military age, and sold the women and children into slavery," leaving the defeated territory nothing but its name until new settlers arrived sometime later.[1]

What has changed, then, is the *ease* of inflicting pain. In this regard, nuclear weapons have had five related and particularly noteworthy effects.

The first change involves the direct economic and social *costs* of destroying or hurting an opponent. While the United States may indeed have had the GNP to slaughter the Japanese population with ice picks, it certainly would have been an economically expensive proposition (especially since complete destruction of the Japanese armed forces would have been required first). Not many nations would have had the GNP for this task. Further and equally important, the slaughter of the Japanese population with ice picks would have traumatized those (large numbers of) individuals called upon to wield them. More than GNP is expended in waging war, and nuclear weapons effect a savings in these other resources as well. Nuclear weapons make destruction *cheaper*—both in terms of economic cost and in terms of psychic strain. Weapons of mass destruction enable states to afford more pain-making potential. Thus, it is more likely to be physically *possible* (rationally or irrationally) to inflict significant pain if one has nuclear devices.

The second change, originally associated with airpower but certainly amplified by nuclear weapons, is that *imposition of pain is no longer directly correlated with military victory.* To be sure, through the use of blockades states historically inflicted costs on opponents they could not invade or militarily defeat. But the shift from war in two dimensions to war in three dimensions and the acquisition of weapons that can inflict substantial pain behind enemy lines dramatically reduced the ability of military forces to provide a shield for the society that fielded them. War was never a zero-sum game: it always entailed high transaction costs. Before airpower, however, there was reasonable hope that the victor's society would be immune to even the threat of direct attack, and before nuclear weapons there was the reasonable hope that it could be assured of safety from massive destruction. In 1962, as the development of invulnerable superpower nuclear arsenals was creating a situation of mutual assured destruction capabilities, Morton Kaplan noted:

> If each opponent were capable of destroying the other even after absorbing a surprise attack, a failure to reach an agreement on some limitations to the conflict would produce utter destruction. This kind of situation never really existed in the past. One side may have had the power to destroy the other, as in the case of Rome and Carthage, but never before in recorded history have two nations had the power to destroy each other simultaneously.[2]

Obviously, this severence of the connection between defeat and pain has enormous implications, first, for states' willingness to engage in war and, second, for the conduct of war. The consequences of mutual vulnerability for states' willingness to use military force were recognized by Bernard Brodie in the immediate aftermath of Hiroshima: weapons of mass destruction meant that the cost of war would soar for the victor and vanquished alike, and that safety would reside only in being able to deter war.[3] As Schelling has elaborated:

> *Victory is no longer a prerequisite for hurting the enemy.* And it is no assurance against being terribly hurt. One need not wait until he has won the war before inflicting "unendurable" damages on his enemy. One need not wait until he has lost the war. There was a time when the assurance of victory—false or genuine assurance— could make national leaders not just willing but enthusiastic about war. Not now.[4]

There is no safety in military victory and the prospect of victory is clearly insufficient for rationally undertaking war. Indeed the traditional attributes of victory—such as occupation of an enemy's homeland—are increasingly irrelevant, since they neither give the "victor" new power to inflict pain on his opponent nor prevent harm to himself.

The fact that victory does not guarantee safety also greatly increases the importance of deliberate restraint in conflict. If there is no expectation or assurance that war can be kept limited, even a state that expects ultimately to "win" may find it irrational to engage in war. Thus wars may be waged in such a way as to ensure limitation rather than victory, and *the prospect of limitation will be even more necessary than the prospect of victory for a rational decision to go to war.* In the nuclear era, conflict limitation becomes an absolutely central intellectual concept. We shall return to it below.

The third basic change associated with nuclear weapons involves the *speed* with which pain can be inflicted. In addition to making destruction cheap and independent of victory, nuclear weapons make destruction fast. They make it *possible* to act in haste, to carry out threats without *having* to take time to think. As Schelling has observed,

> To compress a catastrophic war within the span of time that a man can stay awake drastically changes the politics of war, the process of decision, the possibility of central control and restraint, the motivations of people in charge and the capacity to think and reflect while war is in progress. It *is* imaginable that we might destroy 200,000,000 Russians in a war of the present, though not 80,000,000 Japanese in a war of the past. It is not only imaginable, it is imagined. It is imaginable because it could be done "in a moment, in the twinkling of an eye, at the last trumpet."[5]

Indeed, in a nuclear-armed world the compression of decision time is not simply possible, but highly likely. The speed, or potential speed, of an opponent's actions will *impose* haste on decision-makers. To delay even long enough to assemble additional advisers or brew a fresh pot of coffee is to risk losing the initiative. In the mobilization preceding World War I, military leaders were able to impress upon political leaders that hours were important; in the next world war, generals will impress upon politicians that minutes matter. The nuclear age has created tremendous time pressures, with their attendant problems of stress and organizational control. Thus the possible speed of nuclear war increases the possibility of *ex post* irrational execution of significant negative sanctions.

The fourth change associated with nuclear weapons is the *physical concentration of power* to inflict pain: nuclear warfare requires the acquiescence and involvement of substantially fewer participants. It is revealing that a slang phrase for starting a nuclear war is "pushing the button," an action that one man can do with ease. Obviously this exaggerates. Even the president, acting alone, could not launch a nuclear strike. But far fewer individuals need participate in a war in the nuclear age than in one in the prenuclear day. Nuclear war is war of the few, not war of the many. Napoleon's invasion of Russia in 1812 required 450,000 men; the crew of a B-52 bomber on its way to Moscow numbers six.[6] Nuclear weapons thus make possible dramatically increased centralization of significant power to hurt, either in a single decision center or in multiple, possibly independent, decision centers. Two distinct trends have been at work in the modern era: increasing social organization has made possible the involvement of larger and larger numbers of individuals in war-making efforts, while improvements in technology have permitted smaller and smaller numbers of individuals to wreak more and more damage. The development of weapons of mass destruction appears to have resulted in the dramatically increased importance of this second trend. The proverbial "mad colonel" is a problem unique to the nuclear age: while individuals with different, "nonsensible" values or with irrational decision-making processes are presumably no more likely to exist now than in the past, they now have power to inflict more damage, and the demand on the collective decision-making process to prevent the occurrence of "mad colonels" is therefore greater. Similarly, the danger posed by a few individuals in positions of military or political leadership suffering from situational stress or cognitive failure is far greater now, with so much power concentrated in so few hands.

The fifth and final basic change associated with nuclear weapons is the *increased ease of disrupting normal decision-making processes.* The use of nuclear weapons is likely to put new pressures—physical, psychological, and organizational—on an opponent's decision-making routine. Key nodes for information gathering and analysis and key leadership elements, while located well behind the front and protected from conventional attack, may be vulnerable to nuclear attack. Even if not deliberately subject to attack, they may accidently be destroyed or isolated, particularly given the existence of such poorly understood nuclear effects as electromagnetic pulse (EMP). Desmond Ball, for example, has mused:

> In fact, control of a nuclear exchange would become very difficult to maintain after several tens of strategic weapons had been used, even where deliberate attacks on command-and-control capabilities were avoided. Many command and control facilities, such as early-warning radars, radio antennae and satellite ground terminals would

be destroyed, or at least rendered inoperable, by nuclear detonations designed to destroy nearby military forces and installations, while the widespread disturbance of the ionosphere and equally wide-spread generation of EMP would disrupt HF [high-frequency] communications and impair electronic and electrical systems at great distances from the actual explosions. Hence, as John Steinbruner has argued, "regardless of the flexibility embodied in individual force components, the precariousness of command channels probably means that nuclear war would be uncontrollable, as a practical matter, shortly after the first tens of weapons are launched."[7]

Equally important, even if an opponent's decision-making resources are not destroyed or isolated, he is likely to fear that they will be in the near future.

The corollary of this is equally significant: *one's own* decision-making may be disrupted by nuclear war. It may be disrupted by the opponent's use of nuclear weapons. It may even be disrupted by one's own use of nuclear weapons: natural forces such as electromagnetic pulse do not discriminate by nationality. Thus, the possibility of nuclear war is likely to cause stress on decision-makers, and the actual occurrence of nuclear war is likely to disrupt organizational structure, threatening to result in organizational dysfunction.

The Implications of Nuclear Weapons for Coercion

Our concern, of course, is with the implications for coercion of these changes in the ease of inflicting destruction. The development of nuclear weapons and the subsequent evolution of a balance of terror in which the United States and the Soviet Union each maintain secure capabilities to devastate the other's society have affected the possibility of coercion in three ways.

First, nuclear warfare capabilities increase the likelihood that the opponent will have a contingent strategy. The pain that can be inflicted with nuclear weapons—through efforts at punishment, retaliation, or denial—is so great that very few goals are worth the price.

Second, the existence of a balance of terror based on mutual assured destruction capabilities greatly increases the difficulty that a rational coercer faces in credibly committing himself. In a nuclear world, military advantage and even the prospect of ultimate military victory no longer ensure the protection of one's homeland from massive attack. Just as there are very few objectives that are worth the devastation of an unlimited nuclear war to an opponent, there are very few objectives worth such a war to a coercer.

Since the cost of engaging in an unlimited nuclear exchange is likely to be unacceptably high, the expectation of limitation—the expectation that one's opponent will not inflict all the possible pain at his disposal—will usually be necessary for rational execution of threats against a nuclear opponent. A rational actor will not enter into hostilities or undertake escalation against a nuclear opponent unless that actor intelligently calculates that the likelihood of significant conflict limitation is acceptably high. We will return to this point in a moment.

Third, the existence of nuclear weapons increases the possibility of irrational decision-making and of commitment-through-irrationality to coercive strategies. The vulnerability of decision-making assets and the possibility that threats will be carried out quickly and by a few individuals creates new potential for nonintelligent calculation, inconsistent evaluation, or unreasoned choice—particularly caused by stress and organizational dysfunction.

The argument here is not that the existence of nuclear weapons increases the likelihood of irrational behavior during ordinary times or even during crisis: obviously, as has frequently been argued, nuclear weapons are likely to have a wonderfully "clarifying" effect on decision-makers' thinking. Rather, the point is that the increased speed of warfare, the concentration of power to inflict pain, and the increased vulnerability of normal decision-making processes mean that rational control will be difficult to maintain during an actual conflict. Nuclear arsenals increase the risk of *contingently* irrational behavior, a notion we shall return to in chapter 7.

CONFLICT LIMITATION

As we noted above, a rational decision to use nuclear weapons is, for most plausible sets of American values, likely to require an acceptable likelihood that conflict can be kept limited. Bernard Brodie noted back in 1959:

> The coming of the modern thermonuclear bomb was bound to give a great new impetus to an idea that had already suggested itself to some with the coming of the first atomic bombs: *the prospect of a large-scale mutual exchange of nuclear weapons on cities reduces war to a suicidal absurdity.* It is difficult to imagine a set of positive national objectives that could be realized in such a war by the side

that was "victorious" (the word is put in quotation marks only to remind us that it has lost its former meaning and needs redefining). Certain objectives can be spoken of as though they make sense even under the new conditions, but these usually have to be presented negatively, that is, as the preservation of values the loss of which would presumably be worse than death.[8]

This led Brodie to conclude that "if we assume reasonably secure retaliatory forces, unrestricted thermonuclear war seems to be at once much too destructive and too unpredictable to be invoked in any but the most dire straits."[9] Credible commitment-through-rationality has therefore become closely linked to the problem of conflict limitation in the nuclear age.

The Nature of Conflict Limitation

Conflict limitation has traditionally had two different meanings. One describes limitation in terms of the *ends* for which war is fought. These may be limited, rather than extensive. Survival is not at stake, or unconditional surrender is not required. Since the ends of war are ultimately political, we may think of this version of conflict limitation as *political* limitation. Alternatively, though, conflict limitation is often understood as limitation of the *means* employed by the combatants. War may be limited in "the means of war (weapons, categories of targets, troop levels)" or in "the scope (geographic or numbers of participating nations)."[10] Since decisions on the means employed are in some sense military ones, we can describe this sort of limitation as *military* limitation.

A third understanding of conflict limitation is possible, however. Conflict may be limited in terms of its *consequences*.[11] It is possible to think of conflict limitation as a limitation of destruction. Valued goods may be left undestroyed. Indeed, for the purpose of discussing coercion, the limitation of military conflict is best understood as the choice by an actor not to inflict pain that he is capable of inflicting. Limitation reflects the difference between possible pain and pain actually imposed. By this standard, limitation is a negative measure of pain: it measures *destruction withheld*.

This conception of limitation has some interesting implications. It suggests, for example, that a Soviet-American conflict with 100 Dresden-type bombing raids—in which massive conventional bombing results in fire storms that destroy entire cities—would be no more limited than one involving 100 Hiroshimas: the fact that nuclear weapons are not involved in the former is immaterial. "Nuclear" is not synonymous with "unlimited," nor "conventional" with "limited." Argentina and Chile would not be prevented from waging unlimited war by their nonpossession of nuclear weapons, nor would the United States (or the Soviet Union) need to use them in an unlimited war unless the opponent was large or strong enough to make total and complete extirpation impossible without a resort to nuclear effects. The maximum destruction of unlimited war is simply made greater by the possession of nuclear weapons and other weapons of mass destruction. Because the maximum possible destruction is greater but the maximum tolerable pain has not similarly grown, the magnitude of possible limitation and its importance increase.

Dimensions of Conflict Limitation

If conflict limitation is understood in terms of consequences, limits can be defined in four dimensions. That is, there are four dimensions in which pain or destruction can be withheld.

This dimensional approach to defining limitation is based on the logic that any act of destruction can be described in four ways. It can be described in terms of *what* was destroyed; *where* the destruction took place; *how thoroughly* the destruction was carried out; and *when* the destructive act occurred. Any particular act of destruction, any imposition of pain, involves all four attributes. If one wishes to think graphically (and can imagine four dimensions), every act of destruction can be defined as a point in four-space, with four coordinates. The possible pain one actor can inflict on another describes a four-dimensional universe of points. The destruction or pain that occurs in a conflict can be described as some set of points within this universe. Conflict limitation suggests that this set of points is not identical to the universe of possible points. The *dimension* of limitation describes *which* coordinate has a range of excluded values.

The first of the four dimensions is vertical limitation. Some specific *types* of target sets placed at risk may deliberately not be harmed. Exclusion is based on what the target is. These excluded targets may, for example, be of social or economic value—e.g., hospitals, prisons, oil refineries, power plants, fertilizer factories, or cities—or they may be of principally military significance—e.g., air bases, vulnerable ICBM silos, or military command posts. The U.S. No Cities doctrine enunciated in the early 1960s provides an example of vertical limitation: cities were to be held as continued hostage rather than destroyed.

The second dimension, horizontal limitation, reflects the possibility of withholding destruction by geographic region. Exclusion is based on location. Superpower homelands, for example, may be treated as sanctuaries, or conflict may be restricted to a single theater even though the actor has the power to escalate it into a multitheater one. The decision by Communist forces in the Korean War to eschew attacks on UN bases in Japan can be described in terms of horizontal limitation, as can restraints against attacking military targets in China.

The third dimension is limitation in depth of destruction. An actor may choose to destroy some of the cities or oil refineries or missile silos he holds vulnerable, but not all of them. He may engage in decimation rather than total extirpation, though the latter is within his power. In a popular fictionalized account of the impending Third World War written by General Sir John Hackett and other top-ranking NATO generals and advisers, NATO forces respond to the destruction of Birmingham by destroying only Minsk, though the capacity to devastate the entire Soviet Union was theirs—clearly a limitation in depth of destruction.[12]

The final dimension is temporal limitation. The cessation of hostilities prior to the absolute exhaustion of the actor or the complete destruction of his opponent can be understood as a dimension of conflict limitation. Temporal limitation may involve some sort of negotiated surrender or an explicit or tacit cease-fire. In World War II, Japan surrendered—ending its imposition of pain on the United States—while its armies were still largely intact. In October 1973, Egypt and Israel halted military action even though each had the wherewithal to continue (with more or less effectiveness).

Significance and Possibility of Limitation

Both the *significance* of limitation in each of these dimensions and the *possibility* of achieving it have varied over time. These variations have reflected two types of changes in the world. First, the significance and possibility of limitation have varied in response to changes in the nature of state actors and the international system. Second, they have varied in response to changes in military technology—most importantly, of course, the introduction of nuclear weapons.

At any point in time, norms of limitation are likely to reflect the nature of existing state actors and of the state system as well as the capabilities of available military technologies. During the European dynastic wars of the eighteenth century, for example, vertical and temporal limitation were common and of tremendous social and political importance. Significant efforts were made to place noncombatants and nonmilitary targets off limits, and wars were generally ended by treaty long before either side was completely defeated.

That changes in the nature of states and the international system should affect conflict limitation is hardly surprising. If—as we shall suggest—rational conflict limitation results from the calculation by a decision-maker of a common interest he shares with his opponent (that is, from the calculation that inflicting certain types of pain on an opponent will decrease one's own utility), then changes in the nature of states (and therefore in what yields state decision-makers utility) and in the nature of the international system (and therefore in the nature of interdependencies) should be expected to alter the type of limitations pursued. At the simplest, I—or my opponent and I—may avoid inflicting pain in certain dimensions because such infliction undermines my—or our—domestic social organization. Temporal limitation would have been objectively rational for German and Russian decision-makers, if not for all the participants, in World War I: continued war resulted in revolution and the delegitimation of the state.[13] Similarly, the willingness of individual nobles to serve the Crown in campaigns of conquest during the High Middle Ages may be inseparable from the medieval vertical limitation against killing "enemy" knights (or being killed by them), and instead seeking to take captives and ransom them for a profit.

As the nature of the relationship between the state decision-maker and those it governs and between it and its opponents changes, so too will the nature of conflict limitation. Conflicts between peoples are likely to take a different form—that is, to have different limits—than contests between governments: the rise of nation-states and popularly legitimated governments since the French Revolution appears to have been an important factor in reducing the likelihood of vertical and temporal limits.[14] Revolution of social organization has meant both that the distinction between combatant and noncombatant (and the parallel one between military and civilian industry) has become less clear and that the aims for which war is waged are more likely to involve destruction of an opposing government, state, or social organization and are therefore less amenable to temporal limitation.[15]

The most striking changes in patterns of conflict limitation during the last half-century, though, have occurred as a result of changes in military technology. Technology affects the possible scope of violence in each of the four dimensions, either by increasing the amount of

damage a victor can inflict or by giving the loser the option of imposing substantial pain. Technological changes thereby affect the *importance* of limitation. But by affecting the possibility of behaving rationally and of actually controlling and discriminating in the imposition
of pain, new technology—especially nuclear weapon technology—
has also dramatically affected the *ability* of decision-makers to limit
conflict in the various dimensions.

For example, nuclear weapons have made vertical limitation both
more significant and more difficult. Long-range nuclear weapons have
increased potential violence in this dimension. Whole classes of targets—such as population centers—are now much more vulnerable.
Indeed, with current missile capabilities, anything and everything
that can be located can be destroyed—a far cry from the situation
when only battlefields were vulnerable. The variety of things that can
be destroyed has dramatically expanded. At the same time, though,
discrimination among targets is more of a problem: it is difficult to
discriminate between hospitals and military bases when the two fit
under one fireball. Only the grossest sorts of vertical limitation—such
as not hitting major metropolitan areas—are likely to be possible;
even here (and even setting aside the danger of missiles being mistar-
geted or straying off course) fallout and other nuclear effects, ranging
from electromagnetic pulse to climatic change, mean that the distinction is hardly as definite as was the case with conventional warfare.

The development of long-range air power clearly increased the
significance of horizontal limitation. Interior regions or remote targets across wide oceans were rendered vulnerable. In World War I, if
New York and London remained undamaged it was not because of a
willful decision by the German government to leave them so (indeed,
the German armed forces did subject London to zeppelin attacks). In
the post-World War II era, however, no region of the globe is out of
range of the superpowers' military might. As a result, any future war
between the United States and the Soviet Union which spared their
homelands—any conflict in which destruction, either conventional or
nuclear, was limited to Europe or some portion of the periphery, for
example—would necessarily require horizontal limitation.

Similarly, the development of nuclear weapons has vastly increased the importance of limitation in the depth of destruction. In
the prenuclear age, without tremendous military superiority usually
only very small target sets could be destroyed completely. During
World War II, the Germans could damage various British industrial
facilities and urban areas, but they could not completely destroy an

entire industry or all of Britain's major cities; likewise, Allied strategic bombing efforts against key German war-making industries—such as petroleum and ball-bearings—failed to halt production in these industries. Today, however, it is easy to imagine the complete destruction of a superpower's oil refinery capacity, steel production facilities, or major population centers. True, these target sets could have been completely destroyed in the prenuclear world if one of the parties was completely victorious. After their defeat of Germany, the Allies had the option of completely "pastoralizing" Germany, as the Mongols had had the option of depopulating the territories they conquered. Today, though, such an option simultaneously exists for both superpowers, even if neither is able to achieve a complete victory.

But limitation in depth may be difficult to maintain in a nuclear conflict, if for no other reason than that it is difficult to predict or gauge accurately the depth of destruction that is occurring. It may be difficult during a nuclear war to tell the difference—not to mention to act rationally on the difference—between an attack aimed at weakening an opponent and one aimed at disarming him, or between the destruction of ten cities and one hundred. This is particularly likely to be true because the indirect physical, organizational, economic, and environmental consequences of nuclear exchanges are difficult to measure or predict and are unlikely to be estimated in a consistent fashion: the direct destruction of one command node may lead to the incapacitation of an entire military structure just as the destruction of one city may yield environmental catastrophe and economic dislocation that ripple throughout the nation.

By contrast, changes in military technology have reduced both the importance and the possibility of temporal limitation. While technological innovation increased the scope of possible destruction in the other three dimensions, by increasing the concentration and reach of firepower it had an inverse effect in this dimension: it reduced the time frame required for imposing substantial hurt. Since nuclear wars need not necessarily go off "like one big string of firecrackers," temporal limitation may still retain some significance.[16] (Indeed, it is precisely on this possibility that the idea of controlled nuclear retaliation is based: retaliatory strategies are built on the idea that nuclear war can be halted after it has begun but before unbearable destruction has occurred.) The speed with which nuclear war may be conducted is, however, likely to reduce greatly the importance and potential range of temporal limitation. If cities have already been destroyed, it makes little difference whether war is terminated after an hour or a month—although, to be sure, one might argue that if war lasted for enough months or years it might hinder whatever recovery might otherwise have been possible. The difference between conflict in the prenuclear age and in the nuclear age is striking: in the prenuclear era, combatant states could count on being able to sue for peace before massive devastation of their societies occurred. The suit might not be accepted or the terms demanded might be too harsh. But it had never been the case that it took longer to communicate explicit proposals for mutual temporal limits than to inflict (or experience) unendurable pain.

The *possibility* of temporal limitation—the possibility of terminating a conflict before destructive potential is exhausted—is also physically limited in the case of nuclear conflict. Two reasons are involved. On the one hand, the conflict is likely to have damaged the physical and bureaucratic infrastructure necessary to carry out explicit negotiations with the opponent. On the other hand, the conflict is likely to have damaged the infrastructure necessary to halt one's own activities. In addition to these physical obstacles, however, there may be other reasons why temporal limitation of nuclear conflict will prove impossible *even for rational actors* in an anarchic system. If, after nuclear war has begun and some damage has been inflicted, offense becomes dominant over defense—that is, if there is a significant military advantage to pressing the offense rather than assuming the defense—then states are likely to be skeptical of temporal limitation. Since a halt would leave each side vulnerable to a resumption of hostilities by the other, states are unlikely to engage in temporal limitation. And indeed, once a nuclear conflict has begun, offense is extremely likely to become dominant over defense: as bombers are forced by fuel constraints to land and by mechanical constraints to undergo servicing, and as missile-carrying submarines are forced to return to port for provisions, the ability of a state to maintain an assured second-strike capability is likely to be degraded—particularly if bases and support facilities have been destroyed or damaged. Just as crisis instability threatens to make a decision to go to war rational, cease-fire instability threatens to make a decision to resume war rational.

In sum then, given the potential speed and irreversibility of nuclear destruction, the three particularly important dimensions of nuclear conflict limitation are vertical, horizontal, and depth. If nuclear war is to be undertaken rationally, *there has to be some reasonable assurance of significant limitation in at least one of these three dimensions.*

Of these, the horizontal dimension appears to be the easiest in which to achieve limitation: it is the only dimension in which, given limited information and time and considerable psychological pressure, it is likely to be clear that limitations are being observed.[17] It is, in addition, the dimension in which accidental breaches are least likely.

Reasons for Conflict Limitation:
Noncontingency, Contingency, and Mutual Contingency

But why would limitation occur? If actors are rational, limitations are observed out of self-interest. Conflict involves mixed motives. Refraining from destroying some target may yield greater utility than destroying it. I may feel better about myself for having shown mercy to you, or my survival and prosperity may ultimately depend on your survival and prosperity, or I may simply find it more profitable to exploit you than kill you.[18]

The benefits which accrue to an actor from limiting conflict—and thereby influencing him rationally to choose to limit conflict—may be either contingent or noncontingent. They may depend on the opponent's behavior or exist regardless of it. If noncontingent benefits are the sole or critical factor in an actor's rational decision to limit conflict, then limitation is a dominant strategy: whatever the opponent does, it is in the actor's own best interest to observe certain limits. For example, moral injunctions, such as those voiced by the National Conference of Catholic Bishops or by George Kennan against the killing of noncombatants[19] encourage noncontingent vertical limitations that place cities out of bounds.[20]

Of the contingent reasons to limit conflict, the most obvious is reciprocity. The United States may observe limitations identical or similar to those observed by the Soviet Union. The United States may, for example, observe a cease-fire, refrain from attacking cities, or regard the entire Soviet homeland as a sanctuary because the Soviets have similarly limited their destructive behavior. Reciprocal limitation merely suggests that the U.S. decision-maker estimates that it is in his best interest to mimic certain Soviet behavior. Reciprocal limitation by the United States does not necessarily require that Soviet limitation be contingent on U.S. behavior, much less on U.S. reciprocity. The U.S. decision-maker may, for example, find it morally unacceptable to attack Soviet cities before U.S. cities are attacked, regardless of the reason for Soviet restraint.

Nonreciprocal contingent limitation is also possible. For example, the United States might rationally engage in vertical limitation, avoiding Soviet command-and-control facilities anywhere in the world, as long as the Soviets engaged in horizontal limitation, avoiding targets in the continental United States. Such nonreciprocal but contingent limitation might make perfect sense. So long as the United States is not under attack, the U.S. desire to be able to negotiate a complete end of hostilities may dominate U.S. calculations; once the United States comes under attack, though, the need to disrupt Soviet coordination in order to limit damage may be the critical factor in the U.S. utility function. Similarly, U.S. willingness to withhold attacks on Soviet ballistic missile submarines (a vertical limitation) may be contingent on Soviet restraint in expanding a war to the Atlantic (a horizontal limitation). What should be clear from these examples is that contingent limitation involves a commitment to escalate destruction if certain actions are taken by one's opponent.

Obviously, one's opponent might also engage in contingent limitation. The establishment by an opponent of a credible commitment to escalate destruction in certain contingencies may affect the utility of one's own various options. Indeed, this raises the possibility of *mutually contingent* limitation. Limitation by each side may require limitation by the other. An abandonment of limitation by either side would cause an abandonment by the other. The most obvious examples of mutually contingent limitations are reciprocal temporal ones: cease-fires, truces, and peace treaties. In these cases each side's willingness to stop inflicting pain on the other, after an agreed point in time, depends on the other's willingness to do the same.

Mutually contingent limitation may occur in other dimensions as well, though. For example, U.S. willingness to avoid attacking Soviet war-making industry may depend on a Soviet commitment to respond by attacking U.S. war-making industry; at the same time, Soviet willingness to avoid attacking U.S. war-making industry may depend on a U.S. commitment to respond by attacking similar Soviet facilities.

Most important limitation in a nuclear conflict will probably be mutually contingent. Our self-interest in exercising restraint in a nuclear war is likely to be a function of the opponent's restraint, and his is likely to be a function of our restraint. To say, as we have, that for the use of nuclear weapons to be rational there must be some sufficient prospect of significant vertical, horizontal, or depth limitation is to say that there must be some sufficient prospect that mutually contingent (though not necessarily reciprocal) limitation in these dimensions can be maintained.

Mutually contingent limitation is unique in that it requires communication, either explicit or implicit. Each party must be able not only to estimate how the other will respond, but must also be able to communicate how he himself will respond.

More critically, the maintenance of mutually contingent limitation is likely to require rational behavior. Rational behavior, of course, does not guarantee that mutually contingent limitations that are mutually advantageous will not break down: even rational actors may miscalculate, be misinformed, or be unlucky. In an actual conflict, the United States might, for example, fail to realize either that some particular Soviet limitation is being observed or that it is contingent upon some particular U.S. restraint. We may not understand that the Soviet failure to destroy, say, U.S. West Coast port facilities is a deliberate response to our not bombing conventional military targets in the Far East and is contingent upon that restraint.

In the absence of rational behavior, however, mutually contingent limitation is most likely to prove impossible to maintain. If, for example, each side prefers to place cities off bounds so long as the other does so, but Soviet rational central control over its missile force breaks down when the United States attacks targets other than cities, this particular mutually contingent limitation is likely to fail. Nonproscribed actions may interfere with the ability of one or both sides to observe limitations that, because of their mutually-contingent character, each side would rationally prefer to observe.

Conflict Limitation and Rational War

A certain irony exists here. A limited war may be rational to undertake if one's own continued rationality and the rationality of one's opponent can be ensured, but, given the structure of decision-making processes, many imaginable limited wars are likely to destroy future rationality. They are likely, in particular, to create substantial situational stress and to interfere with the normal function of the state organization, thus causing organizational dysfunction. As we noted above, one of the three principal implications of nuclear weapons is that rationality during war may be particularly difficult to maintain.

In sum, then, nuclear war fought for less than essential aims is likely to be irrational unless it can be kept limited, but it probably can be kept limited only if the participants can remain rational. The ability to achieve commitment-through-rationality to nuclear threats requires that nuclear war not interfere with one's own and one's opponent's ability to behave rationally. Fulfillment of this requirement, however, seems dubious.

This conclusion holds even if one ignores the organizational and psychological effects of nuclear war and considers only the probable physical ones. Bruce Blair has examined the U.S. strategic command and control system and studied the effects of nuclear war on it. His conclusions are bleak. Even in response to a clearly limited Soviet attack on the United States, the United States would face overwhelming difficulties in responding in undertaking a controlled response:

> In formulating a strategic response to a focused attack on U.S. forces, decisionmakers could not determine that the attack is indeed of this character. They would confront a situation in which there would be considerable damage to the ground portion of the command system, which would remain under threat of sudden and total destruction. Other relevant considerations are that the attack would trigger the launch of command aircraft and initiate an operation of relatively short endurance, that a coherent airborne network would be difficult to establish and maintain, that communications would be very difficult to establish, that reconstitution of the network would be highly improbable, that the capacity of communications channels would preclude delivery of detailed instructions, and that the communications subsystems that could be patched together would allow only one-way communication. Under these conditions, *a radical departure from any plausibly rational course of action seems a foregone conclusion.* . . . Regardless of what calculations political leaders might make at the time, they would come under intense pressure to choose without delay an option that would provide for all that they would ever expect to accomplish in retaliation to an attack of uncertain dimensions. There would be strong incentives to order early and comprehensive retaliation, a response contrary to one that would correspond to the scale of provocation and extend deterrence into war itself.[21]

The implications of this inability to act rationally are that

> The postulated limited Soviet attack would carry a high risk of triggering an all-out nuclear war. Although decisionmakers might prefer a limited response, a technical-organizational bind would create strong pressure to respond massively: decisionmakers could

not reliably determine if the attack were indeed limited, and in any case they could not expect to exercise positive control over whatever forces they decide to withhold.[22]

Paul Bracken has reached similar conclusions:

One thing emerges repeatedly when we examine nuclear command and control: there are seemingly insurmountable barriers to maintaining political control in a strategic war. The breakup of communications after attack leads to decentralized assessment and to joint decision making among the isolated islands of forces, with pathological strategy implications. War plans themselves are not structured for centralized political control. Rather, they are based on preplan attacks in which a dead-reckoning control mechanism further increases the likelihood of unstoppable salvoing in a communications-disrupted environment.[23]

Within Europe these same problems are recreated on a smaller scale. Pointing to problems of decentralized and delegated control of nuclear weapons, the ambiguity of command authority, and the complexity of management in a wartime environment, Bracken has concluded that "if a war occurs it is likely to be intrinsically uncontrollable because the NATO command system has not been designed to provide such control."[24] Moreover, the presence of long-range systems in the European theater makes it difficult to ensure that even horizontal limitations can be imposed.

Summary

Building on the preceding chapters, we have reasoned deductively that nuclear weapons and a situation of mutual assured destruction affect coercive power in three ways. First, they increase the likelihood of an opponent's being coercible. Second, they decrease the likelihood that execution of a coercive strategy will be rational. Third, they increase the likelihood of irrational behavior.

In the MAD era, for a coercive strategy to be rational to execute, there will have to be an acceptable prospect of maintaining significant limits in at least one of three critical dimensions: vertical, horizontal, or depth. Such limitations would likely be mutually contingent. The difficulties of maintaining such limitations are extraordinarily great. Particularly given the difficulties of nuclear command and control during war, the prospect for significant limitation is therefore bleak.

This analysis of the implications of nuclear weapons for coercion and of the concept and difficulties of nuclear conflict limitation raises the question: How can coercers such as the United States take advantage of the two possible benefits of a nuclear world (the increased likelihood of a contingent coercee strategy and the increased likelihood of contingently irrational behavior) while avoiding the problems for rational commitment created by a MAD world? What combination of coercive strategy and mode of commitment is suited to the nuclear age? In chapter 7, we will approach this question by developing more fully the notion of contingently irrational behavior. Before doing so, however, it is useful to undertake a brief exploration of the implications of commitment-through-denial-of-choice and commitment-through-irrationality in the nuclear era by drawing on the concept of a Doomsday Machine.

6

DOOMSDAY MACHINES

THE PRECEDING discussion of commitments not involving *ex post* rationality and of the impact of nuclear weapons on coercion is likely to have generated a certain amount of unease. It may have occurred to the careful reader (particularly one who has vivid memories of the late Peter Sellars in Dr. Strangelove's wheelchair) that in the nuclear age, commitment-through-denial-of-choice and commitment-through-irrationality can yield what has become known as a Doomsday Machine. Before dropping from public attention entirely, the notion of a Doomsday Machine received much criticism and little or no serious advocacy.[1] And yet, the model of a Doomsday Machine clearly deserves more careful review and analysis. As a logical construct, it represents a useful tool for thinking about nuclear conflict in an era of mutual assured destruction capabilities. It serves as a *description* of a situation that may arise and yield extended deterrent power in a MAD world; as a descriptive tool, it may also prove heuristically useful in developing a *prescription* for deterrence policy.

THE NATURE OF DOOMSDAY MACHINES

The essence of a Doomsday Machine, like that of any coercive device that involves commitment-through-denial-of-choice or commitment-through-irrationality, lies in the inability of its owner rationally to control his own actions once his opponent has engaged in some particular provocation. The pain and destruction of the negative sanction are imposed not because either side rationally wills them to be imposed but despite the fact that both wish they were not. Once a Doomsday Machine is triggered, the conduct of war ceases to be a rational endeavor and becomes a senseless exercise in destruction; the point of a Doomsday Machine is that as a consequence of this transformation of war, rational opponents are deterred from taking actions that would trigger the Machine.

When people think of a Doomsday Machine they usually imagine a mechanical device that responds automatically to provocation.[2] And clearly, the conceptually easiest way to achieve the absence of rational control is by yielding all control to an actual machine—that is, by building and installing a tamper-proof black box that carries out the threat automatically. As we noted in chapter 4, however, it is likely to prove quite difficult credibly to deny oneself any choice at all: given that the United States would have every incentive to bluff about whether the black box actually had been installed and actually worked, the Soviets would likely be extremely skeptical of the commitment.

Because the existence of the Doomsday Machine in *Dr. Strangelove* was never communicated, either implicitly or explicitly, the United States did not perceive the Soviet Union as credibly committed to a deterrent doomsday threat. But even if the Soviet Union had announced the existence of a Doomsday Machine, it seems implausible that the Soviets would have been—in the eyes of U.S. decision-makers—credibly committed to inflict doomsday in the event of U.S. aggression. Given that the Soviets as well as the Americans would rationally prefer that the Machine never go off, regardless of the provocation,[3] and given that the Soviets could not demonstrate that every wire everywhere in the machine was actually connected, why would U.S. leaders have believed that the claimed Doomsday Machine was actually functional? The Machine could not be made technically unambiguous—a necessary condition for the "rationality of the irrational" so long as the Soviets could not bluff that they actually preferred doomsday.

Logically, however, there is a second principle on which a Doomsday Machine may operate. A Doomsday Machine may also be based on a commitment-through-irrationality. Indeed, where a technically unambiguous commitment involving a *mechanical* black-box Doomsday Machine may be extraordinarily unlikely, an *organizational* Doomsday Machine may be quite likely and quite credible. The equivalent of the hidden wiring of a mechanical black box is the (largely visible) decision-making process (including equipment and procedures for command and control) and the (uncertain but largely predictable) effects of situational stress.

Unique Characteristics of Doomsday Machines

A Doomsday Machine, whether based on mechanical commitment-through-denial-of-choice or on organizational commitment-through-irrationality, has three special characteristics which differentiate it from other cases of commitment-through-denial-of-choice or commitment-through-irrationality. The first special characteristic is that a Doomsday Machine threatens a response that involves massive destruction—something that will be considered "doomsday" by one's opponent. Nuclear weapons make this possible.

The second characteristic is one that makes a Doomsday Machine so unappealing: the owner of the Machine cannot expect to escape the massive destruction his Machine causes. In the event the Doomsday Machine is activated and generates doomsday, it generates doomsday for everyone, including the nation that built it. The earliest Doomsday Machines conceived involved a threat directly to destroy oneself as well as one's opponent—to shroud the whole earth in radioactivity or such. If the worst estimates of the "nuclear winter" phenomenon are accurate, then the use of even a few hundred nuclear weapons against an opponent's urban centers would act as a Doomsday Machine, causing massive climatic change that would devastate both superpowers indiscriminately.

But clearly a state has created a Doomsday Machine just as effectively if it relies on the reaction of its opponent to bring the destruction back home and to spread the devastation around evenly. If my opponent will respond to my destruction of his society by destroying mine (and the collateral damage of our exchange will destroy everything else that matters), then I can succeed in building a Doomsday Machine even if I do not threaten myself directly.[4]

The third peculiarity of Doomsday Machines is really a function of the first two: Doomsday Machines are fundamentally devices for inflicting punishment.[5] While other deterrence tactics involving commitment-through-denial-of-choice or commitment-through-irrationality may involve coercive threats of denial or retaliation, the principal effect of a Doomsday Machine is punitive. To be sure, Doomsday Machines may also succeed in denying an opponent his objective—for example, the destruction of all societies in the Northern Hemisphere may prevent the Soviet Union from exploiting German industry and technology or from reimposing meaningful political control over Eastern Europe—but it is the punishment aspect of doomsday that is likely to prove the dominant consideration.[6] The pain of doomsday is greater than mere denial of some gain for which one had undertaken aggression.

Equally important, a Doomsday Machine is not likely to be a satisfactory device for carrying out retaliation. It is unlikely to provide intraconflict compellent power. To be sure, a Doomsday Machine could conceivably serve as a retaliation device, but only if doomsday was inflicted slowly or (more likely) repeatedly in a probabilistic fashion.[7] Even then, a Doomsday Machine could serve as a retaliation device only if it could be turned off after it had been turned on. And if the Doomsday Machine could be turned off in response to eventual compliance by the opponent, would the opponent find it credible that the Machine could *not* be turned off in the *absence* of his compliance? That is, if the Doomsday Machine could be turned off in the event of compliance, would the denial of rational control in the event of noncompliance be credible? More fundamentally, a repeated-play probabilistic Doomsday Machine is likely to fail to deter by threat of retaliation because it is unlikely that during the period between the original failure of deterrence and the actual imposition of doomsday the Machine will do anything to increase an opponent's rational estimate of the likelihood that doomsday will actually occur, to increase an opponent's surprise aversion, to increase a surprise-averse opponent's uncertainty about final outcomes, or to alter the likelihood of irrational behavior by the opponent. As a consequence, a rational opponent either would never fail to be deterred by the Machine in the first place or would never be compelled eventually to comply, unless, of course, temporary noncompliance permitted him to gain his political goals.

There are three important characteristics that are *not* required of a Doomsday Machine. The first was hinted at in the paragraph above. While by definition a Doomsday Machine must involve the *threat* of doomsday, it need not involve the *certainty* of doomsday should the opponent fail to be deterred. Instead, it may be designed to execute a mixed strategy. It may leave something to chance. Be it mechanical or organizational, a Doomsday Machine may threaten the risk rather than the certainty of massive destruction. A Doomsday Machine might, for example, be designed to yield doomsday a half or a quarter of the time it is triggered. Indeed, as a practical matter, any Doomsday Machine constructed will in fact be a probabilistic one: as we noted in our discussion of threats that leave something to chance, even when it is claimed that pain will be imposed with certainty, given the inherent unreliability of all decision-making processes and tools of destruction, the actual commitment is to inflict pain with some probability less than one.

Second, Doomsday Machines need not be built deliberately to be Doomsday Machines. The fact that they were built, or came about, without intention makes them no less Doomsday Machines.

And third, Doomsday Machines may exist and be effective even if they are not called Doomsday Machines. A Doomsday Machine by any other name—or by no name at all—would logically have the same impact on a rational opponent, although it might be less controversial in the nation that owned it.

THE EXISTENCE OF DOOMSDAY MACHINES

If Doomsday Machines need not involve the certainty of doomsday, need not be built deliberately, and need not be called Doomsday Machines, is it possible that they already exist? Despite the "unacceptability" of Doomsday Machines, is it possible that we have been living happily and more or less securely in a world that has such devices? Indeed, is it possible that we have been *relying* on one of them for our security?

As Doomsday Machines are defined above, the United States currently owns and operates an unacknowledged probabilistic one. The principal stimuli that would cause the U.S. Doomsday Machine to "go off" in a probabilistic fashion are a Soviet nuclear attack on U.S. territory or major Soviet aggression in Europe. There exist probabilistic psychological and organizational "triggers" for the U.S. doomsday nuclear arsenal in both of these contingencies. This is the flip side to our discussion above about the difficulties of retaining rational control of nuclear forces in the event of a nuclear attack on the United States, and the flip side of the noted difficulties in preventing the loss of central negative control over nuclear forces in Europe in the event of a major Soviet attack.[8]

Consider the European case. As Bracken has noted about the NATO nuclear force posture:

What some observers see as a disorderly and thoughtless development of highly differentiated nuclear forces is in fact precisely the kind of force structure needed for a deterrence strategy whose implementation would be suicidal. Although debates among nuclear specialists have broken out over the years about the need for conventional forces, tactical nuclear warfighting postures, and other alternative foundations for NATO security, what has been ignored is that command structure in this particular case is deeply related to political strategy. The NATO strategy of relying on nuclear weapons is politically and militarily credible because the governing command structure is so unstable and accident-prone that national leaders would exercise little practical control over it in wartime. What other command mechanism could possibly be built to invoke a nuclear conflict that, for all practical purposes, is tantamount to a regional doomsday machine?[9]

In the event of Soviet aggression, there exists some significant probability that rational decision-making about the use of U.S. nuclear weapons deployed in Europe would break down; in the absence of rational control, there is some significant probability that these weapons would be used; given such use, there is some significant probability of uncontrolled escalation to unlimited nuclear war, a war equivalent to doomsday. In other words, given the deployment of U.S. nuclear forces in Europe, given the existence of a command-and-control process that (due primarily to the effects of stress and organizational dysfunction) would make rational control over these forces difficult to maintain, given the difficulty Soviet and U.S. decision-makers would encounter in controlling nuclear war once begun, and given the superpowers' possession of nuclear capabilities that if unleashed would yield doomsday, the U.S. nuclear posture in Europe can be comprehended in terms of a Doomsday Machine.[10]

Note that the irrational use of nuclear weapons by the United States by no means makes doomsday certain, nor need it do so for a probabilistic Doomsday Machine to exist. The irrational use of nuclear weapons merely generates a *risk* of doomsday. U.S. commitment-through-irrationality to the use of nuclear weapons thus engages two probabilistic factors—two superimposed threats that leave something to chance. First, commitment-through-irrationality imposes some risk of the irrational use of nuclear weapons. Second, use of nuclear weapons imposes some risk of escalation to doomsday.

Whether the probability is large or small that this probabilistic U.S. Doomsday Machine in Europe will actually trigger doomsday if the Soviets attack NATO is an important factual question. Whether it *should* be large or small remains an important—indeed, the central —policy question for the Alliance. There is no reason to assume that the Doomsday Machine that has evolved without much oversight over the decades is optimally designed or is, on balance, desirable.

But without eliminating the capabilities for mutual annihilation, the possibility that nuclear war would escalate uncontrollably once begun, and the possibility that stress, organizational dysfunction, or other causes of irrationality might result in the irrational initiation of nuclear war given certain stimulation, *it is impossible to eliminate entirely the existence of Doomsday Machines.* One can greatly reduce the risk that an organizational Doomsday Machine will actually trigger doomsday but one cannot stop it from ticking entirely. It is neither a question of whether to build a Doomsday Machine nor of how to unbuild one. Doomsday Machines are with us, whether we like it or not. The critical question is how best to live with them.

This question can be broken down into two basic but interrelated policy questions. First, how much power will one attempt to derive from the existence of a Doomsday Machine? Second, what is the optimal design of the Doomsday Machine?

THE EXPLOITATION AND DESIGN OF DOOMSDAY MACHINES

Given the unfavorable reviews that Doomsday Machines have received, it is not particularly surprising that the United States has neither acknowledged the existence of a Doomsday Machine nor sought to make it the cornerstone of its deterrence strategy. Doomsday Machines are frightening. Especially when survival is at stake, it is natural instinctively to prefer rational control over actions to lack of rational control. And in the 1950s, when the concept of Doomsday Machines was first explored and the notion introduced to the public and policymakers, the United States still possessed the nuclear superiority necessary to make it conceivable that the United States could rationally carry out its nuclear threats. Even given the extended leverage over Soviet behavior that the United States sought to gain from its possession of nuclear weapons, nuclear superiority at least appeared to make denial of rational control unnecessary. The U.S. need for a Doomsday Machine was very small.

As we suggested in chapter 1, however, in a MAD world rational control appears incompatible with the objectives of U.S. deterrence strategy. The United States has found it impossible to structure costs and benefits so as to make it rational to carry out nuclear threats in the event of a Soviet attack on Europe or even a limited nuclear blow against the United States. Continued U.S. reliance on a nuclear threat to achieve political goals, therefore, drives the United States to take advantage of Doomsday Machines' potential for tremendous coercive power rather than to seek simply to minimize the risk of doomsday.[11]

Given the desire to employ nuclear power resources for a range of political ends, it is worthwhile, therefore, to examine carefully the dangers of Doomsday Machines. Beyond the instinctual distaste they generate, Doomsday Machines pose four problems for their owners.

Design Dangers

The first two problems deal with the existence of a contingent coercee strategy. First, it is possible that a rational opponent may lack a contingent strategy associated with the Machine's threat. Conceivably, the negative sanction of the Doomsday Machine may be of insufficient magnitude to create a rational preference to yield. Obviously, if the Doomsday Machine is not a probabilistic one, then this is an unlikely contingency and probably represents the least of the problems facing the Machine's owner: given the large disutility of doomsday, the absence of a rational preference to yield is unlikely. It is difficult to imagine a situation or a plausible set of values in which the certainty of doomsday is rationally preferred over being deterred. Doomsday presumably does not have an *infinite* negative utility, but it is bound to have an extremely large one.[12] On the other hand, however, if the Doomsday Machine threatens only the *risk* of doomsday, then it is possible to imagine objectives worth the expected disutility. For example, the Soviet Union might conceivably undertake some limited aggression in Central Europe, calculating that the risk of doomsday was low enough to be outweighed by the more probable gains of aggression. The opponent may *rationally* prefer to go ahead and trigger the Doomsday Machine, knowing that the Machine will impose only a small chance of doomsday even if triggered.

Second, an opponent may not be able rationally to choose to be deterred. He may be unable to act upon his rational preference to yield. An opponent may trigger the Doomsday Machine because his own actions are outside his rational control. In this case, doomsday may result because of the opponent's inability to respond rationally to the existence of a Doomsday Machine. Computers and other machines may fail in the opponent's organization, causing an accident that triggers the Doomsday Machine. Or the opponent may fail to use information intelligently and therefore not recognize the existence of the Doomsday Machine and its implicit threat; he may evaluate costs and benefits in an inconsistent fashion; or he may engage in unreasoned, random policy choice. That is, the opponent may *irrationally* trigger the Doomsday Machine.

The third danger from Doomsday Machines stems from the difficulty of credible commitment. The existence and operation of the Machine may not be credible to the skeptical opponent. Three distinct problems are possible. First, the opponent may not believe that rational control has in fact been surrendered in the contingencies the coercer wishes to deter: the opponent may not believe that the particular "triggers" the coercer claims actually exist, or he may even doubt whether a Doomsday Machine exists at all. Second, the opponent may not believe the probability the coercer claims for the Doomsday Machine—he may think it less likely that the Machine will actually go off, given the provocation, than is in fact the case. Third, the opponent may doubt that the pain threatened would constitute doomsday. If there is an actual commitment to doomsday (if the Doomsday Machine really *is* in place) and the opponent believes it is a bluff, the possibility of catastrophe is obviously present.

The fourth source of danger associated with Doomsday Machines is that even if the Machine actually deters, it may malfunction and carry out the threat. There is always a risk that the Machine, be it mechanical or organizational, will trigger itself even if the opponent does not act provocatively.

Steps can of course be taken in designing a Doomsday Machine to alleviate each of these four problems. The value of steps taken to alleviate any of these four problems, however, must be weighed against both the aggravation these "solutions" cause for the other three problems and the value the decision-maker assigns to any marginal loss in coercive power associated with such steps. To be sure, there may be design features that are unambiguously desirable—improved sensors that make it possible for the Machine to tell with greater certainty that the opponent has failed to comply, for example—but for the most part design improvements will have costs.

Thus, in the abstract, there is no such thing as an "optimally designed" Doomsday Machine. Optimal design depends on circumstances—on such factors as how much deterrence is worth to the coercer, how much the objective seems to be valued by the opponent, how rational the opponent seems to be, how much information is available to each side and on what subjects, how good or bad the best available technology is, and how vulnerable the coercer can be made to stress and organizational dysfunction.

It should be clear, however, that decisions on such matters as whether to improve command, control, and communication for nuclear forces, whether to deploy intermediate-range theater nuclear forces in Europe, or whether to install permissive action links (PALs) —safety locks—on submarine-launched ballistic missiles can be interpreted as Doomsday Machine design decisions. We may downplay the existence of the Machine. We may even design the Machine to minimize the probability of its going off in the event of the Soviets *fail* to yield—that is, to minimize the chance of irrational initiation and escalation of nuclear war even given Soviet provocation. If we do so, however, we increase at the margin the risk that deterrence will not hold; equally dangerous, we increase the danger that alternative policies for deterrence—such as the pursuit of military superiority— which may prove even more threatening to international stability and safety will seem necessary to us or our allies.

Ex Ante Policies and Ex Post Irrationality

If the existing Doomsday Machine is based on the potential for irrational behavior, what does this suggest about the factors that will be critical in analyzing policy options? That is, what design factors need to be considered in redesigning and optimizing the existing (and unavoidable) probabilistic organizational Doomsday Machine? As we noted in chapter 2, deviations from rationality may occur as a result of personality disorder, cognitive failure, situational stress, or organizational dysfunction. The likelihood that significant deviations from rational decision-making do in fact occur can thus be adjusted *ex ante* through policies that affect these four sources of irrationality. Indeed this likelihood can be adjusted upwards as well as downwards. Notoriously hot-headed individuals with a history of acting first and thinking later can be given authority to launch nuclear weapons. Leaders may be taught that history demonstrates that aggression must be resisted with all means available, that war must be taken to the enemy's homeland with as much violence as possible, and that in victory is safety—regardless of the objective plausibility of such a historical interpretation. The decision-making process can be structured in such a way that during a crisis individuals in key positions will find important values at stake and perceive the need for immediate action—or despair of discovering minimally acceptable policies. Or decisions may be decentralized, thus permitting various agencies of the state to behave according to their own particular interests.

While all four of these approaches to varying the manifest likelihood of irrational behavior are possible, as a practical matter two of them—situational stress and organizational dysfunction—seem especially important. Stress and organizational dysfunction deserve particular study for two reasons: first, they appear to be the critical potential causes of irrationality in the existing Doomsday Machine and, second, they are most easily subject to manipulation in an open democracy.

Decisions to use weapons of mass destruction in situations in which one's own society is vulnerable are likely to be potentially stressful, to say the least. Situational stress can be manipulated *ex ante*, however, by adjusting factors such as the amount of hope, time, information, and support available to deal with problems. Most simply this can be achieved by altering the physical conditions under which decisions must be made, particularly the survivability of the decision-maker and decision-making resources. In the present U.S. case, for example, the National Command Authorities would have to make a decision within minutes, hours, or (at best) days in the event of an attack on the United States—a far cry from the deliberate and presumably temperate process, involving extensive debate and even a division of power, used to make other decisions of national importance.[13] In Europe, following a Soviet attack, NATO's supreme allied commander (SACEUR) would quickly face a choice between using, losing, or—perhaps most frightening—losing control over his nuclear forces. Battlefield commanders to whom control might devolve would face the same types of pressures.

Similarly, the organization of decision-making can be designed to be more or less likely to break down in certain contingencies. Or, looking at it another way, the continued rational functioning of the organization in certain contingencies may or may not be regarded as a high-priority objective in the design of the organization. Important links necessary for collectively rational decision-making can be left vulnerable, as they have been in the U.S. case. Redundancies may be eschewed or eliminated. The nuclear trigger can be designed without extra "safety catches" or with "safety catches" that are likely to fail in certain situations. It can be done. Indeed it has been done. Ballistic missile submarines, for example, currently set to sea carrying on board everything physically needed to launch their missiles; no effective physical safety catch to prevent the submarine's crew from launching nuclear weapons without authorization exists, although such a permissive action link could easily be installed.

In sum, the United States appears to have, without any explicit intention, created a decision-making process in which stress and organizational dysfunction have a not inconsiderable likelihood of leading to irrational use of nuclear weapons in certain contingencies. Further, it seems quite possible for a liberal, open democracy to design a nuclear decision-making process that would have a greater or lesser vulnerability to stress and organizational dysfunction. Equally important, as we will explore in the following chapter, there is considerable potential to make stress and organizational dysfunction result in *contingently irrational* behavior—that is, irrational behavior that would occur only if the Soviet Union failed to be deterred.

Obviously, in emphasizing the importance of stress and organizational dysfunction in explanations of Doomsday Machines, we cannot entirely overlook the other two sources of irrationality: cognitive failure and personality disorder. But while cognitive failure may play a role in the working of the existing Doomsday Machine (and may have played an even more substantial role in the past), it does not appear particularly amenable to policy manipulation. It is not clear, for example, how one goes about "creating" a false belief system, particularly in an open, democratic society. One might, of course, attempt to exploit more fully existing cognitive failures—that is, to employ those existing rigid belief systems held by portions of the body politic which do not fully reflect new information. Fortunately for the avoidance of nuclear war, but unfortunately for the ability to threaten irrationally to wage such a war, the tremendous negative utility of nuclear war is hard to overlook or significantly underestimate. Since the immediate postwar period, an understanding of the vast destructiveness of nuclear warfare has increasingly permeated American consciousness at all levels: the American people have come to recognize that there would be no winners in a large-scale nuclear war. Equally important, it appears (as we noted in chapter 1) that the United States has come to recognize that even limited use of nuclear weapons would be likely to lead to unacceptable consequences. The erosion of a belief system that suggested the possibility and acceptability of limited nuclear conflict is likely to be accelerated by the gradually growing literature on the fragility of command, control, and communications and by the discovery of the potential for a nuclear winter and massive climatic change resulting from even limited nuclear use.[14] These intellectual trends will be difficult for an open democracy to slow, halt, or reverse.

As for personality disorder, it appears to play a negligible role in the existing Doomsday Machine and appears logically doomed to that negligible role. Two points deserve to be highlighted. First, as we will note further in the next chapter's discussion of contingently irrational behavior, there is likely to be some difficulty in getting psychopathological individuals to behave irrationally only when one *ex ante* wanted them to—and not frightening the opponent into launching a preventive war. Second, there may be some difficulty in electing or appointing such persons in a democracy: individuals who are manifestly irrational enough to frighten the opponent are likely to frighten their own constituents. Much has been made of Richard Nixon's understanding that an appearance of not being sensible is valuable in coercing international opponents: "If the adversary feels that you are unpredictable, even rash, he will be deterred from pressing you too far. The odds that he will fold increase greatly, and the unpredictable President will win another hand."[15] Though Nixon may have convinced international opponents that he valued successful resolution of the war in Vietnam very highly, there is little or no evidence that he impressed these opponents with his irrationality as we have defined it. He seemed to be able to handle new information intelligently, exhibit reasonably constant preferences, and select decisions that promised to maximize expected utility. A better case can be made, however, that Nixon frightened the American public into suspecting that he might have a psychopathological personality and that this was a key factor in his loss of public support and ultimate removal from office.

Placing the Trip Wires

If the *likelihood* that decision-makers will suffer situational stress and organizational dysfunction is one of the key issues in the design of a Doomsday Machine, then the other is *when* decision-makers will suffer from this stress and organizational dysfunction. What provocations or international tensions will lead to stress or organizational failure triggering the Doomsday Machine?

The dangers of a Doomsday Machine that is triggered by international crisis, rather than solely by the appropriate *casus retaliati*, are self-evident. Such a Machine is definitionally crisis-unstable and is likely to promote crisis instability in the opponent as well.

Any optimal Doomsday Machine—whether designed to maximize deterrent power, to minimize the chance of its going off, or to balance these two objectives—will have to be designed to keep low the likelihood that an international crisis alone will cause an irrational decision to use nuclear weapons. Situational stress and organizational dysfunction must be made contingent on war, not on the threat of war. This is actually an easier task than it sounds.

Stress results from the perceived need to make an important decision. The potential for stress during a crisis can therefore be reduced by eliminating this need: if, on the one hand, decision-makers possess an assured capacity for imposing some kind of retribution and, on the other hand, they lack any attractive options for preemptive blows, stress in decisions on nuclear use will be minimized. Attractive preemptive options—the kind one conceivably might rationally want to execute—are dangerous. They make irrational behavior during crisis more likely. Only in the wake of unacceptable Soviet aggression should decision-makers be in a position in which they perceive themselves as faced with real and difficult decisions.

Organizational dysfunction can be made contingent on Soviet aggression, of course, by structuring the decision-making process so that tight central negative control is lost through wartime degradation of communication systems. Peacetime "safety catches" against the use of nuclear weapons can be designed to be eliminated not by alert procedures but by actual wartime conditions, including the destruction of communication networks.

The design of Doomsday Machines thus must take into account the need to minimize the danger that occurrences less or other than the *casus retaliati* will trigger irrational execution of punishment. The practical consequences of this in terms of the geographic deployment of nuclear weapons and the design of command-and-control systems will be sketched out in chapter 8. Logically, however, this is no different than insisting that a mechanical Doomsday Machine be triggered by the actual detonation of nuclear warheads on one's country rather than by early-warning reports of possible missile launches.

NUCLEAR WEAPONS AND IRRATIONALITY

In sum, in this chapter our argument has been that nuclear weapons and the potential for irrational behavior yield the ingredients of a probabilistic organizational Doomsday Machine. And while it is possible to redesign the existing unacknowledged Doomsday Machine to reduce the likelihood that it will go off, it appears impossible to eliminate its existence entirely, at least so long as significant nuclear arsenals exist. The key variables in optimizing the design of the nuclear deterrent Doomsday Machine appear to be the situational stress and organizational dysfunction decision-makers are likely to encounter in the contingency. Optimization requires balancing the risk the Doomsday Machine will fail to deter or will go off despite the opponent's yielding against the political gain (including the maintenance of peace and the preservation of "vital" interests) that may accrue from its implicit threat.

These conclusions are consistent with those of chapter 1—that while U.S. decision-makers believe the Soviets are deterred from attacking the United States or undertaking aggression in Europe by a credible probabilistic threat to use nuclear weapons, the *rational* U.S. execution of nuclear threats is in fact in doubt. It is in doubt principally because of the fear that after U.S. use things would indeed get out of hand. The impossibility of effective damage limitation, the risk of escalation to unlimited war once U.S. nuclear use occurs, tremendous uncertainty about final outcomes, and doubt that nuclear use would guarantee the values at stake make the use of nuclear weapons irrational in response to any Soviet attack short of one that threatened the immediate destruction of American society. If technically unambiguous denial of choice were possible, such U.S. threats might be effective but, as we noted, as a practical matter such credible denial of choice is impossible.

We are thus driven to the conclusion that in an era of mutual assured destruction the key to employing nuclear weapons to gain coercive power is the ability to commit oneself to act in an irrational fashion *ex post*. This conclusion harks back to Schelling's observation that it is "perfectly clear that it is not a universal advantage in situations of conflict to be inalienably and manifestly rational in decision and motivation."[16] Nuclear threats that would yield significant coercive power if they were credible are prohibitively difficult or simply impossible to make *ex post* rational to execute. Since opponents may be able to determine that actual commitment-through-rationality does not exist, "It may be perfectly rational to wish oneself not altogether rational, or—if that language is philosophically objectionable—to wish for the power to suspend certain rational capabilities in certain situations."[17]

.   .   .

The crucial phrase here is "in certain situations." Nuclear deterrence rests on the threat to behave irrationally and use nuclear weapons in certain contingencies. More precisely, it rests on the threat to behave irrationally if the opponent fails to be deterred. Irrational behavior must be *contingent* on the opponent's failure to yield. The logic of the Doomsday Machine is the logic of *contingently irrational behavior*. The coercer's behavior is rational so long as deterrence holds; if deterrence fails, however, rational behavior may fail as well. For this reason, we turn in the following chapter to the logic and practice of contingently irrational nuclear deterrent behavior.

7

COERCION AND CONTINGENTLY IRRATIONAL BEHAVIOR

WE HAVE argued that nuclear deterrence of less than all-out attacks on the United States and of aggression against U.S. allies rests on the existence of a commitment-through-irrationality to the probabilistic execution of punishment. We have described the current U.S. deterrence posture in terms of a probabilistic organizational Doomsday Machine. This conceputalization has both positive and normative implications. It allows us to understand the factors that give the United States political leverage from the possession of the secrets of atomic fission and fusion. It also allows us to identify the critical trade-offs facing policymakers in fine-tuning an organizational Doomsday Machine that cannot—at least so long as mutual assured destruction capabilities and the potential for irrational action exist—be completely eliminated.

To understand the workings of an organizational Doomsday Machine, it is necessary to return to our ideas about irrationality and irrational behavior. Since the idea of a Doomsday Machine is that doomsday, or the probabilistic infliction of doomsday, is *contingent* on the opponent's unacceptable behavior, it is necessary to think through the logic of *contingently* irrational behavior. Four topics need to be addressed. First, we must explore the concept of contingently irrational behavior and its relationship to irrational decision-making processes. Second—in the same way we examined the possible types of irrationality in chapter 2—we must examine the possible types of contingently irrational behavior. Third, we must investigate the potential causes of contingently irrational behavior and determine both which of these possible causes explain the existence of a probabilistic

Doomsday Machine and which can be manipulated in efforts to fine-tune the existing machine. Finally, we must discuss the implications of contingently irrational behavior for possible modes of coercion.

CONTINGENTLY IRRATIONAL BEHAVIOR

In chapter 2, we distinguished between "irrationality" and "irrational behavior." We observed that an actor is irrational if he makes decisions in an irrational way. Irrationality represents a failure of the *decision-making process:* it is a condition in which the actor fails to engage in intelligent calculation, consistent evaluation of expected utility, or reasoned choice. It represents a failure of the decision-making process to select policies that represent an intelligent attempt to maximize expected utility.

By contrast, irrational behavior was defined as behavior that is significantly different from that which would have been produced by the actor if he were rational. An irrational actor—that is, an actor with an irrational decision-making process—may *behave* rationally some or all of the time. Though his decision-making process involves nonintelligent calculation, inconsistent evaluation, or unreasoned choice, an actor's behavior may yet be the same as it would have been had these flaws not existed. By luck or chance an actor may do the optimal thing even though his decision process is nonoptimal. I may refrain from shooting my neighbor because I understand that murder will be punished and I therefore rationally choose to express my hostility in some other fashion or because, in my rage, I simply cannot remember where I left my gun. The United States may refrain from initiating a nuclear war this afternoon *because* it has a rational decision-making process or *despite* the fact that it does not.

If irrational *behavior* on a particular policy issue occurs, it must occur either continuously or noncontinuously. That is, if behavior on some matter is ever irrational, it is either irrational all of the time or only some of the time. As an irrationally unneighborly homeowner,[1] I may act irrationally to harm my neighbor or his property at every opportunity or only on special occasions. If irrational behavior on a particular policy is continuous, then it clearly is not contingent upon the opponent's behavior. If I always irrationally strike my neighbor at every opportunity, my behavior cannot be because of some novel action he has taken.

On the other hand, if irrational behavior on a particular policy is not continuous, then it can be described as being either *contingent* or *noncontingent* on the opponent's failure to yield to coercive demands. Irrational behavior will be either correlated or uncorrelated with the opponent's behavior on the issue at stake. I may irrationally break my neighbor's windows when I see him in my garden—or I may do it when the moon is full or when I suffer from stomach upset from overeating. In the first case, my irrational behavior and the damage it produces are contingent upon my neighbor's trespass; in the other cases, they are not contingent upon anything over which my neighbor has control. The United States might irrationally launch an all-out nuclear blow against the Soviet Union because Soviet aggression disrupted command-and-control procedures and placed decision-makers under stress. Or the United States might irrationally launch an all-out nuclear blow against the Soviet Union because a 50–cent computer chip failed or because U.S. early-warning systems misidentified flocks of geese, prompting U.S. standard operating procedures to launch on warning. In the first case, the irrational nuclear blow can be described as contingent on Soviet aggression; in the second set of cases, the same irrational behavior is correlated only with occurrences beyond Soviet control (the failure of computer chips or the flight of geese).

A Doomsday Machine involves contingently irrational behavior.[2] Whether a mechanical one, reliant on commitment-through-denial-of-choice, or an organizational one (like the one we are concerned with), reliant on commitment-through-irrationality, a Doomsday Machine threatens some probability of contingently irrational behavior of cosmic scope. A Doomsday Machine requires that the opponent believe that an unacceptable probability of irrational escalation will exist if he does not yield and will not exist if he does. In the situation that exists today, deterrence rests not on the Soviet perception that the United States has denied itself the ability to act rationally in the use of nuclear weapons all of the time, but on the perception that it has *ex ante* denied itself that ability *if and only if* the Soviet Union carries out some specific actions that endanger fundamental U.S. interests.[3]

Contingent Occurrence and Contingent Manifestation

Because irrationality and irrational behavior are not synonymous, neither are contingency in irrationality and contingency in irrational behavior. Contingently irrational behavior may arise in two ways.

First, and most obviously, contingently irrational behavior may reflect the contingent *occurrence* of irrationality. An actor's inability to make decisions in a rational fashion may not be a continuous problem, but occur only occasionally; indeed, irrational decision-making (nonintelligent calculation, inconsistent evaluation, or unreasoned choice) may be contingent upon the opponent's failure to yield. Irrationality may be triggered directly or indirectly by the opponent's behavior. Consider, for example, the case in which I, as a homeowner, shoot my neighbor because when I see him in my garden I am seized by an ungovernable fit of temper that causes me to disregard the consequences of my behavior (to evaluate inconsistently the disutility of being put in jail). In this case, my contingently irrational behavior (I shoot only when he trespasses) is a result of my contingent irrationality (I find myself unable to engage in rational decision-making only when he trespasses). Analogously, if the U.S. decision-maker acts in haste or fury in response to a Soviet attack on, say, Berlin, without intelligently calculating costs and benefits or without evaluating disutility and utility in a consistent fashion, both irrationality and irrational behavior can be said to be contingent upon the attack. Irrational behavior is contingent because irrational decision-making is contingent.

Second, however, contingently irrational behavior may also reflect the contingent *manifestation* of irrationality. Contingently irrational behavior may occur as a consequence of a noncontingently (indeed, even continuously) irrational decision processes. For example, suppose I continuously suffer from a cognitive failure that leads me irrationally to believe that a neighbor's trespass will mysteriously but certainly cause a death in my family. In this case I may behave as if I were rational—as if I possessed a rational decision-making process—except when I see my neighbor in or near my garden. While my decision-making process is continuously irrational, my behavior is only contingently irrational. My decision-making process always suffers from a cognitive failure. Disregarding available evidence, I stubbornly and continuously choose to believe that a neighbor's trespass will cause a death in my family. My behavior, though, is only contingently irrational. Despite the fact that my reasoning is always flawed, my irrationality is manifested in my behavior only when I see my neighbor in my garden or when I believe he is about to enter it. The rest of the time my behavior is quite rational, however warped or misguided my thought processes. Analogously, a U.S. decision-maker might, because of some cognitive failure, irrationally believe that the survival of the United States depends on Western control of Berlin.

Such a U.S. decision-maker would behave rationally except on occasions when Berlin is threatened. This decision-maker would be willing to intervene more massively and run greater risks to prevent or defeat an attack on Berlin than would a rational U.S. decision-maker. Though a Soviet assault on Berlin would do nothing to *make* the U.S. decision-maker irrational, it would *reveal* the irrationality of U.S. decision-making.

TYPES OF CONTINGENTLY IRRATIONAL BEHAVIOR

Thus, contingently irrational behavior may occur either because the circumstances arising as a consequence of the opponent's failure to yield affect the rationality of the coercer's decision-making process or because they expose that process' otherwise hidden irrationality.[4] In either case, however, contingently irrational behavior may involve any of the three types of failings of rational decision-making that we noted in chapter 2: nonintelligent calculation, inconsistent evaluation, or unreasoned choice. The cases of contingently irrational behavior most relevant to understanding the functioning of the U.S. probabilistic organizational Doomsday Machine are those involving nonintelligent calculation and those involving inconsistent evaluation in situations with multiple decision centers. To reach this conclusion, however, it is useful to investigate briefly all types of contingently irrational behavior.

Unreasoned Choice

At its simplest, contingently irrational behavior may involve unreasoned choice. That is, contingently irrational behavior may be a consequence of random or reflex choice. Consider a gun-toting homeowner with a nervous trigger finger that twitches uncontrollably. Despite the fact that discharging his weapon is irrational—that is, despite the fact that the expected utility of shooting is negative—the homeowner may nonetheless fire. More to the point, his action may be contingent upon misbehavior by a neighbor even though the neighbor's misbehavior does not alter the fact that it is not rational for the homeowner to fire. On the one hand, the neighbor's provocation may prompt the anger or excitement that makes the finger twitch. In this case, the neighbor's trespass *creates* the decision process involving unreasoned choice. On the other hand, the marksman may suffer from a degenerative nervous disease that makes his finger twitch randomly, but this probabilistically irrational decision-making process is made manifest only by circumstances that lead him to handle his weapon. In this case, the trespass merely *reveals* the marksman's inability rationally to control his actions by creating a situation in which the uncontrolled finger is in proximity to the trigger. In both of these cases, policy choice—the actual pulling of the trigger—is disconnected from a calculation of utility; in both, the irrational shooting of the neighbor is contingent on his trespass.

It is actually possible to imagine an organizational decision to use nuclear weapons which could best be described as unreasoned choice. The nuclear decision-making process could be organized in such a fashion that low-level military officers had standing instructions to use nuclear weapons in response to certain external stimuli—conventional assault, radar warnings of intercontinental attack, or such. The execution of a nuclear response in such a case would be disconnected from any *ex post* calculation of national costs and benefits by the state. This, however, is not a satisfactory description of U.S. decision-making or of the U.S. posture at any point in the nuclear era,[5] so to understand what is actually involved in the U.S. Doomsday Machine it is necessary to move on to other explanations.

Nonintelligent Calculation

In addition to involving unreasoned choice, irrational behavior may, of course, involve faulty calculation of costs and benefits. We have already considered a hypothetical case in which contingently irrational behavior arises as a consequence of *contingent manifestation* of nonintelligent calculation. If, contrary to available evidence, I believe that a neighbor's trespass will cause a death in my family, I routinely fail to use evidence intelligently. This cognitively caused failure to calculate intelligently is manifest only contingently, however. It is manifest only in the event that my neighbor trespasses. In general, if cognitive failure results in contingently irrational behavior, it is likely to be precisely because a continuous failure to gather and process information intelligently is manifest only contingently. If U.S. military planners possess a cognitive belief structure that suggests nuclear war can be precisely controlled—can be fought as what Thomas Schelling has called "coercive war," as distinguished from "a war of risk"[6]—and resist the available evidence that nuclear war would be likely to interfere with command and control, an irrational decision-making process exists all the time but will be manifest in actual behavior only if a nuclear *casus belli* arises.

By contrast, *contingent occurrence* of nonintelligent calculation is likely to take place in two situations. First, it may arise if the opponent's failure to yield creates situational stress. Psychological stress, alone or in combination with organizational dysfunction, can, in certain very specific circumstances, prevent a decision-maker from dealing effectively with his environment. When I see my neighbor cross my property line and I realize that despite my warnings he has chosen to violate the sanctity of my private property and that I must now find some appropriate response, I may experience stress. I may, as a consequence, suffer from hypervigilance and therefore fail to use the time and other decision-making resources available to me to their full marginal value in assessing my options. I may "feel the pressure"; think, but not as long or as well as I intelligently should; grab my shotgun; and come out shooting even though better options are available. The U.S. National Command Authorities (NCA), composed of the president and Defense Department officials responsible for authorizing nuclear actions, might engage in nonintelligent calculation when they receive unexpected notification of a Soviet ICBM attack. In this example a contingently irrational decision process might result either because individual participants in the decision-making process panic or become exhausted (e.g., the president experiences psychological collapse[7]) or because the stress interrupts the operations of a nonunitary actor. Important information available to some portions of the decision-maker may not be circulated, or orders may not reach their destinations. In other words, inputs and outputs in a nonunitary decision-making process may get lost as a result of stress.

Second, a contingent occurrence of nonintelligent calculation may also arise as a consequence of organizational dysfunction even without the additional burden on decision-making of situational stress. It is possible, of course, to imagine organizations that are *always* rationally dysfunctional in some policy area—organizations that because of their design never permit the intelligent use of information on some policy issue. It is also possible, however, to imagine organizations whose normal ability to engage in intelligent calculation on some matter is destroyed by an opponent's failure to yield.[8] When "failure to yield" implies war or aggression such contingent organizational dysfunction is particularly easy to imagine. Major military operations, most especially if they involve nuclear weapons, carry considerable risk of destroying critical communication links within the target nation's political-military organization. Intelligent collection and analysis of information may be disrupted because the organization is not designed to function without the North American Air Defense Command (NORAD), or without the Joint Chiefs of Staff, or without the president.

Inconsistent Evaluation

Even if choice is related to a consideration of consequences and even if consequences are intelligently estimated, irrationality may still occur. Indeed, perhaps the most complicated and most interesting types of contingently irrational behavior are those involving inconsistent evaluation of the utility of various costs and benefits. As we noted in chapter 2, inconsistent evaluation of the total utility associated with particular costs and benefits may arise in either unitary or nonunitary actors, although the latter case is more intriguing.

In the simpler situation of a unitary actor, contingently irrational behavior stemming from inconsistent evaluation may arise as a consequence of value extension associated with the psychological stress of a crisis.[9] It may also be a product of contingent manifestation of continuous cognitive problems. Individuals may be unable successfully to reconcile competing values—say, liberty and peace—in a utility function, but this inability to develop a single, consistent utility function is hidden except when an opponent's action calls one of the two values into question.

In the case of a nonunitary actor, inconsistent evaluation may be caused by either of the two types of nonunitary decision-making we noted in chapter 2. First, it may arise as a result of collective decision-making in which power is shared among several groups or individuals in a single decision center. Second, it may arise because the decision-maker consists of multiple decision centers, each of which wields independent power.

Inconsistent Evaluation Caused by Shared Power

Where shared decision-making power exists, contingently irrational behavior reflecting inconsistent evaluation can come about in three ways. The first two involve contingent occurrence of inconsistent evaluation. The third reflects the possibility of contingent manifestation.

First, contingent inconsistent evaluation will occur if individual participants in collective decision-making fail to evaluate utility in a consistent fashion, either across time or issue areas. The failure of the opponent to yield alters the values of some of the participants. In this case, *collectively* irrational behavior arises in the contingency because the contingency results in *individually* irrational behavior.

Second, inconsistent evaluation by a collective decision-maker will occur contingently if the failure of the opponent to yield changes the identity or relative power of participants in the coercer's decision-making process. "Learning"—the updating of probability assessments about the opponent's values and capabilities and about causal relationships—does not alter one's own values; it may, however, lead to change in the membership of the decision-maker, and thus alter collective values. After my neighbor begins his trespass, my wife and I may begin to listen—or to listen more seriously—to the advice of my mother-in-law (either because she always mistrusted my neighbor and warned us against him or because she owns a shotgun we now think we may have a use for).[10] Thus, the failure of the opponent to be deterred may alter the composition, and therefore the values, of the collective decision-maker. This change may affect policies actually chosen—that is, actually affect behavior. This is likely to be most strikingly apparent in the evolution of war aims to reflect the expanding circle of individuals involved in decision-making. If war requires a democratization of foreign policy and war aims—because the society as a whole is called upon to shoulder extraordinary burdens in defense of state interests and may therefore demand from the state an extraordinary voice in defining state aims—then objectives may balloon from status quo to reformist, or from revisionist to revolutionary.[11] Consequently, evaluation of costs and benefits is likely to be inconsistent across time.

Broadly speaking, a shift in the participants involved in decision-making or in their relative power may occur either because the failure of the opponent to yield changes the decision-maker's definition of the problem or because it discredits or enhances the reputation of particular participants or potential participants. In the former case, new or different expertise or resources are needed. In the latter case, less astute or lucky participants are replaced by others who are more prescient or fortunate in predicting the interaction between one's own collective behavior and that of the opponent. Once my family has defined the relationship with our neighbor as one of conflict and potential physical violence, the advice of my cousin the mob enforcer will be treated relatively more seriously and my own professorial input will be given relatively less weight; similarly, if I have been optimistic about my neighbor's intentions and the possibilities of avoiding confrontation through skillful diplomacy, my power to sway the family's decisions may now be greatly degraded. Analogously, military leaders and their advice on how to cope with the international situation may become more important after the outbreak of war either because foreign policy is now viewed as a military problem or because civilian leaders are discredited by their failure to predict or prevent the war.

Third, inconsistent evaluation in a situation of shared power may be contingently manifested, even when the failure to possess a single, consistent utility function exists continuously. My wife and I may never have been able to agree on how to trade off the multiple values involved—the good neighborliness I value because it allows me to borrow tools or the toughness she values because it protects the garden. Our inability to formulate a single, consistent family utility function remained unapparent, however, until the particular contingency arose. Similarly, the U.S. Congress, as a collective decision-maker, may be unable to aggregate consistently the rival values of, say, peace and overseas political interests in deciding whether to declare war. Or the NCA may be unable to aggregate consistently the rival values of early nuclear use (which would maximize military effectiveness) and late use (which would increase the possibility of avoiding nuclear conflict entirely). So long as the opponent yields and does not challenge either value, the fact that the decision center inconsistently aggregates values in its collective utility function does not affect actual behavior.[12]

Inconsistent Evaluation Caused by Independent Power

The possibility that contingently irrational behavior reflecting inconsistent evaluation will arise is even greater if nonunitary decision-making involves division of power among multiple, independent decision centers, rather than simple sharing of power within a single decision center. In a situation of independent power, as in one of shared power, contingently irrational behavior involving inconsistent evaluation may occur in three ways. Again, the first two involve contingent occurrence of inconsistent evaluation and the third involves contingent manifestation.

The first way multiple decision centers may cause contingent problems for evaluation is if the failure of the opponent to yield *changes the values of some of the independent decision centers.* After all, two decision centers may normally be independent of each other yet not result in inconsistent evaluation for the decision-maker as a whole if they share the same values. If decision centers' values change as a consequence of the opponent's behavior, however, inconsistent evaluation occurs. (Since each decision center may involve shared power, such a situation might arise if the occurrence of the contingency altered the composition or relative power of participants within any decision center.) In my family's troubled dealings with my neighbor, my son may routinely represent an independent decision center, since he is as stubborn as I am and I lack coercive sanctions that would lead him to follow my instructions. Since, ordinarily, we share the same values, the fact that his decision is independent of mine is moot. If, however, the neighbor's trespass leads my son to engage in value extension while it leaves me unaffected, the independence of his decision contingently affects our family's behavior.

The second way multiple decision centers may cause contingent problems for evaluation is if *the independence of decision centers is itself contingent* on a failure of the opponent to yield. Even if decision centers routinely fail to share utility functions, inconsistent evaluation may be contingent if secondary decision centers become independent when the opponent fails to yield. As our definition of independent decision centers in chapter 2 suggests, this would occur if the failure of the opponent to yield eroded the coercive power of the central decision center vis-à-vis secondary centers. There are two reasons why coercive power might disappear.

First, the secondary decision center may, in the given contingency, cease to be coercible. This may occur if the secondary decision center remains individually rational (i.e., if the secondary decision center still intelligently calculates its own expected costs and benefits, evaluates these costs and benefits using some consistent utility function, and acts to maximize this expected utility). The moral, legal, and physical rewards and punishments available to the central decision center may no longer be sufficient to induce the secondary center to remain subservient; on the one hand, the resources available to the central decision center may be diminished as a consequence of the failure of the opponent to yield and, on the other hand, the failure of the opponent to yield may raise the value of independence to the secondary decision center. Once war breaks out, the value of behaving contrary to the wishes of the central decision center (e.g., using nuclear weapons in self-defense) may so outweigh the sanctions still available to the central decision center (e.g., the possibility of demotion, ostracism, imprisonment, and psychic guilt after the war ends), that the secondary decision center may for the first time find it individually rational to act in a fashion that is irrational for the decision-maker as a whole. Further, however, the failure of the opponent to yield may result in an *individually irrational* decision by a secondary decision center to act independently and ignore the sanctions of the central decision center: in the heat of the moment, a military commander may unrealistically downgrade or entirely overlook the penalties that may be imposed on him for disregarding orders, or he may evaluate the disutility of these penalties differently, or he may simply respond by rote without making any reasoned choice at all.

Second, even if the secondary decision center remains coercible—that is, even if there are still sanctions available to the central decision center that would make the secondary center choose to obey—the central decision center may be unable to maintain a credible commitment to the threatened sanctions in the event the opponent fails to yield. Maintenance of credible commitment, as we noted in chapter 4, requires both communication and the establishment of credibility. The failure of the opponent to yield may interfere with communication between decision centers. For example, in the event of a Soviet nuclear attack on military bases in the continental United States, it may become difficult for the NCA to communicate with individual missile, bomber, and submarine commanders. Similarly, it may become progressively more difficult for them to communicate with commanders of nuclear weapons in Europe as a Soviet invasion of Western Europe continues. Even if the sanctions for disobedience have been implicitly (i.e., historically) communicated to the secondary centers, explicit communication may be necessary to convey what it is the central decision center wants done. The commander of a missile submarine may know that he will face stiff penalties if he disobeys the NCA, but he may not know whether the NCA want him to launch or not.

Even if communication is successful, the credibility of the central decision center's threats may be dependent on the opponent's yielding. It may be that in the event the opponent fails to yield, the central decision center would no longer carry out the sanctions it can inflict on the secondary center. In the middle of a conflict, a state may prefer not to replace commanding officers. Or it may be that the secondary decision center rationally or irrationally believes that the central decision center will not carry out its sanctions, even though this belief is objectively incorrect.

The third way in which contingently irrational behavior might arise among multiple decision centers is if the failure of the opponent to yield *reveals existing but hitherto hidden differences in values between independent decision centers.* A battlefield commander might always value his own survival highly enough to use nuclear weapons in self-defense, even in defiance of the NCA. But unless the enemy fails to yield—that is, unless the enemy attacks him—this inconsistency between the commander's preferences and those of the NCA will not affect behavior. The failure of the opponent to yield means that values that were not in conflict before—such as individual survival and escalation control—now are in conflict. Prior to the failure to yield, central and secondary decision centers might pursue the same policy, though for different reasons; after the failure to yield, the different reasons result in different policies.

Probable Failures of Rationality and the U.S. Doomsday Machine

Before going further, it seems useful to highlight two basic insights about the U.S. Doomsday Machine provided by this exploration of the various types of failures of rationality. First, the difficulties of intelligent calculation of costs and benefits during a contingency may be critically important in explaining the U.S. Doomsday Machine. A contingent failure of rational behavior stemming from nonintelligent calculation may potentially arise in two very different fashions. On the one hand, contingent occurrence of nonintelligent calculation may follow as a consequence of situational stress and organizational dysfunction. The task of calculating the probable consequences of various rejoinders to Soviet aggression may be rendered insurmountable by the psychological and organizational strains created by that aggression. On the other hand, it is conceivable that contingent manifestation of nonintelligent calculation might also be a problem—or, at least have been a problem in earlier days when the consequences of nuclear weapons were not so fully reflected in cognitive belief systems. To whatever extent that decision-makers continue rigidly to rely on the outdated, inappropriate, and inaccurate models for assessing the controllability and survivability of major war that were widely accepted in the first decades of the nuclear era, contingent manifestation of cognitive failure could play a role in the Doomsday Machine's functioning.

Second, in its nuclear decision-making the United States faces the potential for massive problems of contingent occurrence and manifestation of inconsistent evaluation. Decision-making on the use of nuclear weapons in the wake of major Soviet aggression will involve not only shared decision-making power, with all its potential for inconsistent evaluation, but independent decision-making power as well. Inconsistent evaluation may arise in a number of ways, but situational stress and organizational dysfunction occupy central positions in most explanations of how it might yield the contingently irrational behavior of an organizational Doomsday Machine.

Perhaps the most important service provided by our analysis of the types of failures of rationality that may be involved in the U.S. Doomsday Machine, then, has been to focus our attention on the probable *causes* of contingently irrational behavior. This discussion of the failings of rational decision-making involved in the U.S. Doomsday Machine has suggested that an understanding of the various causes of irrational behavior may have important implications for the trade-offs that can and must be made in developing an optimal deterrence posture.

SOURCES OF CONTINGENTLY IRRATIONAL BEHAVIOR

Logically, there are four possible underlying causes of contingently irrational behavior—the four causes of irrationality we discussed in chapter 2. These are: personality disorder, cognitive failure, situational stress, and organizational dysfunction. In our examination of Doomsday Machines in the preceding chapter we anticipated this discussion by observing that the two critical sources of contingently irrational behavior, at least as far as our study of commitment-through-irrationality to nuclear deterrent threats is concerned, are stress and organizational dysfunction. In order to support this conclusion, it is worth our while to examine briefly all four potential sources.

Personality Disorder

It is hard to imagine personality disorders coming and going quickly with the ebb and flow of international events. But personality disorders might result in contingently irrational behavior through contingent manifestation of a continuous or nearly continuous problem. Key

members of the decision-making process may have psychopathological personalities that routinely prevent them from gathering and using information intelligently, from aggregating values in a consistent
fashion, or from making reasoned choice, but these problems may
only become apparent once the opponent fails to yield. I may have a
psychological problem that renders me unable to deal appropriately
with setbacks, but unless someone refuses to yield (for example, refuses to stay out of my garden), I will exhibit the same behavior I
would if I were rational.

This seems unlikely, however, to be useful in explaining commitment-through-irrationality to nuclear threats for three reasons. First,
the particular action to be deterred is not likely to be entirely unique:
other stimuli in the environment would also be likely to reveal the
problems inherent in the decision-maker's personality. A psychopathological decision-maker is likely to exhibit irrational behavior in a
variety of situations. It appears unreasonable, though, to expect that
democratically elected leaders who behave irrationally will be toler-
ated very long.[13]

Second, if the individual does *not* reveal his personality disorder
and irrational decision-making process—that is, if his psychopathol-
ogy is kept hidden, a secret—then its existence will be unlikely to be
credible to an opponent. Why would my neighbor believe that I am
psychotic and that I will behave in a psychotic fashion if I have never
done so before? Why would Soviet leaders believe that U.S. leaders
are psychotic if U.S. leaders do not behave in a psychotic fashion—
and, indeed, are so clearly not psychotic that the American people
trust them enough to elect them or tolerate their appointment.

Third, nations with advanced systems of state and governmental
legitimation are unlikely to entrust decisions on national survival to
a single individual. To be sure, as we observed in chapter 5, nuclear
weapons—along with fears of being disarmed in a surprise attack
because of cumbersome political controls—have indisputably resulted in a tremendous concentration of real power in a few hands. In
the nuclear era, there is no longer a presumption that the president
would wait for a congressional declaration of war before ordering
nuclear use. In response to a Soviet attack, or perceived Soviet attack,
the president might involve the United States in a massive military
engagement without consulting with or obtaining authorization from
other elected officials. Even in this situation, however, the president
does not wield solitary power. The National Command Authorities
are not composed of a single individual; except by force of personal-

ity, probably no single psychopathological individual can cause the United States to use its nuclear arsenal.[14]

For the same reason, the nightmare of a single mad colonel starting a nuclear war is probably just that: a nightmare, not a plausible reality. The modern state protects itself against irrational action by single psychopathological individuals by structuring its decisional organization so that power is shared. While the precise capability of the commanding Air Force general aboard "Looking Glass," the Strategic Air Command (SAC) airborne command post, is unclear from the unclassified literature, it is possible that even his capability to initiate a nuclear strike is not entirely unfettered. And at lower levels of command, ICBM launch officers, sane or mad, require external inputs in order to launch a missile; even SSBN commanders require the cooperation of other officers on board the submarine.

None of this is to say that individuals with personality disorders may not come to positions of national prominence and dramatically influence the course of their nation's history (and that of their neighbors). Hitler is a historical fact. The point being made is somewhat simpler: there is no empirical evidence that U.S. nuclear deterrent leverage has depended on the existence of such personalities in positions of leadership and there are good deductive reasons for expecting that leaders with manifest personality disorders will be fairly rare and that states will guard against them. Thus, in *descriptive* terms, the possibility of personality disorder does not seem to take us very far in explaining the existence of an American organizational Doomsday Machine. And in *prescriptive* terms—in terms of advice on how to fine-tune the existing Doomsday Machine—personality disorder seems equally unhelpful.

Cognitive Failure

On first inspection, cognitive failure seems at least somewhat more useful in explaining the contingently irrational behavior threatened by the U.S. Doomsday Machine. After all, if a cognitive failure exists, one would not be surprised if it were manifested contingently: one would expect a cognitive failure to be reflected in policy only when specific, relevant policy issues arise, and such issues may well arise as the result of an opponent's behavior.

Indeed, contingent manifestation of cognitive failure seems to explain at least part of the threat posed by the U.S. Doomsday Machine in the past. In 1961, reflecting on the U.S. Massive Retaliation strategy, Glenn Snyder observed:

> One should not underestimate the capacity of democratic governments to practice self-deceit or uncalculated irrationality. For example, it would not be too much of an exaggeration to say that U.S. military budgets between 1954 and 1961 were based on the premise that the resources available for military use were limited, that the limited resources should be allocated so as to produce the maximum firepower, that maximum firepower could be obtained by concentration on nuclear weapons, and that nuclear weapons were therefore the most efficient means of fighting wars of any size larger than a mere incident or "brushfire." . . . There is impressive evidence that the government committed itself so thoroughly to the nuclear deterrent thesis that by a certain process of psychological repression it failed to consider thoroughly the consequences of having to carry out the deterrent threat. If this habit of thinking continues, the government may not be able in time to disengage itself from its own preconceptions and act rationally when the *casus retaliati* arises.[15]

It is less clear, however, that cognitive failure provides as much insight into why the United States might irrationally use nuclear weapons today.

The point here is one noted briefly in earlier chapters: it appears increasingly unlikely that there exist today significant cognitive failures that would lead the National Command Authorities to authorize nuclear use. U.S. leaders—like the American public as a whole—apparently realize that nuclear war would be extremely destructive and recognize that once the United States undertakes nuclear war, escalation is likely to get out of control.

Further, as far as the prescriptive implications of the possibility of cognitive failure are concerned, there seems little practical way of slowing or reversing this declining likelihood of cognitive failure on nuclear issues, even if one wanted to. Belief structures tend to evolve naturally over time to reflect more appropriately and adequately the new reality. As time passes and—through generational change, if nothing else—it becomes accepted that prenuclear modes of thinking about war provide an inadequate framework for considering security problems in a MAD era and that we do indeed live in a MAD era, the credibility of a threat to use nuclear weapons because of a rigid conceptualization of nuclear war in prenuclear terms will fade. The steps an open democracy can take to alter or adjust this process seem somewhat limited. The state may, of course, attempt to train its employees—in particular, its military establishment—to believe that nuclear war can be controlled, and could therefore rationally be undertaken in circumstances in which U.S. survival was not directly and immediately threatened. The state could, for example, mandate military training and exercises that create a psychological presumption among both military and civilian officials that nuclear weapons could, should, and would be used in response to a variety of Soviet provocations. The inculcation of such beliefs would run directly counter to societal interests and pressures, however, and the practicality of such efforts, at least in the long run, must be considered doubtful.

Equally—indeed, perhaps more—important, it is difficult to imagine manifestation of cognitive failure being contingent on precisely the right thing. In the example we have used of a homeowner and his trespass-prone neighbor, we observed that if the homeowner believed that the neighbor's trespass would mysteriously but certainly cause a death in the family, this nonintelligent belief system might be manifested contingently. But it is likely to be manifested in contingencies well short of trespass. If the neighbor even approaches near the property line, the homeowner is likely to behave irrationally; as a consequence, crisis is likely to be uncontrollable. Similarly, a cognitive belief system suggesting the controllability or winnability of nuclear war would threaten to lead to an irrational resort to nuclear weapons even when Soviet aggression had not occurred. Such a belief system would likely be manifested during crisis, when nuclear use appeared to offer some benefits (by reducing uncertainty, if in no other way), rather than only when Soviet aggression had actually occurred. The Doomsday Machine would respond to the wrong trigger. If, because of cognitive failure, nuclear war is conceived as "doable" in response to limited Soviet aggression, it is likely to be seen as "doable" preemptively, in response to an expected or feared Soviet aggression. The consequences of this possibility for crisis stability and the functioning of deterrence are clear.

Situational Stress

By contrast, it is easier to imagine how a decision-making process can be designed so that crisis is rendered relatively less stressful and actual conflict relatively more. Indeed, since the failure of the opponent to yield is quite likely to be perceived as threatening important values and calling for some sort of decision or reaction, situational stress seems a likely generator of contingent irrationality in the U.S. Doomsday Machine. It is intuitively obvious that my neighbor's invasion of my garden—or a major Soviet attack on the United States or its close allies—will contingently create stress. In such a situation, as we observed in chapter 2, hypervigilance seems a probable pathology.

The usefulness of stress, in terms of establishing a commitment-through-irrationality to a nuclear threat, is that it permits a credible commitment to a punitive action in situations where either the central decision center or forward-located secondary ones suddenly come under a great deal of pressure, as they would following the outbreak of war. As the NCA learn that Soviet missiles have hit the United States, who knows how they will respond? They must make a decision, a decision of cosmic importance, one that will mean life or death for millions and determine the social, political, and economic conditions under which the survivors live. Similarly, as exhausted commanders in Europe come under attack, they will—if they have the physical ability to use their weapons—have to make what they may reasonably regard as the most important decision of their lives. Even if it is irrational for them as individuals to authorize nuclear use— and even if they lack the psychopathological personality or cognitive framework that would justify nuclear war-fighting—situational stress makes nuclear use possible. Minds under pressure do not always work clearly.

Obviously, if irrational behavior is to be contingent upon Soviet aggression (as is necessary for the organizational Doomsday Machine to function properly), then crisis alone, in the absence of actual Soviet aggression, must not create situational stress that would lead to irrational use of nuclear weapons. Decision-makers who are likely to experience stress during a crisis—that is, decision-makers who see important values at stake and feel pressure to make a decision—must not represent independent decision centers or dominate in collective decision-making on nuclear matters. And decision-makers who do make nuclear decisions during time of crisis must be shielded from stress. Thus, on the one hand, vulnerable military commanders who might experience "use-them-or-lose-them" pressure during a crisis must be prevented by command-and-control procedures from making nuclear decisions. And, on the other hand, central authorities must not be given any meaningful or attractive options that would be lost at the outbreak of war. For those who do have control over nuclear decisions during a crisis, there must be no significant incentive for getting in the first blow, and therefore no psychological pressure to do so. It must be the Soviet attack itself, not the threat of an attack, that creates the need (or ability) for decision.

As this implies, it is extremely important exactly where and when in the decision-making process situational pressure is felt. What irrational behavior, if any, occurs will depend on who in the decision-making process is under stress. Four points are worth making.

First, as we have observed, stress, like organizational dysfunction, has the potential to make decision centers independent. Secondary decision centers that ordinarily would not be independent because they could be coerced may either cease to be coercible or cease to find the central decision center's threats credible as a consequence of stress. Wartime stress suffered by battlefield commanders, for example, may prompt inconsistent evaluation of the values at stake or a temporary failure to consider the psychological or physical sanctions associated with defying central authority. Commanders may, as a consequence, be conditionally independent.

Second, the probability of some sort of irrational behavior increases as the number of independent nuclear decision centers suffering the effects of situational stress increases. A decision-maker can, *ex ante*, increase the likelihood that an irrational act will be executed in some *ex post* contingency by increasing the number of independent or contingently independent decision centers likely to suffer situational stress during an actual conflict.

Third, while stress may make irrational behavior possible, it may also interfere with a decision-maker's capacity for coordinated action. Stress among lower-level military decision centers may interfere with the effective execution of complex operations. This point is an important one: by increasing the number of independent decision centers and by leading decision centers to act irrationally, stress may greatly increase the likelihood of the irrational execution of simple actions, but it may at the same time reduce the probability of successful (rational or irrational) execution of complex ones.

Fourth, while stress is likely to result in contingent irrationality and contingently irrational behavior, it is far less likely to result in *continued* irrationality or irrational behavior. As decisions are made —for better or for worse—stress recedes. By its nature, stress is more a transient phenomenon than a chronic condition.

These four points have important descriptive and prescriptive implications for U.S. nuclear deterrence. In the first case, they help to explain the possibility of an irrational response to a Soviet attack and (as we shall explore later in this chapter) why an irrational deterrent response is likely to have to be punitive, rather than retaliatory or denying. They focus attention on the number of independent or conditionally independent decision centers capable of initiating or escalating nuclear conflict and on the psychological pressures these secondary decision centers experience due to a failure of deterrence. They also focus attention on the psychological pressures building at the center.

In terms of prescription, these four points suggest the possibility of fine-tuning the Doomsday Machine both by altering the number of independent and conditionally independent decision centers with potential control over nuclear forces and by altering the amount of stress these decision centers will face during the contingency. Stress may be manipulated by controlling the time frame and decision-making resources available to and perceived by decision-makers.

Organizational Dysfunction

Given our interest in explaining commitment-through-irrationality to nuclear threats, perhaps the most important potential source of contingently irrational behavior is organizational dysfunction. Organizational dysfunction may result in contingently irrational behavior either because the event itself causes an organization to break down or because it uncovers structural failures in the organization that otherwise are not revealed in policy.

The failure of an organization to function correctly may result in any of our three types of failures of rational decision-making. The organization may, for example, fail to provide information to its full marginal value. Critical information and analysis may not make its way to central decision-makers: the North American Air Defense Command may fail to provide critical information on a Soviet attack, or the Strategic Air Command may fail to inform national political leaders of the full range of possible responses and their probable consequences. The organization may not be designed to provide in a timely and intelligible form the information needed by decision-makers in their calculations of costs and benefits, even though such information is available at an acceptable shadow price.

Even more interesting, though, is the possibility that organizational dysfunction may result in inconsistent evaluation. In the event of Soviet aggression, the failure of the organization to prevent the independence of decision centers or to provide the means successfully to reconcile values within and between decision centers may result in the pursuit of policies by individual decision centers—policies such as using nuclear weapons—that are irrational for the decision-maker as a whole. It may be that the Soviet aggression itself may cause the independence of the decision centers: the organization may fail because the Soviet aggression destroys the command-control-communications facilities either that physically prevent the secondary decision centers from doing what they will or that allow the central decision center to coerce secondary ones. Or the Soviet aggression may simply reveal existing independence by engaging different values: Soviet aggression may expose the fact that coordinated action had been based on a temporary commonality of purpose among decision centers rather than on shared values or subordinance. A decision center in Germany, for example, might value revenge for the destruction of, say, Heidelberg (with its population of U.S. dependents) much more highly than do the National Command Authorities. Similarly, a battlefield commander might value the benefits associated with use of tactical nuclear weapons more highly than do central authorities— after all, his personal survival may depend on a positive decision to use nuclear weapons.

Situational Stress in Conjunction with Organizational Dysfunction

Situational stress and organizational dysfunction are not mutually exclusive. Indeed, an understanding of the likelihood of contingently irrational behavior requires an appreciation of their interaction. At the simplest, stress may be responsible for irrationality in secondary decision centers, while organizational dysfunction translates that local irrationality into irrational behavior by the collective decision-maker. If the United States wishes credibly to commit itself to the execution of nuclear threats in response to limited Soviet aggression, the critical variables are likely to be the amount of situational stress decision-makers are put under and the likelihood that decision centers will function independently in the event that the Soviets are not deterred.

There is an interaction we have not yet considered, however. This is the interaction between the mode of creating commitment and the type of threat that can be made.

COERCIVE USES OF CONTINGENTLY
IRRATIONAL BEHAVIOR

So far, one of the most interesting implications of our discussion of contingently irrational behavior for U.S. policy has only been vaguely suggested. Why does reliance on the threat of contingently irrational behavior necessarily suggest reliance on a probabilistic organizational Doomsday Machine? We have discussed what contingently irrational behavior is, what it might involve, and what might cause it to occur, but we have not focused on what it means for the types of threats the United States can credibly make. In the U.S. case, does commitment-through-irrationality to contingently irrational behavior dictate reliance on total punitive threats, like those of a Doomsday Machine?

In the abstract, commitment-through-irrationality involving contingently irrational behavior implies nothing about the mode of coercion adopted. The coercer's contingently irrational behavior may, in theory, entail denial, retaliation, or punishment (see chapter 3): as a homeowner, I may respond to my neighbor's trespass in a contingently irrational fashion by beating him back, by breaking his windows until he abandons my garden, or by burning down his house. Analogously, a contingently irrational U.S. response to Soviet aggression aimed at the occupation of, say, West Germany might be to use nuclear weapons tactically to permit NATO forces to retain or regain military control over West Germany; to use nuclear weapons systematically to destroy Soviet military, economic, or political assets until the Soviet Union halted or reversed its aggression; or to use nuclear weapons in a single spasm attack against a full range of Soviet valued assets.

Obviously, each of these modes of coercion implies different demands on decision-making resources and on rational decision-making. Perhaps less obvious, but equally important, is that each of these three modes of coercion places different demands on *irrational* decision-making. As an irrational homeowner, to be committed to a coercive threat of denial I must remember where I left my cudgel and how to use it effectively, and I must be ready to continue to employ it until my neighbor leaves, regardless of his reasoned or honeyed words or his counterthreats. For retaliation, I must remember where I keep my bricks and how to toss them through my neighbor's windows, and I must be ready to keep throwing the bricks for as long (and only as

long) as my neighbor trespasses—again despite his reasoned or honeyed words or his counterthreats. For punishment, I must remember
where I left my incendiary supplies and how to use them, and I must
be ready to start the fire.

Commitment-through-irrationality requires not only that the coercer will behave irrationally, but that he will irrationally carry out an
effective coercive strategy.[16] If, in the event of a trespass, I irrationally
howl at the moon, I am behaving in a contingently irrational fashion
just as if I irrationally beat my neighbor, break his windows, or burn
down his house. However credible, though, the threat of howling at
the moon is unlikely to deter my neighbor from entering my garden.
My howling is an exercise in contingently irrational behavior; it does
not, however, indicate that I have achieved commitment-through-
irrationality to an effective coercive strategy.

A threat to attempt *unsuccessfully* to beat my neighbor, break his
windows, or burn down his house has far more in common with a
threat to howl at the moon than with a threat to do any of these
hurtful things *successfully.* If my flawed decision-making process means
that I will be unable effectively to beat my opponent while I am
behaving irrationally, or to break his windows, or to burn down his
house, then my implicitly threatened behavior is unlikely to represent
an effective coercive strategy. This is true regardless of whether or not
my contingently occurring or contingently manifested irrationality is
credible. The fact that my contingently irrational behavior is *aimed*
at hurting my opponent is far less important than the fact that it will
clearly fail to accomplish this aim.[17]

Given the difference in the decision-making capabilities required
for effective denial, retaliation, and punishment, the type of coercive
threat being made is likely to be critical in establishing whether
commitment-through-irrationality is possible. We will proceed, therefore, by examining the requirements of each type of nuclear coercion
with an eye to the types of failure of rationality that might be necessary—and to the causes of irrationality which this implies. The conclusion to which we will be driven is that while in theory all three
modes of nuclear coercion are possible, in practice it may be unacceptably difficult to achieve commitment-through-irrationality to effective strategies of nuclear denial or retaliation. This difficulty results, first, from the complexity of the action threatened in denial and
retaliation and, second, from the protracted period of time which may
be required for the execution of the strategy.

Denial

In general, the threat to use nuclear weapons for denial purposes is a threat to carry out a highly complex set of military operations, requiring the participation and coordination of a large number of decision centers. Consider the case of using nuclear weapons to deny the Soviets control of Western Europe. A hypothetical U.S. Army scenario for using nuclear weapons to destroy a Soviet tank formation called for the coordinated use of nuclear land mines, nuclear artillery, short-range nuclear missiles, and Air Force-delivered nuclear bombs.[18] For such an operation to succeed, commanders would need timely intelligence on Soviet movements as well as the ability to react with coherence and dispatch. Even assuming that all operations were executed by U.S. personnel without the involvement or interference of allied forces or governments—not necessarily an easy assumption to make—not only would a number of distinct military units be involved, but the U.S. Army and U.S. Air Force would have to coordinate their actions. This coordination for an attack on a single Soviet tank formation might have to be repeated a number of times to halt a major Soviet axis of advance even temporarily and would have to be multiplied by the number of major Soviet axes of advance. Since the various possible axes lie in different corps sectors, even within a single military service effective nuclear use would require coordination at high levels.

Coordination and execution of complex operations like this one would require that irrationality not go very deep—that is, that irrationality be limited to upper levels of command. It is hard to imagine such well-coordinated behavior in the event of a failure of rationality at the front line. Decision centers at the national or theater level would need to be irrational enough to order the use of nuclear weapons, but the military organization at the front would need to remain rational enough to use them effectively. The organization could not malfunction in carrying out irrational decisions. Nor could stress be allowed to block the collection and analysis of information on Soviet movements and surviving NATO military capabilities, the distribution of this information, the timing of nuclear blows for maximum military effect, or the preservation of reserves of nuclear firepower for follow-up blows.[19]

It is possible to imagine such a failure of rationality in national or theater decision centers arising if the cause of irrationality were personality disorder or cognitive failure. If the NCA consisted of deeply disturbed individuals or if the collective U.S. decision-maker failed to understand the tremendous dangers of nuclear war, then authorization of the use of nuclear weapons in a manner that would be effective for denial might be conceivable. And there may even have been a time when this second situation existed: until the 1960s, the difference between nuclear and conventional weapons apparently remained underappreciated by high-level decision-makers, and their inappropriate cognitive framework might have led to an irrational authorization of the use of nuclear weapons.[20] But without calculated action to increase the likelihood of their occurrence, these causes seem fairly unlikely to result in irrational use of nuclear weapons in the 1990s. Further, as we have observed, even if one wished to increase the likelihood of these causes of irrationality, as a practical matter it is not clear how one could do so successfully.

Irrational use of nuclear weapons on a European battlefield might of course also stem from situational stress—but such stress is likely to be at least as great at secondary decision centers as at higher levels. Intuitively, hypervigilance seems more likely to occur in the isolated, hard-pressed, and war-ravaged hedgerows of Germany than in the comparatively safe Pentagon or airborne command post. And if local commanders begin acting irrationally, effective execution of the threat might be impossible: I cannot irrationally beat back my trespassing neighbor if my irrationality means that I cannot control what my hands and arms do.

Similarly, irrational use of nuclear weapons on a European battlefield might result from organizational dysfunction. And again, it is difficult to imagine *effective* use of nuclear weapons for denial purposes once organizational control fails.

Looking at our other problem case of nuclear deterrence, the use of nuclear weapons to deny the Soviets their objective in undertaking a limited attack on the United States is, if conceivable at all, a tremendously complex task. If, for example, the Soviet Union seeks to gain an advantage in "the nuclear balance" or in ability to mobilize and transport military forces to the European theater (or some critical region in the third world), the use of nuclear weapons by the United States for denial purposes would require extensive and coordinated U.S. counterforce strikes against Soviet bases. Such extensive and coordinated strikes might result from irrationality, but only if the irrationality occurred at the highest levels *only*. Successful denial— difficult to imagine under any circumstances—becomes virtually impossible to imagine if one contemplates the growing independence of decision centers due to organizational dysfunction and situational stress.

In addition to this problem of complexity, denial also encounters the problem that the necessary nuclear use might need to be protracted over days or weeks. Critical targets might not be identified or become vulnerable until after the conflict had begun, and possibly not until well after its nuclear phase commenced. This protracted time frame raises two difficulties.

First, the decision-maker may have to continue to choose to use nuclear weapons even though their use continues to be irrational. True, it is at least logically conceivable that later nuclear actions may be rational once the first irrational nuclear step has been taken. But, since the continuation of a nuclear conflict poses a continuing risk of escalation to unlimited war, it is quite probable that later nuclear steps will also be irrational. Thus, for commitment-through-irrationality to exist, the decision-maker may have to guarantee credibly not only that he will behave irrationally in the event that the opponent fails to yield but also that he will continue to behave irrationally. This is a difficult task. A state that just used nuclear weapons might, considering the dangers posed by continuing use and given time to reflect, begin to deal intelligently with the surrounding world, to aggregate values in a consistent way, and to choose policies in a reasoned fashion. If the initial decision was made because of personality disorder, the psychotic leader may be removed. If the decision reflected a cognitive failure, the shock of nuclear use and its consequences might result in the alteration of belief systems. If the decision was a consequence of organizational dysfunction, the decision-maker might act to correct its flaws, eliminating independent decision centers and taking whatever other steps might be necessary.

Second, in addition to continuing to behave irrationally, the decision-maker must continue to have the power to use nuclear weapons. In the case of denying Soviet control of Western Europe, the nuclear assets necessary to deny the Soviet objective may be destroyed or fall into the hands of U.S. allies. These allies may rationally or irrationally choose not to permit the United States to continue to fight a tactical nuclear war in Europe. Given that tactical nuclear war would be "fought" in the villages, towns, and cities of central Europe, it would not be particularly surprising if Europeans developed rather negative feelings about continued U.S. battlefield use of nuclear weapons, nor is it altogether inconceivable that they might take forcible action to end it. Further, even if nuclear weapons remain under the control of U.S. decision centers, central coordination may very well be degraded. The vulnerability of command-control-communication systems to nuclear effects has already been noted.

In brief, the prognosis for irrationally but effectively using nuclear weapons for denial seems rather bleak. To be sure, the Soviets may fear that irrationally undertaken efforts to deny may escalate to involve retribution, but this possibility must be understood as a commitment-through-irrationality to nuclear retaliation or punishment.

Retaliation

If anything, the difficulties of achieving commitment-through-irrationality to threats of retaliation are even greater than those of achieving commitment to threats of denial. Although acts of retaliation need not be highly coordinated (perhaps a city bombed at two o'clock today, an oil refinery at ten o'clock tomorrow, and a dozen army bases on Thursday or sometime next week) or involve large numbers of participants (presuming their vessel survives counterattacks, one missile submarine crew alone has the theoretical potential to cripple a half-dozen cities every business day for a month), they do have to be controlled temporally.

The negative sanction involved in retaliation is the infliction of pain *until* the adversary yields. The "until" is critical. It differentiates retaliation—with its intraconflict compellence—from punishment. "Until" has two components: first, the pain will be continued for the *duration* of noncompliance; second, the pain will be *stopped* when compliance occurs.

As with denial, there may be difficulty in ensuring that the coercer will remain irrational over an extended period and that, while irrational, will continue to inflict pain. As we mentioned, this difficulty is somewhat eased by the fact that the number of necessary participants in nuclear decisions to retaliate may be limited. But irrationality may be a temporary—even momentary—aberration, particularly if caused by stress or by easily remediable organizational dysfunction. Unless, as we noted above, once nuclear war has begun it becomes rational to continue it (despite the continuing and even increasing risks of escalation to unlimited conflict), the prospect of momentary irrationality will not be sufficient to achieve credible commitment to retaliation. Even if a central decision-maker cannot *coerce* secondary decision centers into halting continuing nuclear use, it may be able to act *directly* to stop such use, particularly given a time span of many days or weeks.

More importantly, there may be difficulty in ensuring that retaliation will stop when the opponent ceases his noncompliance. One cannot assume the retaliation will be halted simply because the opponent yields—it has, after all, been rational all along for the coercer to eschew retaliation.

None of these problems disappear if the retaliation involves probabilistic rather than real incremental imposition of pain. That is, these problems remain even if retaliation's gradual imposition of pain for compellent purposes is accomplished by creating some continuing or increasing risk of grave hurt rather than by actually imposing some continuing or increasing pain. Either way, firm temporal control over irrational actions is required.

It is hard to imagine that this temporal control over the imposition of pain would or could be maintained—and would or could be credible to an opponent—if the irrational decision process involved stemmed from situational stress or organizational dysfunction. Once again, personality disorder or cognitive failure might allow commitment-through-irrationality, but these sources of irrationality in the use of nuclear weapons seem unlikely to occur.

Punishment

A punitive nuclear strategy avoids these problems associated with commitment-through-irrationality. The required behavior need not be complicated (as in denial), nor need it be protracted (as in both denial and retaliation), nor need it be terminated in response to the opponent's compliance (as in retaliation) for it to be effective. With nuclear weapons, "burning down the house" is easy for a decision-maker to do irrationally. A few individuals, rational or irrational, freed from constraints by organizational dysfunction, may start the blaze. Or stress may result in hypervigilance at the critical moment and cause a failure to calculate intelligently or evaluate consistently the comparatively high costs of burning down the house.

When we introduced the idea of punishment in chapter 3, we noted that punishment need not be all-out in effect or unlimited in effort. A court that sentences a convict to life in prison with no possibility of parole is engaging in punishment even though it does not mete out the death penalty. Burning down my neighbor's house is an act of punishment whether or not he owns a detached garage (or second home) that I leave untorched.[21] Similarly, the United States could threaten punishment without threatening doomsday. To say that commitment-through-irrationality involving contingently irrational behavior means that the United States will be limited in its effective sanctions to threats of punishment is not to say that the United States will be limited to probabilistic doomsday threats.

It is possible, however, to continue the argument we have been making and arrive at precisely the conclusion that the United States is indeed limited to probabilistic doomsday threats. Stress and organizational dysfunction mean that it will be relatively easy to start an all-out conflagration and relatively difficult to burn only select targets. Stress and organizational dysfunction imply not only that the effective sanctions available to the United States are likely to be limited to punitive ones, but that the punitive sanctions available will tend to have a high probability of involving massive destruction, even by nuclear standards. Regarding existing U.S. strategic command-and-control capabilities, for example, Bruce Blair has noted that

> In the short time available for decision, national policy officials are ... bound to focus on a single, one-time plan of retaliation. This restriction encourages comprehensive retaliation. Whatever the SIOP [Single Integrated Operating Plan] may be, the U.S. *control system* thus has been geared historically to a spasmodic, indiscriminate response.[22]

Eliminating these organizational and psychological pressures for a "spasmodic, indiscriminate response" may be difficult in any case, but eliminating them while leaving manifest pressures for some sort of punitive response seems unimaginable.

To the extent that nuclear use is made possible or encouraged by organizational dysfunction, nuclear use and irrational behavior are likely to be mutually reinforcing, since nuclear use (not to mention any reaction by the opponent) is likely to interfere with organizational behavior. Likewise, nuclear war is likely to generate situational stress as well as to follow from it. The same absence of control that makes it difficult to imagine "turning off" retaliation is likely to make it difficult to keep punishment to levels meaningfully short of all-out devastation.

CONTINGENTLY IRRATIONAL BEHAVIOR AND THE U.S. DOOMSDAY MACHINE

Our argument on entering this chapter was that U.S. nuclear forces offer the ability to deter a variety of Soviet transgressions—not simply the ability to deter the destruction of American society—because the United States has the capability credibly to threaten to behave irrationally. Indeed, in chapter 6 we observed that the U.S. nuclear posture could be likened to a probabilistic organizational Doomsday Machine. The United States is committed by its posture to act in a contingently irrational fashion.

This chapter's argument has suggested that this threat of contingently irrational behavior involves the possibility of nonintelligent calculation of costs and benefits or inconsistent evaluation of the utility associated with them. The prime culprits in causing this potential for the contingent occurrence or manifestation of irrationality are situational stress and organizational dysfunction—although, at least historically, cognitive failure may also have played a role. Among the implications of this key role of stress and organizational dysfunction are that the United States is likely to be limited in its choice of coercive strategies to punishment and limited in its choice of nuclear punishments to largely unconstrained ones. As a practical matter, the mode of commitment dictates the mode of coercion. Not only is the existence of some sort of probabilistic organizational Doomsday Machine inevitable (at least so long as the capabilities for mutual assured destruction exist), but in deriving political leverage from the existence of nuclear weapons, the United States has no alternative but to rely on a Doomsday Machine.

What the United States retains is the capability to design or redesign its Doomsday Machine. The United States has the option of maintaining, reducing, or increasing the amount of political leverage it seeks to derive from essentially omnicidal nuclear capabilities. It can maintain, retrench, or expand its nuclear commitments. The United States also has the ability to alter the probabilities that its Doomsday Machine will actually be triggered in the event of various proscribed *casus retaliati*. The United States can, at least roughly, relate the contingent probability of doomsday to its assessments of the motivations of adversaries. And it can also act to reconfigure its nuclear arsenal to reduce the likelihood that adversaries perceive nuclear war as inevitable or U.S. objectives as unacceptable—or are driven to make irrational decisions. The United States can, without reducing the effectiveness of a Doomsday Machine as a deterrent device, reduce pressures on the Soviet Union for a rational or irrational decision to rush into war.

The notion that the United States has, and will continue to have, a Doomsday Machine and that it is this Doomsday Machine which yields us political power from our nuclear forces should not, therefore, give rise to fatalism. The range of policy choices that can and must be made is great. It is just not the same range that has been discussed in the counterforce and coupling debates.

8

THEORY AND POLICY

THIS BOOK has explored the logic of deterrence but has deliberately left uninvestigated the implications of this logic for U.S. policy. Our analysis has dealt with logical generalizations about coercive power in MAD situations rather than with particular circumstances, and it has dealt with what *is* rather than with what *ought to be*. It has avoided both delving into the specifics of U.S. forces and making recommendations about what those forces should be in the future.

However, theoretical and positive analysis on a topic as immediate, important, and controversial as nuclear deterrence begs to be translated into prescriptive terms. If the U.S. deterrence posture can be understood as a probabilistic organizational Doomsday Machine, what implications does this have for policy? What does the logic of contingently irrational action suggest about how U.S. policymakers can or should deal with the pressing problems of coupling, counterforce, and strategic defense?

This final chapter is appended because interesting implications follow from the logic of the preceding chapters. These final pages are in no sense a conclusion to the book: the logical-deductive explanatory task of the book has been completed. This chapter is, rather, an afterword on policy, designed to identify new trade-offs and possibilities. Though it provides no definitive answers, it should serve to stimulate a new, more fruitful debate.

The Underlying Logic

In the opening pages of this book, we asked: *In an era of MAD capabilities, what qualities of the U.S. nuclear force posture make it possible for the United States to use the threat of nuclear response to deter not only massive Soviet nuclear attacks on American cities, but also carefully limited Soviet nuclear attacks on U.S. targets and major Soviet nuclear or conventional aggression against close U.S. allies?* We inquired, in other words, what credibly commits the United States to using its nuclear weapons in response to any provocation less than an all-out attack on U.S. society. Given the (at least potentially) suicidal nature of nuclear war, how does the United States derive a range of deterrent power from its nuclear arsenal? In pursuit of an answer to this question, we began by examining the logical difficulty posed for U.S. strategy by the existence of mutual assured destruction capabilities and reviewing the attempts of U.S. policy analysts to deal with this difficulty. In chapters 2 through 7 we deductively developed a novel answer by exploring the nature of rationality and the logic of nuclear deterrence.

Our analysis suggested that to deter Soviet aggression against allies and limited attacks on the United States itself, the United States relies on the existence of a probabilistic organizational Doomsday Machine. The United States has established a commitment-through-irrationality to the execution of punitive nuclear threats.

Current counterforce and coupling debates assume that credible commitment depends on the existence of options that would, *ex post*, be rational actually to execute. Our argument has been quite contrary. We have joined with critics of current policy in arguing that it would not be rational for the United States to execute its nuclear threats. We have gone on, however, to argue that deterrence does not depend on rational options. U.S. nuclear threats are credible and provide deterrent power because the United States is committed to the *irrational* execution of its nuclear threats. The qualities of the U.S. nuclear posture that make the nuclear threat credible as a response to a variety of provocations are the vulnerability of U.S. decision-making to the effects of situational stress and the existence of organizational dysfunctions that would be created or manifested contingently. The U.S. deterrent posture can be understood as a probabilistic organizational Doomsday Machine that cannot be eliminated but whose design can be optimized.

THE RELEVANCE FOR POLICY

But does this analysis—or ought this analysis—make any difference for policy? After all, U.S. nuclear deterrence posture may pose a threat of contingently irrational behavior even if the authors of U.S. strategy and formulators of U.S. policy do not comprehend this reliance upon irrationality or do not actively seek to employ or manipulate this threat. Indeed, this is the case today. U.S. policies are aimed explicitly at making possible a rational decision to use nuclear weapons. But the net effect of these policies is that the Soviet Union faces a considerable risk that the United States might irrationally respond with nuclear weapons if deterrence failed. As we have noted, the Doomsday Machine cannot be altogether eliminated, at least so long as nuclear weapons exist. If the threat of irrational use of nuclear weapons is always with us, why do we need to worry about the logic developed in this book? Why should we explicitly recognize that the potential for irrationality provides the real foundation of our deterrence policy?

There are two reasons for explicitly recognizing the role of commitment-through-irrationality and for rejecting policies that, though perhaps reliant on some assumed "existential" deterrent effect, are motivated by a strategy of commitment-through-rationality. First, continued attempts either to create rational nuclear responses or to limit nuclear threats to those that could rationally be executed are likely to generate unnecessary financial and political costs. Put simply, failure to recognize and deliberately build on the threat to behave irrationally is *wasteful*. It creates unnecessary costs, both in terms of unnecessary expenditure of national resources and in terms of unnecessary risks of international instability and war. Whether the United States pursues policies aimed at controlled response, nuclear superiority, nuclear retrenchment, or political retrenchment, insistence on equating *ex ante* rationality with *ex post* rationality imposes a false and unnecessary constraint on optimization efforts.

Second, failure to recognize explicitly the role played by irrationality in the maintenance of deterrence may result in policies that are not only wasteful but *counterproductive*. On the one hand, pursuit of an ability to carry out nuclear deterrent threats rationally, if taken far enough, may not only make America poorer and the world less stable but may actually reduce the credibility of deterrent threats. It may convince the Soviet Union that the United States would be as able to exercise rational self-restraint after an attack as before it. On the other hand, pursuit of the ability rationally to carry out nuclear deterrent threats may reduce or eliminate the coercibility of the opponent. It may make it rational for an opponent to initiate war or to strike "preemptively" during a crisis rather than leave himself vulnerable, or—even more likely—it may make it difficult for an opponent to act on a rational preference to yield.[1] The final deterrent posture thus may be less likely to deter the Soviet Union and more likely to result in nuclear war.

The final third of this chapter examines some of the controlled response policies that are wasteful and counterproductive. In this way our theoretical exploration of the role played by irrationality in nuclear deterrence has a payoff: it permits us to identify current policies that are unnecessarily costly and dangerous.

There is, however, another and more basic reason for thinking about the logic of power, irrationality, and MADness before trying to develop policy. The thorough examination of the role of irrationality provides the foundation for the construction of a new strategy from which logically consistent policies can be derived. By doing so, it opens the door for an escape from the impasse of the current policy debates, debates far richer in criticism than in constructive suggestions.

Scholars and analysts have been successful in identifying the logical failings of the controlled response strategy, the implausibility of achieving meaningful nuclear superiority and the dangers of attempting to achieve it, and the potential costs of political and military retrenchment. This success, however, has not been matched by progress in finding new alternatives. Critics of controlled response, nuclear superiority, and nuclear or political retrenchment have had very little useful to suggest for U.S. policy. Colin Gray has made a fair complaint, observing that

Critics. . . appear to believe they have said something profound and helpful when they remind us of the all-too-obvious possibility of nuclear catastrophe that lurks in the present security system. Understandably, responsible officials tend to be impatient with those who tell them what they know already—that they have a problem. The officials cannot lament the difficulty of relating the energy yield of nuclear weapons to the securing of political objectives—that is, the difficulty of accommodating nuclear weapons in *strategy*—and throw up their hands in despair. Unlike the extragovernmental critic, they must do the best they can in making security sense of a weapon that cannot be disinvented.[2]

Without a thorough consideration of the positive contribution of irrationality as a mode of commitment, deterrence scholars and policy analysts are able to do little more than announce their angst, musing as Robert Jervis has done, in the closing paragraph of his recent work on U.S. nuclear strategy, that

> no nuclear strategy can be fully rational. . . . There is something horribly irrational about a strategy which turns on the inherently uncertain possibility of unleashing the destruction that everyone wants above all to avoid. But without defenses that would repeal the nuclear revolution, this possibility cannot be excised. The countervailing strategy fails because it tries to escape from the resulting dilemmas. But if the realization that one must build a strategy on the risks and uncertainties inherent in nuclear bargaining can avoid many of the errors and dangers of current policy, it cannot bring back the rational relationship between force and foreign policy that previously existed. We will have to find new and different paths. G.K. Chesterton said, "I have seen the truth and it makes no sense." I do not claim that the arguments I have made here are the truth. But I do think that nuclear weapons have so changed our world that much of the truth does not make sense.[3]

The frustration of any policymaker asked to build policy on the advice that "much of the truth does not make sense" would seem fully justified.

Can we do any better if we recognize that the potential for irrationality can create credible commitments and if we focus on the forces that may lead to contingently irrational behavior? Can the logic of commitment-through-irrationality and of probabilistic organizational Doomsday Machines help us to develop optimal nuclear policies?

This chapter addresses these concerns. It looks at the new questions and trade-offs suggested by the logic of commitment-through-irrationality. By doing so, it confronts Gray's complaint: it suggests a logically consistent way "of accommodating nuclear weapons in strategy" and of "making security sense of a weapon that cannot be disinvented." The effort is designed to demonstrate how we can accept Jervis' criticism of the rationality of current strategy without complaining that "the truth does not make sense" and abandoning the search for optimal nuclear deterrence policies.

The Demands of Policy

But how are we to judge deterrence policies? At a minimum, policies aimed at deterring Soviet aggression against U.S. allies and deterring limited Soviet attacks on the United States must also be compatible with the deterrence of unlimited nuclear attacks. A deterrence posture that deters the Soviets from undertaking limited military attacks while failing to discourage a massive Soviet blow against American society is of dubious utility. To return to the analogy we have used extensively in previous chapters, it will do me little good to succeed in deterring my neighbor from trespassing in my garden if the steps I take to accomplish this lead him to choose to kill me.[4] Indeed, a major complaint about the present U.S. posture has been that the counterforce capabilities being pursued for extended deterrent purposes undermine deterrence of an all-out attack by reducing crisis stability.

The success of any U.S. deterrence posture in meeting these deterrence demands must be judged on two criteria. Both must be satisfied at least minimally. First, a deterrence posture must be *effective*. It must yield the desired outcome. Judgments of effectiveness must take into account not simply the posture's impact on a rational opponent but the posture's impact on his rationality and on an irrational opponent. A deterrence posture that unacceptably increases the likelihood that an opponent will irrationally attack cannot be considered effective.[5]

This means that to be effective, U.S. deterrence policies must avoid placing Soviet decision-makers in situations in which they will be unable rationally to choose to be deterred. If, for psychological or organizational reasons, Soviet decision-makers are unable to act upon a rational preference to yield to U.S. deterrent threats, U.S. efforts to create a rational Soviet preference to yield will be for naught. As we will observe below, this means that effective deterrence policies may involve eschewing the sorts of militarily effective options that are likely to create psychological or organizational problems for the Soviet Union during crisis.

Further, effectiveness must be measured not simply in terms of impact on an opponent. As we noted in our discussion of the ways in which Doomsday Machines could fail, there is always the danger that irrational retribution will be exacted even if the opponent is deterred and does not undertake the *casus retaliati*. Judgments of the effectiveness of deterrence policies must bear in mind the dangers of accidental or irrational initiation of nuclear war in the absence of a Soviet attack on fundamental U.S. interests. To avoid a trade-off between minimizing the danger of peacetime or crisis use of nuclear weapons and maintaining a risk of wartime use, the risk of wartime use must be contingent on Soviet aggression. Any effective posture must, like the present U.S. posture, provide extremely large barriers to the accidental or irrational use of nuclear weapons—barriers that would collapse *only* under the organizational, physical, and psychological weight of wartime operations, destruction, and pressures.

Effectiveness is only the first criterion for evaluating deterrence posture, however. In addition to being effective, U.S. deterrence posture must be *acceptable* to the politically relevant American public and to critical U.S. allies. Acceptability requires that a deterrence posture be neither so frightening that it scares the United States and its allies into foregoing deterrence nor so morally objectionable, politically repugnant, or fiscally costly as to be perceived as intolerable. (On the other hand, a deterrence posture might also be unacceptable because it is so invisible or nonthreatening that a concerned public believes the government has failed to recognize or deal with threats to national interests. The scale of the U.S. nuclear build-up in the early 1960s may be partially explicable in these terms: the U.S. government needed to convince relevant internal audiences that it was indeed striving for an effective deterrence posture.)

The acceptability of any new posture may be much harder to predict than its effectiveness. If history provides any indication, however, the U.S. political elite has considerable capacity to lead and shape public opinion and therefore enjoys broad latitude in policy choice. It is instructive to note that the U.S. government has in the past been able to adopt not only a deterrence posture based on the repugnant notion of killing millions of innocent civilians but also a posture explicitly accepting parity and mutual vulnerability—which left American society hostage to a much-distrusted rival. Indeed, in its declaratory stance, the U.S. government has even been able to boast of the *desirability* of the vulnerability of American cities. While these policy developments reflected sensible responses to changing technological facts and international realities, these policies did not represent the only possible course of action and they involved substantial changes in the way the American people thought about war and international politics.

Weighing the Alternatives

That the strategy on which current policies are based is logically flawed is indisputable. The problem today is not one of acceptability. The problem is that the policies being pursued do not make any sense because the logic on which they are based is faulty. If we cannot—

and both the evidence and our leaders suggest that we cannot—feel at least minimally certain that U.S. participation in a controlled use of nuclear weapons will not escalate to unacceptable levels of violence, then a threat *rationally* to choose to engage in an initially controlled use of nuclear weapons in response to a clearly limited provocation is a bluff. It is a bluff regardless of the details of the relative force balance between the superpowers.

Further, the nostrum of meaningful nuclear superiority appears at present a delusion and a snare. The prospect of achieving an imbalance in forces so great that the United States would possess the ability to destroy Soviet society without fearing such a fate in return is so distant and so dubious as to make discussion of it purely hypothetical.

In deterring attacks on allies, the real choice facing the United States today is between continued reliance on the threat to use nuclear weapons irrationally on the one hand and political or nuclear retrenchment on the other. Policies aimed at retrenchment of U.S. commitments involve a dramatic step into the political unknown. If one sees many dangers for world peace and for the American nation in a world in which Western Europe is not covered by a U.S. nuclear umbrella, then the risks of continued reliance on a threat to behave in an irrational fashion seem small by comparison. But in any case, the cost of retrenchment needs to be compared to the real cost of maintaining an effective and acceptable extended deterrence posture. This cost can be fairly gauged only after considering how commitment can be achieved and then logically deriving the necessary posture. *The United States should not be rushed into nuclear or political retrenchment because of the unnecessary costs of controlled response or superiority, nor should it be dissuaded from retrenching its commitments by some false promise of controlled nuclear wars or of the ability to "win" an all-out nuclear exchange.*

Not even this choice exists when it comes to strategies for deterring limited attacks on the United States itself. It is hard to imagine circumstances in which the Soviet Union would be seriously interested in launching a limited attack on the United States. But if such circumstances were to arise, the only effective coercive strategy available to the United States would be one of nuclear retribution, and the only available mode of commitment to such a strategy is commitment-through-irrationality. As with extended deterrence in Europe, if the United States is concerned about the possibility of a limited Soviet attack on its territory, it needs to make the real trade-offs and pay the real costs involved, rather than delude itself with logically unsatisfactory notions of controlled response or pursue will-o'-the-wisps like nuclear superiority.

NEW QUESTIONS, REQUIREMENTS, AND TRADE-OFFS

Our theoretical analysis in the preceding chapters permits a change in the question to be addressed by policymakers: "How can the United States make it rational to carry out coercive nuclear threats?" gives way to "What makes it credible that the United States will be irrational enough to carry out those coercive threats that it would not be likely to carry out rationally?"

This change is important because it shifts the ground of the debate about defense policy. As a practical matter, the first question is an impossible one to answer; the second is not. Critics of current policy have been frustrated in developing a logically consistent alternative because they have been asking the wrong question. It is not, as Jervis has suggested, that "the truth does not make sense." It is that the assumptions of the present debate do not make sense.

Because it assumes rationality or the desirability of rationality and it overlooks the possibility of deterrence based on the potential for irrational action, the current debate has focused nearly exclusively on issues of weapons capabilities. By doing so, it has failed even to identify the critical requirements and trade-offs facing U.S. decisionmakers.

Weapons capabilities are only one factor in a state's capability to wage nuclear warfare. Other physical assets—such as those command, control, and communications (C^3) resources involved in waging war or in retaining rational control over it—are also critical to the credibility of threats to use nuclear weapons. In addition to physical assets, a capability for nuclear warfare requires the possession (or lack) of particular organizational, political, and psychological resources. This simply reflects the fact that the capability—and perceived capability—to wage nuclear war depends not only on the weapons at hand but also on the ability to choose to employ them or to refrain from employing them.

Though they have escaped debate, assets other than weapons have not entirely escaped comment. John Steinbruner has drawn attention to the need for survivable C^3 in deterring Soviet counterforce attacks and to its contribution to strategic stability, while Paul Bracken and Bruce Blair have studied the demands placed on C^3 by strategies of controlled nuclear war.[6]

But there has been little recognition or practical discussion of how the possession of decision-making resources and particular physical assets other than weapons may also serve to *decrease* coercive power and U.S. ability to deter.[7] Policy debate has not extended into these areas.

It is revealing that the only relatively uncontroversial portion of the Reagan administration's strategic program has been investment in C^3. The Scowcroft Commission, for example, devoted only three sentences to C^3 in its recommendations for strategic force modernization:

> Our first defense priority should be to ensure that there is continuing, constitutionally legitimate, and full control of our strategic forces under conditions of stress or actual attack. No attacker should be able to have any reasonable confidence that he could destroy the link between the President and our strategic forces. The Commission urges that this program continue to have the highest priority and urges the investigation of ways in which the planned improvements could be augmented by low-cost back-up systems.[8]

Improved peacetime and crisis C^3 is indisputably beneficial. Reducing the danger of irrational or accidental use of nuclear weapons during peacetime or crisis not only reduces the risk of catastrophe, but enhances deterrence of war by assuring the opponent that the nuclear sanction can indeed be avoided by the making of concessions.

Improved wartime C^3, however, cuts two ways. While improved wartime C^3 may make it more certain that the United States will be able to respond rationally to Soviet aggression, by the same token it will make it more difficult credibly to threaten to carry out an irrational response and use nuclear weapons while U.S. cities remain hostage.[9] There is a trade-off here and it needs to be recognized. Improved wartime C^3 may increase U.S. confidence that the United States will be able to exercise rational self-restraint in the wake of a Soviet attack, but it also reduces the probabilistic punishment the Soviets face for aggression. If one estimates Soviet incentives for attacking the United States or NATO as small (as, indeed, this author does), one may be willing to proceed with improving wartime C^3. There is, nonetheless, a trade-off.

Similarly, the complex interplay between decision-making resources and deterrence has been largely ignored in the policy debate. To the extent that resources such as time and freedom from physical and psychological stress during war are considered at all, they are considered as necessarily desirable.[10] If, however, deterrence of the Soviet Union stems from the prospect of irrational U.S. behavior, then the possession of these resources in some situations may undercut effective deterrence.

Deterring a Limited Attack on the United States

As we have observed throughout this book, the critical difference for deterrence purposes between an all-out attack on the United States and a limited one is that in the latter case it is not likely to be rational for the United States to respond by using nuclear weapons. Deterrence of an all-out attack thus poses a logically simpler problem. It requires that the United States possess nuclear forces that can—without provoking a rational or irrational Soviet first strike—remain under rational negative control during peacetime and crisis, survive a Soviet attack, penetrate Soviet defenses, and inflict unacceptable damage on the Soviet Union. Deterrence of a limited attack requires all this as well, but it additionally requires that the U.S. nuclear posture create an unacceptable risk of contingently irrational behavior. How much risk might be "acceptable" to Soviet leaders in various situations—and how much contingent risk of doomsday the United States must therefore build into its deterrence posture—remains an open question, of course. The features of the current U.S. posture that generate the risk of contingently irrational behavior on which deterrence rests can be identified, however, as can be measures that increase or decrease that risk. It is thus possible to identify the principal requirements and trade-offs facing U.S. policymakers in deterring a limited Soviet nuclear attack.

There are at least four plausible paths by which the current posture might lead to an irrational use of nuclear weapons in response to a limited Soviet nuclear attack. First, central political authorities may act irrationally because of situational stress associated with an actual Soviet attack. U.S. leaders may see their options rapidly disappearing and suffer from hypervigilant decision-making. As a consequence, when informed of a Soviet attack they may act in a hasty and ill-conceived fashion. As Richard Ned Lebow has put it:

> This [hypervigilant] pattern of coping is . . . likely to be adopted if the time pressures are such that the policy-maker does not even believe it possible to initiate a search for an acceptable alternative. Hypervigilance is characterized by indiscriminate openness to all information and a corresponding failure to determine whether or

not that information is relevant, reliable, or supportive. . . . In its most extreme form, panic, decisions are formulated in terms of the most simple-minded rules, e.g., "Do what others around you are doing." This is why a fire in a theater may prompt the audience to rush irrationally toward only one of several accessible exits.[11]

If nuclear decision-making remains structured so that important values appear at stake, time seems extremely limited, and the simplest, easiest, or most obvious thing to do is to reply "in kind" (i.e., with strategic nuclear weapons) to a Soviet attack, then a danger of contingently irrational response will continue to exist.

Second, central political authorities may irrationally authorize a nuclear response because of organizational dysfunction. Organizational failures during a Soviet attack may result in the NCA lacking critical information available to the organization as a whole. Graham Allison has suggested a historical example of this sort of organizational dysfunction. He has argued that during the Cuban missile crisis the president and Executive Committee were not informed of the true ability of the U.S. Air Force to conduct a surgical strike. As a consequence, central decision-makers acted under the misapprehension that a disarming strike was not possible.[12] The organization was unable to apprise central decision-makers of their true options.

In these first two scenarios, an irrational nuclear response results from the irrationality of central political authorities. The two other scenarios involve the elimination or incapacitation of the NCA—that is, the failure of C^3. These other scenarios are important because they suggest that the Soviets could not disable the Doomsday Machine with a "decapitation" attack.

The third path to irrational use involves organizational breakdown and individually rational action resulting in collectively irrational behavior. Organizational dysfunction may result in the independence of military commanders with utility functions different from the national one. A Soviet attack, even if not aimed at the U.S. NCA nor designed to interfere with the normal operation of the U.S. military command, would risk disrupting the negative control exercised by central political authorities over nuclear weapons. The survivability and endurance of the airborne command post for top political officials, for example, is limited. Devolution to military officers of authority, as well as physical ability, to order nuclear retribution is likely. Further, communication links that because of their redundancy are sufficient to ensure extremely good negative control over strategic forces in peacetime may be of dubious reliability following even a limited nuclear attack.[13] Control procedures that rely on communication to prevent independent nuclear action by secondary decision centers thus create a possibility of a contingent failure of central control. ICBM commanders might rationally conclude that their personal interest in revenge for the deaths of family members outweighs other considerations, or senior military officers on board airborne command posts might rationally conclude that their professional duty requires them to authorize retribution. If, as in these examples, nuclear use is individually rational for military commanders, then independence of decision-making by itself might result in a contingently and collectively irrational use of nuclear weapons.

Far more probable than this third scenario is a fourth: given the decentralization of nuclear control, some secondary decision centers may begin behaving in a fashion that is *individually as well as collectively* irrational. Organizational dysfunction may leave individuals with the capacity to launch nuclear weapons; cognitive failure or, more likely, situational stress may lead them to make irrational decisions to do so. The traditional SAC idea that in war "the whole idea is to *kill* the bastards" may conceivably linger yet and, if central negative control is eliminated, may yield a nuclear response.[14] More probably, situational stress may cause secondary decision centers to suffer from hypervigilance. Even if hypervigilance does not occur, the second type of maladaptive behavior associated with decision-making under stress—defensive avoidance—may also lead officers to use nuclear weapons: seeing no attractive alternatives available to them, individuals may avoid coming to grips with the costs of the most obvious policy—using the strategic weapons in their charge.

As these four scenarios suggest, one capability of the U.S. nuclear force is essential for deterrence of limited attacks: it must be clear that if central political authorities are killed or isolated, some combination of military commanders will be able to carry out preprogramed responses against the Soviet Union, even in the absence of instructions to do so. This capability presently exists. The crews of ballistic missile submarines can launch their weapons; procedures for using Air Force weapons in the event of the incapacitation of the NCA apparently also exist.

Four additional "problems," however, also contribute to the U.S. commitment to respond to limited attacks. The first is the manifestly dubious survivability and endurance of the NCA and their communication links. This vulnerability increases the likelihood of situational stress at the center of decision-making.[15] The second is the limited access of central decision-makers to information. The third is the risk that a limited Soviet nuclear attack on the United States, even one not aimed at destroying C^3, would interrupt the NCA's negative control over nuclear weapons. The fourth is the manifestly dubious survivability and endurance of military commanders and the risk that secondary decision centers will be subject to considerable psychological pressure to use nuclear weapons.

These "problems" exist, at least to some substantial degree, at the present time despite the U.S. pursuit of the ability to wage nuclear war rationally. In his review and critique of existing U.S. C^3 capabilities, Blair has argued forcefully that

> regardless of Soviet targeting doctrine, a nuclear war could not be controlled. The rudimentary design and short endurance of our control system nullifies the entire conception of multiple, time-phased strategic campaigns undertaken in pursuit of bargaining advantage. Such campaigns are purely intellectual constructions, metaphors really, that have no place in serious threat assessment and planning.[16]

Rather than being an unmitigated liability, however, it is precisely this frailty of C^3 that provides the basis for deterrence of limited attacks. In the four scenarios sketched out above, the United States, for organizational or psychological reasons, would be unable to distinguish between a limited and an unlimited attack. "Solutions" to U.S. deterrence problems which do not focus on this critical inability will be no solution at all; more hardware, more throw-weight, more accuracy, and more flexibility are likely, at best, to be irrelevant.

The United States does indeed face trade-offs in its deterrence policies, but these do not—as the current counterforce debate would have led us to conclude—involve questions of enhanced flexibility and hard-target kill capability. Rather, the trade-offs facing the United States in deterring limited Soviet intercontinental attacks involve strategic decision-making capacities. How much contingent frailty need strategic C^3 have, and how much contingent pressure need central decision-makers be under? Given Soviet incentives for attacking the United States, can these be reduced? Contingent frailty and pressure decrease the likelihood of deterrence failing, but they do have a price: they increase the risk that the Doomsday Machine will actually trigger doomsday if deterrence fails. This is the trade-off that policymakers must face in dealing with present C^3 problems.

Deterring an Attack on Major U.S. Allies

As a direct consequence of geography, the practical working of the Doomsday Machine in Europe is somewhat different. A Soviet attack on Europe is unlikely to interfere with strategic C^3, nor is it likely to place central political authorities under severe time pressure in their decisions on the use of strategic forces.

Extended nuclear deterrence logically works, however, because there are at least two scenarios in which an irrational U.S. decision to respond with nuclear weapons to Soviet aggression might occur. First, the NCA might be forced to make a decision on nuclear use in the opening hours or days of a war, during a period when surprise, shock, or anger at the Soviet action might temporarily interfere with intelligent calculation or consistent evaluation. This possibility exists because nuclear weapons are deployed in the theater in such a fashion as to require a rapid decision on their use.

Second, irrational use of nuclear weapons might occur due to loss of central control over forces deployed in the theater. A Soviet attack, even while not significantly affecting strategic C^3 or the ability of strategic force commanders to behave in an individually rational fashion, threatens to disrupt C^3 within the theater and place theater commanders under significant stress.[17]

In practical terms, then, the key to the probabilistic organizational Doomsday Machine in Europe is the deployment of theater nuclear weapons in such a fashion that they create demands for immediate use and that they risk escaping central political control during a conflict. To serve as an effective deterrent, theater nuclear deployments need not create effective military options or result in some sort of controlled escalation ladder. Quite to the contrary, theater deployment is important because it manifestly creates possibilities for contingently irrational behavior. Theater deployment employs the military requirements and physical destruction of an actual war to put decision-makers under stress and to strain the organizational structure.

This understanding of why theater deployments deter has four important implications for the design of a crisis-stable and effective organizational Doomsday Machine for Europe. These four implications reflect the four possible ways in which Doomsday Machines may fail. As we observed in chapter 6, Doomsday Machines may fail because the opponent does not have a rational preference to yield associated with the Machine's threat; because the opponent cannot act on a rational preference to yield; because the Doomsday Machine fails to represent a credible commitment to an effective coercive strategy; or because the Doomsday Machine goes off in the absence of provocation.

The first implication for U.S. and NATO posture, then, is that it not make Soviet aggression rational. The theater nuclear force should not invite a *rational* Soviet attack. The deterrent threat must not be vulnerable to timely Soviet military action. The Soviets must not have the prospect either of being able to eliminate the U.S. capacity to inflict punishment or of being able to eliminate the U.S. capacity to act irrationally. If the Soviets possess either prospect, then a decision during a crisis to strike preemptively may be rational and the Doomsday Machine will have failed. Thus, even if the total number of theater nuclear weapons is kept small, the number of storage sites should be maintained and sites should be hardened to prevent destruction without a substantial Soviet nuclear attack. Procedures for rapid dispersal are important, as is the continued existence of a nuclear quick-reaction alert (QRA) aircraft force that creates the risk of irrational response to attacks on nuclear storage sites and airfields.

Equally important, this demand that U.S. and NATO forces not make a Soviet attack rational suggests that the Western posture should not appear to give NATO the ability to "win" a conflict or gain some decisive military advantage by striking first. If Soviet leaders are not to see a preemptive blow as rational, they must not only be denied the ability to disarm the West but must be given some assurance that the West will not consider war the optimal choice in a crisis. In the absence of this assurance, a Soviet preemptive blow—undertaken in desperation, not out of optimism—might indeed be rational. This suggests not only the dangers of attempting to match or overmatch Soviet conventional capabilities but also that an extensive, modern, and militarily effective theater nuclear arsenal able to destroy front-line Soviet forces, disrupt the movement of follow-on units, and result in a NATO victory on the ground is a liability rather than an asset. Indeed, for precisely the sorts of reasons military analysts dislike them, nuclear land mines and artillery may be more desirable than large stockpiles of tactical missiles and air-deliverable ordnance.

Second, U.S. theater nuclear forces should not encourage an *irrational* Soviet decision to strike. As we noted in chapter 3, the requirement that the opponent be coercible implies that deterrence may fail because an opponent is unable to act upon a rational preference to yield. Certain U.S. theater nuclear force deployments may increase the likelihood of an irrational Soviet decision to attack. Three factors may be involved. First, badly conceived U.S. force deployments may increase the Soviets' perceived need to make decisions hastily. U.S. deployments should be aimed at reducing time pressure and situational stress for Soviet decision-makers during crises. Second, U.S. deployments may reinforce incorrect Soviet cognitive frameworks that suggest that NATO has offensive intentions, that conflict with the United States is inevitable, or that striking first makes a difference, thus increasing the likelihood of an irrational Soviet decision to attack. At a minimum, U.S. deployments should not enlarge the cognitive blinders that might cause Soviet decision-makers to overlook or underestimate the possibility of peaceful crisis resolution. Third, by threatening the survival of central military control during conflict, U.S. deployments may encourage *ex ante* decentralization of Soviet decision-making and predelegation of authority, thus increasing the danger of organizational dysfunction in time of crisis.

Third, U.S. posture must create a credible commitment to an effective coercive strategy. The Doomsday Machine must be credible. As a consequence, theater nuclear weapons must have a significant capacity for retribution or create a risk of further irrational escalation to strategic war. Longer-range theater systems—the so-called "intermediate-range nuclear forces" (INF)—capable of reaching into the Soviet Union seem ideally suited for this role.

Shorter-range "tactical" nuclear systems, designed to be used directly on the battlefield, also have an essential role to play in making nuclear punishment unacceptably likely, however. In the wake of Soviet aggression, an irrational use of battlefield nuclear weapons is easier to envision than the use of INF. It is easier to imagine for a variety of reasons, including the greater number of battlefield weapons, their dispersal to greater numbers of units and to front-line areas where C^3 is most vulnerable and decision-makers may be under greatest stress, their real utility to local commanders, the potential for decision-makers under stress to repress psychologically the consequences of authorizing their use, and the existence of lingering cognitive failures about the consequences of tactical nuclear war.[18] A tactical nuclear conflict, in turn, would add to the confusion of the situation, increasing the likelihood of organizational dysfunction and the stress suffered by decision-makers throughout the organization. This trigger role suggests that the bulk of tactical nuclear forces should have extremely short range, threatening to interfere with NATO's own ability to control escalation once the nuclear threshold is crossed. As long as the use of tactical nuclear forces by NATO threatens to interfere with the United States' own communications and to create stress on other U.S. nuclear decision-makers, this requirement is met. Again, nuclear land mines, now eliminated from NATO's arsenal, and nuclear artillery, long in disfavor, are ideal sorts of weapons for the very reasons they have been unpopular with the military.

Fourth, U.S. theater nuclear forces must be designed so that if deterrence holds, doomsday is not mistakenly triggered. U.S. forces should minimize the potential for accidental or irrational use of nuclear weapons during peacetime or crisis. This minimization may be pursued even at the cost of military effectiveness, since deterrence does not rest on the existence of militarily effective threats that could rationally be executed.

Irrational use of nuclear weapons must be contingent on Soviet aggression, not on tension or crisis. The probabilistic infliction of doomsday should be contingent on actual attack, not on Warsaw Pact or NATO mobilization. As a consequence, it should be war itself—not either side's preparation for war—that generates a risk of irrational U.S. behavior. The NCA should not be under psychological pressure to use nuclear weapons during a crisis, nor should alert procedures interfere with effective central political control. Psychological pressure will be reduced if plausible options for nuclear preemption are not perceived as existing; effective central control requires redundant negative controls vulnerable only to the physical and organizational impact of wartime operations.

This requirement that irrational behavior not occur in the absence of provocation also has important implications for the geography of nuclear deployment. Deployment in the Federal Republic is necessary if the U.S. Doomsday Machine is to protect Germany: deployment there means that any Soviet advance might both interfere with the central control over nuclear weapons and place field commanders under a great deal of stress. Deployment of U.S. INF in Britain also appears useful, not because it provides any new military capability but because it complicates Soviet planning and makes a Soviet disarming attack more difficult. With such deployment, a preemptive attempt to destroy U.S. theater nuclear forces risks generating a British decision to respond with its national nuclear forces.

Other locales lack these justifications, however. The United States may rationally choose to run a risk of nuclear annihilation in order to deter Soviet aggression in central Europe, but this does not imply that the United States should scatter triggers for nuclear holocaust around the globe. This suggests that it is desirable to cease deploying nuclear weapons on the territory of other allies and to avoid new deployments.[19]

Equally important, elimination of nonstrategic nuclear forces at sea would reduce the potential for a naval incident, in which fundamental U.S. interests were not at stake, to trigger irrational escalation to nuclear exchange. Such escalation might occur as a result of rigid standard operating procedures or other organizational dysfunctions that permit (or dictate) nuclear self-defense or response against military targets. This elimination would, of course, marginally increase the vulnerability of the U.S. Navy to Soviet conventional and nuclear attack (although its vulnerability to nuclear attack is already monumental). It would not, however, reduce the credibility of extended nuclear deterrent commitments to allies.

IMPLICATIONS OF ABANDONING THE SEARCH FOR RATIONAL OPTIONS

What this discussion suggests is that recognition of the irrational element in nuclear deterrence and abandonment of the pursuit of rational options would have serious implications for nuclear policy. The controlled response strategy has been wasteful and counterproductive. Understanding what its nuclear leverage derives from, the United States could abandon its Sisyphean task of attempting to match the Soviet Union in real or imagined options for limited war. The United States could afford to reverse the McNamara revolution: it could drastically pare its repertoire of available military options vis-à-vis the Soviet Union.

Controlled Response and Nuclear Thresholds

Abandonment of a strategy of controlled response is likely to be controversial. In particular, critics may complain that it will have the effect of lowering the nuclear threshold and of reducing the controllability of nuclear war. Thoughtful analysis, however, will reveal that this is not the case. The use of U.S. nuclear weapons, except in response to an all-out attack on U.S. society, is not presently rational despite the existence of a plethora of nuclear and conventional escalation options. Acknowledgment that the pursuit of options is costly and counterproductive will not make the use of U.S. nuclear weapons rational in the future. Actual commitment to probabilistic contingent use of nuclear weapons reflects the vulnerability of U.S. rational central control to the effects of stress, organizational dysfunction, and possibly cognitive failure. The actual nuclear threshold and controllability of nuclear war are—*both at present and in the event of the abandonment of controlled response*—determined not by the options at U.S. disposal, but by the contingent difficulties of maintaining rational control.

Abandonment of a strategy of controlled response is therefore in no way synonymous with a lowering of the nuclear threshold or a decrease in the controllability of nuclear war. One can recognize the existence of a Doomsday Machine and the futility of trying to make the use of nuclear weapons rational without insisting on an increase in the contingent probability that the Doomsday Machine will go off. Decisions on the height of the nuclear threshold and on the amount of effort spent on making nuclear war controllable are logically separable from the decision to rely on a commitment-through-irrationality rather than on the phantom of "appropriate" nuclear response. If it perceives Soviet incentives for aggression as small, the United States can take steps to reduce the probabilistic threat posed by the Doomsday Machine even while it is abandoning the search for nuclear options. Regardless of the actions taken by the United States to reduce or increase the stress and organizational dysfunction encountered by nuclear decision-makers during conflict, however, the United States can decrease the costs and increase the effectiveness of nuclear deterrence by abandoning controlled response.

Implications for Strategic Forces

In terms of strategic nuclear forces, the controlled response strategy has dictated at least six requirements. First, it has demanded flexibility and responsiveness in nuclear targeting and use—the NCA must have both the equipment and plans for executing a variety of responses. Second, it has required substantial and survivable intelligence capabilities to assess the size and scope of Soviet actions and damage done to the Soviet Union by U.S. strikes. Third, it has required that the United States seek secure and survivable C^3 adequate for a prolonged war.[20] Fourth, it has meant the United States needed an extremely large and diversified nuclear arsenal, one able not only to destroy Soviet society after surviving a Soviet first strike but also to carry out a variety of limited options. Fifth, it has demanded "surgical" nuclear capabilities—the ability to strike at target sets with a high degree of accuracy and reliability, avoiding unsought collateral damage. Sixth, the interpretation of controlled response incorporated into the Countervailing strategy has necessitated extensive hard-target counterforce capabilities to respond in kind to a Soviet attack on strategic forces.

Since these six requirements have served to justify most of the current U.S. strategic force modernization, their abandonment would permit a dramatic curtailment of the ongoing modernization effort.[21] According to the Pentagon's own presentation, the Peacekeeper (MX) missile, the Trident II missile, the Advanced Technology "Stealth" bomber, and the nuclear sea-launched cruise missile (SLCM) programs would lack justification.[22]

It might, of course, still be possible to try to justify the modernization effort in terms of *perceptual* requirements, even if the capabilities it provides are meaningless, unnecessary, or even dangerous. In the medium- and long-run, however, perceptions of military capability are likely to be correlated with educated appraisals of real military capability, not with some simplistic tallying of numbers. Even in the short-run, perceptions of weakness can be combated without senseless arming. As psychologist Steven Kull has argued:

> The answer may be as simple as stating that the emperor has no clothes. Even if perception theorists are entirely correct in claiming that key audiences are caught up in the illusion that the strategic balance is critical or that a nuclear war can be won, it does not necessarily follow that the best response is to enter into this illusion and compete within it. It is possible to play it straight and effectively work to dispel the illusion.[23]

Abandonment of unnecessary strategic modernization efforts would have two major benefits. First, of course, it would result in not insubstantial fiscal savings. Second, it would result in increased crisis stability. Two distinct processes would be involved. First, elimination of programs such as Peacekeeper and Trident II would reduce the stress on Soviet decision-makers during crisis by reducing decisional time pressures. Second, elimination of programs such as nuclear SLCMs would reduce the danger that the United States might irrationally or accidentally use strategic weapons during some minor confrontation in which fundamental U.S. interests were not engaged—and reduce Soviet fears that this might happen. This helps to ensure—and to make clear—that events that do not engage vital interests do not trigger the Doomsday Machine.

These increases in crisis stability are in addition to those caused directly by a change in employment strategy: by moving away from threats to respond in an appropriate fashion, the United States greatly reduces psychological and organizational pressures to act quickly, before confirmation of attack. With controlled response, such pressure may exist either because the weapons or C^3 necessary for the appropriate response are vulnerable or because the targets are ones of opportunity.

Implications for Theater Nuclear Forces

In addition to drastic cuts in strategic modernization, however, abandonment of the search for rational deterrent responses would permit major cuts in theater nuclear forces. If the purpose of theater nuclear forces is solely to create a risk of punitive blows against the Soviet Union, then the total size, diversity, and capability of U.S. theater nuclear forces can be reduced. Indeed, one implication of the above discussion is that extended deterrence in Europe not only does not require but may actually be undercut by militarily effective nuclear capabilities. Militarily effective forces—as distinct from forces capable only of senseless destruction—increase psychological and organizational pressures on the opponent and may possibly increase his rational incentives for rushing into war as well.

Precise numbers, types, and capabilities can be debated indefinitely—particularly since conclusions rest on judgments about perceptions of stress and organizational problems rather than on mathematical calculations derived from campaign analyses. Some rough estimates of a more nearly optimal force can be made, however. A well-designed Doomsday Machine in the European theater might involve four elements. First, 500 or 1,000 rounds of nuclear artillery ammunition would serve as a nuclear trigger. Second, a small force of INF missiles or aircraft based in the Federal Republic of Germany would threaten punishment and the risk of further escalation. Third, an INF force in Great Britain would complicate a Soviet disarming blow. Fourth, the retention of a few hundred aerial bombs for a dedicated force of quick reaction alert aircraft based in Germany and Britain would similarly complicate a preemptive strike.

All in all, with the change in strategy U.S. theater nuclear forces in Europe could be slashed to perhaps 1,500 or less. The cuts would come principally in tactical surface-to-surface missiles and air-delivered ordnance.

Equally important would be the elimination of theater nuclear weapons outside of Europe, especially at sea. The Navy's arsenal of 1,400 nonstrategic warheads could be cut to zero.

While the fiscal savings from these reductions would not be great by Pentagon standards, these cuts would still be extremely beneficial in terms of both acceptability and effectiveness. In addition to impressing domestic critics with U.S. willingness to reduce nuclear stockpiles and thereby making the adoption of the rest of the deterrence policy easier, reductions in theater nuclear forces may improve Alliance harmony by demonstrating to European publics that the United States does not see NATO as a vehicle for fighting a limited nuclear war in Europe. The elimination of naval nonstrategic nuclear weapons would solve an increasingly thorny diplomatic problem for overseas basing and port calls and project a more forthcoming image of the United States to littoral allies. The complete elimination of theater nuclear weapons at sea and in peripheral theaters would also reduce the risk of accidental, inadvertent, or irrational U.S. use of nuclear weapons in situations not involving fundamental U.S. interests. Most importantly, though, the elimination of sea-based theater nuclear forces and reduction of land-based ones would reduce the threat that the United States and NATO pose to Soviet military forces.

That deterrence may be enhanced by reducing the threat posed to the opponent's military forces is somewhat counterintuitive. This reduction would be expected, however, to reduce both the likelihood of an irrational Soviet decision to go to war and the incentives faced by rational Soviet decision-makers for rushing into it. At least three factors are involved. First, the clear absence of a U.S. ability to wage a successful offensive theater nuclear war—to wage a nuclear war with some prospect of defeating Soviet military forces and occupying Eastern Europe—makes it more difficult for the Soviet leadership to maintain or develop an inappropriate cognitive framework suggesting that the West has aggressive intentions. Second, the clear absence of a U.S. ability effectively to wage offensive theater nuclear war has the effect of reducing the stress Soviet decision-makers might face during an international crisis, when Eastern Europe was perhaps in revolt and public opinion in Western Europe favored intervention. Third, a reduction in the NATO offensive threat reduces the incentive for undertaking preemption to prevent a NATO military victory: to the extent that the classical security dilemma exists in Europe, the avoidance by the West of a potentially offensive military capability offers an escape from it.

Implications for Conventional Forces

Recognizing the coercive power stemming from its Doomsday Machine, the United States could also adopt a more relaxed attitude toward the conventional balance in Europe. Nuclear deterrence is neither incredible nor dependent on some hypothetical escalation ladder involving conventional rungs.

While the United States may indeed choose to maintain or even increase its conventional capabilities, conventional forces are expensive and generate troubling manpower requirements. More importantly, they have the potential to create psychological pressures and rational incentives for a hasty Soviet decision to attack during a crisis. These pressures and incentives threaten to undermine Soviet coercibility. Reductions in conventional forces might play an important role in limiting the potential decision-making stress experienced by Soviet leaders during social or political unrest in central Europe, and they might help to reduce any existing cognitive rigidities suggesting a military threat from the West. Further, deliberate limitation of U.S. conventional capabilities would avoid presenting the Soviet Union with a rational reason to strike first and hastily in time of crisis in order to prevent a decisive Soviet military defeat. (This places continued reliance on nuclear deterrence in polar contrast to recent proposals by Samuel Huntington for the development of a conventional counteroffensive retaliatory capability.[24]) Conscious and careful avoidance of meaningful offensive military capabilities would help to prevent an unstable situation like that of 1914, when French and Russian offensive capabilities made it rational for Germany to rush to strike first.

Any diminishment of the U.S. conventional presence in Europe risks upsetting decades of accumulated symbolism, of course, and might raise doubts in Western Europe about the U.S. commitment to the maintenance of the status quo in Europe. If tanks and planes are withdrawn today, may not the nuclear umbrella be withdrawn tomorrow? Reductions in U.S. conventional efforts might be designed in such a way, however, as to avoid raising such concerns. First, while leaving forces currently deployed in Europe unaltered, the United States could cut or reconfigure those deployed in the continental United States and scheduled to be transported to Europe during a crisis or war.[25] Second, the United States could engage in a slowdown or freeze of qualitative improvement rather than in a reduction in quantitative strength: simply terminating a few major procurement items designed principally for use in the European theater (such as the M-1 tank, AH-64 helicopter, Patriot air defense missile, and Bradley fighting vehicle) and their successors would save billions of dollars a year and might significantly reduce Soviet fears of a NATO offensive. Third, reductions could be made as part of negotiated agreements with the Soviet Union or NATO allies.

An understanding of the U.S. Doomsday Machine thus permits a serious rethinking of U.S. conventional force requirements. Without retrenching current commitments, the United States could achieve significant fiscal savings and enhance crisis stability.

Implications for Declaratory Stance

Beyond these possibilities for reductions in force capability, however, abandonment of the pursuit of rational options would also permit beneficial changes in declaratory stance. A controlled response strategy has dictated that the United States publicly indicate a belief in the limitability and potential rationality of nuclear war. Talk comes cheap, of course. Nonetheless, in the long run such a declaratory stance is likely to involve three types of costs. While to date none of these has been unbearable, each has the potential to undermine the foundations of U.S. deterrence strategy. Abandonment of controlled response rhetoric promises to improve both the acceptability and effectiveness of the U.S. deterrence posture.

First, the declaratory stance of controlled response risks generating domestic political opposition. The American people do not believe that a major war is likely to remain limited, and they may regard political leaders who speak of nuclear war as something that can rationally be undertaken as naive or dangerous. Popular political opposition generated by the rhetoric of nuclear warfighting has been limited to the short-lived and remarkably temperate nuclear freeze movement of the early 1980s, but a domestic political backlash against nuclear deterrence policies remains an ever-present possibility.

Second and more important, the declaratory stance necessarily associated with controlled response strategies is likely to prove an irritant within the NATO Alliance. It highlights the difference of interest that exists between Americans and Western Europeans, a difference that is the natural product of geography. A nuclear war that appeared limited to the United States would understandably appear quite total to the European allies. The musings of President Reagan that "I could see where you could have the exchange of tactical nuclear weapons against troops in the field without it bringing either one of the major powers to pushing the button"[26] are unlikely to be particularly comforting to the inhabitants of the field involved. The long-term implications for political discourse within and between Alliance states are uncertain. If NATO is to survive, U.S. declaratory stance must at least minimally reassure the European members. And a declaratory stance which—in order to deter the Soviets—stresses U.S. willingness to reduce Europe to radioactive rubble while the United States and Soviet Union exchange recriminations is unlikely to reassure. It may be that in the long run the nuclear threat cannot, in any case, be made acceptable to Europeans. The notion that one's homeland may be incinerated irrationally is not an entirely reassuring one. But at least at the margin it is likely to be more acceptable than the notion that one's ally would deliberately and willingly undertake the nuclear devastation of one's homeland.

Third, a declaratory stance compatible with either controlled response strategies or nuclear superiority will involve costs in U.S.– Soviet political relations. Continuous harping on U.S. willingness rationally to choose to use nuclear weapons against the Soviets will neither create a very forthcoming image of America nor lead to a very optimistic assessment of U.S. aims and intentions.

POWER AND MADNESS

Despite the benefits of abandoning the futile search for rational nuclear options, the notion of relying on a threat to behave irrationally may, per se, still be a discomforting one. The fact that commitment to *ex post* irrational behavior is *ex ante* rational behavior is a difficult truth. Observing the true nature of the U.S. nuclear commitment to Europe, Paul Bracken has complained:

> What government can possibly announce that its security is dependent on turning nuclear weapons over to a battalion commander who just might pull the trigger even if he were not authorized to do so? Even governmental and academic studies have difficulty comprehending the extraordinary nature of this strategy.[27]

And yet, any other nuclear strategy is even more dangerous and less palatable as a basis for policy. President Reagan—displaying an ability to recognize the obvious, which nuclear strategists often lack —correctly noted in an address to the United Nations that "nuclear war cannot be won, and must never be fought."[28] Nuclear war is not rational to wage. Our best plans and our best weapons are not likely to make it so. Nonetheless, in a world in which nuclear weapons cannot be disinvented—and to which nuclear weapons have brought an element of stability—the threat to use them cannot be totally eliminated and can promote fundamental U.S. interests, including international peace. Understanding our Doomsday Machine is the first step toward living with it or redesigning it to make it easier to live with. Understanding the logic of power and MADness permits us to escape the current coupling, counterforce, and strategic defense debates and to build consistent policies on the basis of a logically coherent strategy.

The idea of exploiting the coercive power associated with irrationality and of basing U.S. policy on limited physical assets and limited organizational, political, and psychological resources runs directly counter to common sense. The counterintuitive nature of the logic presented in this book does not, however, necessarily imply its invalidity or impracticality: the ideas that have driven U.S. deterrence strategy at each key stage in its development have violated traditional views on the nature of conflict. A quarter of a century ago, in a seminal volume exploring the now accepted idea of controlled nuclear retaliation, Thomas Schelling observed that the unfamiliarity and strangeness of new strategic concepts

> provides no immunity; we live in an era of strange power relations, and nothing can be judged implausible just because we have never thought of it before or because it appears to contradict what used to be called common sense. The human foot would seem wildly improbable to a creature that had never seen one. We must judge the concepts and strategies discussed in this book in that fashion—not according to whether they are strange, but according to whether in the strange world of modern weaponry and international relationships they are much more implausible than the conceptions of war and the strategies that we daily discuss.[29]

In the same volume Klaus Knorr reviewed the problems posed for U.S. deterrence by the development of Soviet assured destruction capabilities and cautiously advocated a strategy of controlled and limited nuclear reprisals. His observations about a strategy of controlled nuclear war are equally relevant to a strategy of irrational nuclear response:

I have been told in conversation that this is an absurd war and an absurd strategy. And so, no doubt, it is. From every conceivable point of view it looks like a bad war and a bad strategy. But the question remains whether the available alternatives may not be, or may not come to be, more absurd and worse. . . .[30]

NOTES

Introduction

1. Henry A. Kissinger, "The Future of NATO," *The Washington Quarterly* (Autumn 1979), vol. 2, no. 4. The remark was made at a conference on the future of NATO held in Brussels on September 1–3, 1979.

2. Many persuasive—though frequently irreconcilable—policy pieces have been written in the past few years predicting and prescribing futures for the American security guarantee to NATO. Among those worth serious review are: McGeorge Bundy, George F. Kennan, Robert S. McNamara, and Gerard Smith, "Nuclear Weapons and the Atlantic Alliance," *Foreign Affairs* (Spring 1982), vol. 60, no. 4; Robert J. Art, "Fixing Atlantic Bridges," *Foreign Policy* (Spring 1982), no. 46; Karl Kaiser, Georg Leber, Alois Mertes, and Franz-Josef Schulze, "Nuclear Weapons and the Preservation of Peace," *Foreign Affairs* (Summer 1982), vol. 60, no. 5; Hedley Bull, "European Self-Reliance and the Reform of NATO," *Foreign Affairs* (Spring 1983), vol. 61, no. 4; Josef Joffe, "Europe's American Pacifier," *Foreign Policy* (Spring 1984), no. 54; and John J. Mearsheimer, "Nuclear Weapons and Deterrence in Europe," *International Security* (Winter 1984–85), vol. 9, no. 3. Perhaps the most provocative recent piece, however, is David Garnham, "Extending Deterrence with German Nuclear Weapons," *International Security* (Summer 1985), vol. 10, no. 1. See also the interesting collection of articles: John D. Steinbruner and Leon V. Sigal, eds., *Alliance Security: NATO and the No-First-Use Question* (Washington, D.C.: Brookings, 1983).

3. Among the best contributions to this debate are: Wolfgang K. H. Panofsky, "The Mutual-Hostage Relationship Between America and Russia," *Foreign Affairs* (October 1973), vol. 52, no. 1; Herbert Scoville, Jr., "Flexible MADness," *Foreign Policy* (Spring 1974), no. 14; Ted Greenwood and Michael L. Nacht, "The New Nuclear Debate: Sense or Nonsense," *Foreign Affairs* (July 1974), vol. 52, no. 4; George W. Rathjens, "Flexible Response Options," *Orbis* (Fall 1974), vol. 18, no. 3; Paul H. Nitze, "Deterring Our Deterrent," *Foreign Policy* (Winter 1976–77), no. 25; Robert Jervis, "Why Nuclear Superiority Doesn't Matter," *Political Science Quarterly* (Winter 1979–80), vol. 94, no. 4; Colin S. Gray and Keith Payne, "Victory Is

Possible," *Foreign Policy* (Summer 1980), no. 39; and Spurgeon M. Keeny, Jr. and Wolfgang K. H. Panofsky, "MAD vs. NUTS," *Foreign Affairs* (Winter 1981–82), vol. 60, no. 2.

4. Caspar W. Weinberger, *Annual Report of the Secretary of Defense to Congress, Fiscal Year 1987* (Washington, D.C.: GPO, 1986), p. 40.

5. On the connection between counterforce and coupling, see Earl C. Ravenal, "Counterforce and Alliance: The Ultimate Connection," *International Security* (Spring 1982), vol. 6, no. 4, or Gray and Payne, "Victory Is Possible."

6. The elaboration of official U.S. targeting and procurement strategy can best be found in the annual statements made by Secretary of Defense Harold Brown to Congress and published by the Government Printing Office. Much the same information is also found, for example, in: Walter Slocombe, "The Countervailing Strategy," *International Security* (Spring 1981), vol. 5, no. 4; Warner R. Schilling, "U.S. Strategic Nuclear Concepts in the 1970s: The Search for Sufficiently Equivalent Countervailing Parity," *International Security* (Fall 1981), vol. 6, no. 2; or Lynn Etheridge Davis, *Limited Nuclear Options: Deterrence and the New American Doctrine*, Adelphi Paper no. 121 (London: International Institute for Strategic Studies, 1976). Among the best of the critiques of U.S. doctrine are those of Robert Jervis, Colin S. Gray, and Earl C. Ravenal: See Jervis, "Why Nuclear Superiority Doesn't Matter"; Jervis, "The Madness Beyond MAD—Current American Nuclear Strategy," *PS* (Winter 1984), vol. 17, no. 1; Jervis, *The Illogic of American Nuclear Strategy* (Ithaca: Cornell University Press, 1984); Gray, "Nuclear Strategy: A Case for a Theory of Victory," *International Security* (Summer 1979), vol. 4, no. 1; Gray, "Targeting Problems for Central War," *Naval War College Review* (January–February 1980), vol. 33, no. 1; Gray and Payne, "Victory Is Possible"; Gray, "Presidential Directive 59: Flawed But Useful," *Parameters* (March 1981), vol. 11, no. 1; Ravenal, "After Schlesinger: Something Has to Give," *Foreign Policy* (Spring 1976), no. 22; and Ravenal, "Counterforce and Alliance: The Ultimate Connection." Two excellent histories of U.S. nuclear strategy and strategic thinking are Lawrence Freedman's *The Evolution of Nuclear Strategy* (New York: St. Martin's Press, 1981) and Fred Kaplan's *Wizards of Armageddon* (New York: Simon and Schuster, 1983).

7. The most important of these are probably the works of Thomas C. Schelling. See Schelling, *The Strategy of Conflict* (Cambridge: Harvard University Press, 1960); Schelling and Morton H. Halperin, *Strategy and Arms Control* (New York: Twentieth Century Fund, 1961); Schelling, "Comment," in Klaus Knorr and Thornton Read, eds., *Limited Strategic War,* (New York: Praeger, 1962); Schelling, "Nuclear Strategy in Europe," *World Politics* (April 1962), vol. 14, no. 3; and, largely summarizing his earlier writings, Schelling, *Arms and Influence* (New Haven: Yale University Press, 1966).

Other landmarks in deductive deterrence theory produced during this period include (in chronological order): Bernard Brodie, "Nuclear Weapons: Strategic or Tactical?" *Foreign Affairs* (January 1954), vol. 32, no. 2; Bernard Brodie, "Unlimited Weapons and Limited War," *The Reporter* (November 18, 1954), vol. 11, no. 9; William W. Kaufmann, ed., *Military Policy and National Security* (Princeton: Princeton University Press, 1956); Morton A. Kaplan, "The Calculus of Nuclear Deterrence," *World Politics* (October 1958), vol. 11, no. 1; Albert Wohlstetter, "The Delicate Balance of Terror," *Foreign Affairs* (January 1959), vol. 37, no. 2; Bernard Brodie, *Strategy in the Missile Age* (Princeton: Princeton University Press, 1959); Herman Kahn, *On Thermonuclear War* (Princeton: Princeton University Press, 1960);

Anatol Rapoport, *Fights, Games, and Debates* (Ann Arbor: University of Michigan Press, 1960); Glenn H. Snyder, *Deterrence and Defense* (Princeton: Princeton University Press, 1961); Knorr and Read, eds., *Limited Strategic War*; J. David Singer, *Deterrence, Arms Control, and Disarmament* (Columbus: Ohio State University Press, 1962); Herman Kahn, *On Escalation: Metaphors and Scenarios* (New York: Praeger, 1965); and Klaus Knorr, *On the Use of Military Power in the Nuclear Age* (Princeton: Princeton University Press, 1966).

Although these works generally employ game theory for heuristic rather than formal/mathematical modeling purposes, underlying much of this research was the development of formal game theory. Here it is important to recognize John Von Neumann and Oskar Morgenstern, *A Theory of Games and Economic Behavior* (Princeton: Princeton University Press, 1944, 1953).

An excellent annotated bibliography of most of the literature of the period can be found in Halperin, *Limited War in the Nuclear Age* (New York: John Wiley, 1963), pp. 133–84.

8. "Chicken" suggested an analogy to competitions among teen-age hot-rodders who compete for dominance by racing their cars directly at each other. To swerve in this game, particularly if the opponent does not, demonstrates a lack of courage and involves loss of face. To fail to swerve, however, risks fiery collision and ensures mutual destruction if the opponent fails to yield the right of way. See, for example, Schelling, *Arms and Influence*, pp. 116–25. For a rigorous look at the game, see also Glenn H. Snyder and Paul Diesing, *Conflict Among Nations* (Princeton: Princeton University Press, 1977), pp. 107–22.

9. For an unparalleled discussion of contributions to the development of deterrence theory made during the late 1950s and early 1960s—and earlier and later— see Robert Jervis, "Deterrence Theory Revisited," *World Politics* (January 1979), vol. 31, no. 2.

10. At least five of these contributions—those by Philip Green, Stephen Maxwell, John D. Steinbruner, Patrick M. Morgan, and Jack L. Snyder—remain, for various reasons, worth careful reading. See Green, *Deadly Logic* (Columbus: Ohio State University Press, 1966); Maxwell, *Rationality in Deterrence*, Adelphi Paper no. 50 (London: International Institute for Strategic Studies, 1968); Steinbruner, "Beyond Rational Deterrence," *World Politics* (January 1976), vol. 28, no. 2; Morgan, *Deterrence* (Beverly Hills: Sage, 1977); and Jack Snyder, "Rationality at the Brink," *World Politics* (April 1978), vol. 30, no. 3.

More recently, considerable attention has also been devoted to "formal theory" —applied mathematical game-theoretic modeling. For examples of this burgeoning literature see Steven J. Brams, *Superpower Games: Applying Game Theory to Superpower Conflict* (New Haven: Yale University Press, 1985) or Robert Powell, "Nuclear Brinkmanship with Two-Sided Incomplete Information," *American Political Science Review* (March 1988), vol. 82, no. 1. While the impressive mathematical rigor of much of this recent work in formal theory is beyond dispute, its relevance remains unclear. The utility of formal theory appears to be constrained both by the behavioral assumptions it allows and by the difficulty of translating its numerical findings into predictions and prescriptions useful to policymakers operating in the unquantified world of real life. A graver complaint is that the mathematical artistry of formalization tends to obscure rather than illuminate or test the underlying assumptions and, in the absence of appropriate sensitivity analyses, conveys a false sense of analytic rigor and certainty.

11. It seems fair to argue that in many senses Steinbruner and Jack Snyder came closest, but their cognitive/cybernetic models lack predictive (and therefore prescriptive) power. As Steinbruner himself confesses: "We cannot leap directly to counsel a drastic change in established strategy. . . . Cybernetic analysis is neither sufficiently developed nor sufficiently accepted to carry that degree of responsibility or impact." See Steinbruner, "Beyond Rational Deterrence," p. 242. See Chapter 2 for further discussion of the problems of working within cognitive/cybernetic paradigms and the possibility of incorporating insights provided by such paradigms into constrained rational-actor models. Perhaps the best indication that it is not possible or practical at present to reformulate deterrence theory within a cognitive/cybernetic, rather than analytic, paradigm is that there has been no rush to attempt to do so.

12. Augustinian just war theory suggests that war is immoral unless certain requirements are met in the resort to war (jus ad bellum) and in the conduct of war (jus in bello). For the conduct of war to be morally tolerable, the weapons used must be proportionate to the objective and belligerents must discriminate between combatants and noncombatants. For an excellent summary of just war theory, see National Conference of Catholic Bishops, The Challenge of Peace: God's Promise and Our Response (Washington, D.C.: United States Catholic Conference, 1983), pp. 21– 37. For a fuller treatment of the evolution of just war theory see, for example, James Turner Johnson, Just War Tradition and the Restraint of War (Princeton: Princeton University Press, 1981).

13. The critical pathbreaking work in this regard has been Alexander L. George and Richard Smoke, Deterrence in American Foreign Policy (New York: Columbia University Press, 1974). See also Alexander L. George, David K. Hall, and William R. Simons, The Limits of Coercive Diplomacy (Boston: Little, Brown, 1971); Stephen S. Kaplan and Barry M. Blechman, Force Without War (Washington, D.C.: Brookings, 1978); Stephen S. Kaplan, Diplomacy of Power (Washington, D.C.: Brookings, 1981); and John J. Mearsheimer, Conventional Deterrence (Ithaca: Cornell University Press, 1983). The most insightful study of the unique problems of conventional coercion that I am aware of is Jonathan Shimshoni's Israel and Conventional Deterrence (Ithaca: Cornell University Press, 1988). While the problems inherent in quantification raise some concerns about the meaning of their statistical findings, the research of Paul Huth and Bruce Russett is also worth serious examination: see Huth and Russett, "What Makes Deterrence Work? Cases from 1900 to 1980," World Politics (July 1984), vol. 36, no. 4; Huth and Russett, "Deterrence Failure and Crisis Escalation," International Studies Quarterly (March 1988), vol. 32, no. 1; and Huth, "Extended Deterrence and the Outbreak of War," American Political Science Review (June 1988), vol. 82, no. 2.

14. See, for example, Marc Trachtenberg, "Nuclear Weapons and the Cuban Missile Crisis," International Security (Summer 1985), vol. 10, no. 1, especially p. 163.

15. Bernard Brodie, Escalation and the Nuclear Option (Princeton: Princeton University Press, 1966), p. 74. For a provocative expression of a somewhat dissimilar view, see George H. Quester, Deterrence Before Hiroshima (New York: John Wiley, 1966), especially pp. 172–87. Quester identifies the invention (or imagination) of strategic air capabilities rather than nuclear weapons as the revolutionary event. He balances this judgment and expands his argument to include seapower in The Future of Nuclear Deterrence (Lexington, Mass.: Lexington Books, 1986), pp.

61–68. While Quester's work certainly reminds us of the danger of overestimating the impact of the nuclear revolution, not only does Brodie's summary still seem a fair one, but even at the psychological level the new potential for high-speed total societal destruction appears critical. See Chapter 5 for further discussion of the implications of the nuclear revolution.

16. Particularly valuable in this regard is Robert Jervis, Richard Ned Lebow, and Janice Gross Stein, *Psychology and Deterrence* (Baltimore: Johns Hopkins University Press, 1985).

17. See, for example, James G. March and Herbert A. Simon, *Organizations* (New York: John Wiley, 1958); Richard Cyert and James G. March, *A Behavioral Theory of the Firm* (Englewood Cliffs, N.J.: Prentice-Hall, 1963); and Herbert A. Simon, *Administrative Behavior*, Third Edition (New York: The Free Press, 1976).

18. The best-known representatives of this literature are: Graham T. Allison, *Essence of Decision* (Boston: Little, Brown, 1971); Morton H. Halperin, *Bureaucratic Politics and Foreign Policy* (Washington, D.C.: Brookings, 1974); Richard Neustadt, *Alliance Politics* (New York: Columbia University Press, 1970).

19. Indeed, some of the bureaucratic politics literature foreshadowed later political psychology work by observing that how participants defined the "national" interest was itself colored by their bureaucratic positions.

20. There are, of course, some doubting voices about the ultimate significance of bureaucratic politics and organizational behavior, and about how far such interpretations of state behavior can, should, or need be pushed. Stephen D. Krasner's research offers a good counterperspective. See Krasner, "Are Bureaucracies Important? (Or Allison Wonderland)," *Foreign Policy* (Summer 1972), no. 7; and Krasner, *Defending the National Interest* (Princeton: Princeton University Press, 1978). See also Robert J. Art, "Bureaucratic Politics and American Foreign Policy: A Critique," *Policy Sciences* (December 1973), vol. 4, no. 4; and Lawrence Freedman, "Logic, Politics, and Foreign Policy Processes," *International Affairs*, London (July 1976), vol. 52, no. 3.

21. Recent work by Desmond Ball, John D. Steinbruner, Paul Bracken, and Bruce G. Blair has explored the organizational problems that decision-makers would likely encounter in maintaining rational central control over nuclear weapons during a major war. This work tends to cast doubt on the practicality of nuclear targeting strategies that downplay or ignore command and control difficulties in complex organizations. See Ball, *Can Nuclear War Be Controlled?*, Adelphi Paper no. 169 (London: International Institute for Strategic Studies, 1981); Ball, "U.S. Strategic Forces: How Would They Be Used?" *International Security* (Winter 1982–83), vol. 7, no. 3; Steinbruner, "Nuclear Decapitation," *Foreign Policy* (Winter 1981–82), no. 45; Bracken, *The Command and Control of Nuclear Forces* (New Haven: Yale University Press, 1983); Blair, "Solving the Command and Control Problem," *Arms Control Today* (January 1985), vol. 15, no. 1; Blair, *Strategic Command and Control* (Washington, D.C.: Brookings, 1985). Also of interest in this regard is Scott D. Sagan's "Nuclear Alerts and Crisis Management," *International Security* (Spring 1985), vol. 9, no. 4.

22. Among the most important pieces of research in this field are: Charles F. Hermann, ed., *International Crises: Insights from Behavioral Research* (New York: The Free Press, 1972); Ole R. Holsti, *Crisis, Escalation, War* (Montreal: McGill-Queens University Press, 1972); Janice Gross Stein and Raymond Tanter, *Rational Decision-Making: Israel's Security Choices, 1967* (Columbus: Ohio State University

Press, 1980); Michael Brecher with Benjamin Geist, *Decisions in Crisis: Israel, 1967 and 1973* (Berkeley: University of California Press, 1980); and Richard Ned Lebow, *Between Peace and War* (Baltimore: Johns Hopkins University Press, 1981).

23. Ole R. Holsti and Alexander L. George, "The Effects of Stress on the Performance of Foreign Policy-Makers," in Cornelius P. Cotter, ed., *Political Science Annual* (Indianapolis: Bobbs-Merrill, 1975), p. 257.

24. Although the empirical study of crisis behavior noted above represents an important contribution to this field, research has been much broader. Perhaps the most important works in this area are Irving Janis' and Leon Mann's *Decision Making* and Robert Jervis' *Perception and Misperception in International Politics*, but the literature is extensive and growing: see Irving L. Janis and Leon Mann, *Decision Making* (New York: The Free Press, 1977); Robert Jervis, *Perception and Misperception in International Politics* (Princeton: Princeton University Press, 1976). Daniel Frei summarizes much of the research that is relevant to nuclear deterrence in *Risks of Unintentional Nuclear War* (Totowa, N.J.: Rowman & Allanheld, 1983), pp. 109–55. Lester Grinspoon's brief article also focuses on the implications of these phenomena for nuclear war: see Grinspoon, "Crisis Behavior," *Bulletin of the Atomic Scientists* (April 1984), vol. 40, no. 4. See also Janis, *Victims of Groupthink* (Boston: Houghton Mifflin, 1972); Holsti and George, "The Effects of Stress on the Performance of Foreign Policy-Makers"; Klaus Knorr, "Threat Perception," in Klaus Knorr, ed., *Historical Dimensions of National Security Problems* (Lawrence, Kans.: University Press of Kansas, 1976); Stein and Tanter, *Rational Decision-Making: Israel's Security Choices, 1967*; Alexander L. George, *Presidential Decision-making in Foreign Policy* (Boulder, Colo.: Westview Press, 1980); Lebow, *Between Peace and War*; and (reviewing much of the literature) Jack S. Levy, "Misperception and the Causes of War," *World Politics* (October 1983), vol. 36, no. 1. Pathbreaking in this field was Roberta Wohlstetter's *Pearl Harbor: Warning and Decision* (Stanford: Stanford University Press, 1962). While the full implications of stress and cognitive rigidity for rationality are somewhat broader (see Chapter 2, below), much of the current literature has focused on motivated and unmotivated biases. On the distinction between motivated and unmotivated biases, see Jervis, Lebow, and Stein, *Psychology and Deterrence*, p. 4. On motivated bias, see Janis and Mann, *Decision Making* and on unmotivated bias, Daniel Kahneman, Paul Slovic, and Amos Tversky, eds., *Judgment Under Uncertainty: Heuristics and Biases* (Cambridge, UK: Cambridge University Press, 1982).

The effect of psychopathological personalities on the course of international affairs has long been studied—unlike bureaucratic politics or social and cognitive psychology, it is not a new field. The classic case study of the role of personality disorder in irrational decision-making is provided by Alexander L. George and Juliette L. George in *Woodrow Wilson and Colonel House* (New York: Dover, 1956). Sidney Verba's analysis of the rationality or irrationality of apparently psychopathological behavior is excellent. See Verba, "Assumptions of Rationality and Non-Rationality in Models of the International System," *World Politics* (October 1961), vol. 14, no. 1.

25. See Schelling, *The Strategy of Conflict*, pp. 16ff, and Glenn Snyder, *Deterrence and Defense*, pp. 1–50.

26. Schelling, *The Strategy of Conflict*, p. 4.

27. For a different explanation of the link between deterrence theory and realism, see Jervis, "Deterrence Theory Revisited," pp. 289–90. Quite apart from

realism, deterrence theory's assumptions of rationality may also have their roots in the neoclassical economic training of some of the early theorists.

28. Schelling, *The Strategy of Conflict*, p. 4. Schelling, of course, goes on to caution: "Whether the resulting theory provides good or poor insight into actual behavior is, I repeat, a matter for subsequent judgement." This word to the wise has been overlooked in more recent efforts to formalize deterrence theory.

29. Klaus Knorr, *The Power of Nations* (New York: Basic Books, 1975), p. 42.

30. Richard M. Nixon, *The Real War* (New York: Warner Books, 1981), p. 176. This conclusion is not unique to Nixon but is, rather, a commonly held premise within the U.S. national security community. See, for example, Secretary of Defense Caspar Weinberger, *Annual Report to Congress, Fiscal Year 1984* (Washington, D.C.: GPO, 1983), p. 52.

31. Schelling, *The Strategy of Conflict*, p. 18.

1. MAD AND THE NUCLEAR DETERRENCE PROBLEM

1. For fairly recent work see, for example, Lawrence Freedman, *The Evolution of Nuclear Strategy* (New York: St. Martin's Press, 1981); Fred Kaplan, *The Wizards of Armageddon* (New York: Simon and Schuster, 1983); Colin S. Gray, *Nuclear Strategy and Strategic Planning* (Philadelphia: Foreign Policy Research Institute, 1984). A great deal of original archival work has been done during the 1980s, much of it by David Alan Rosenberg. See, for example, Rosenberg, "The Origins of Overkill: Nuclear Weapons and American Strategy, 1945-1960," *International Security* (Spring 1983), vol. 7, no. 4.

2. See, for example, Kaplan, *The Wizards of Armageddon*, pp. 291-306.

3. Albert Wohlstetter, "Letters from Readers: Morality and Deterrence," *Commentary* (December 1983), vol. 76, no. 6, p. 16. Emphasis in original.

4. Robert S. McNamara, "The Military Role of Nuclear Weapons," *Foreign Affairs* (Fall 1983), vol. 62, no. 1, p. 72. McNamara's views on the lack of military utility of nuclear use have been shared by a wide variety of other informed observers, including senior NATO military officers. See, for example, Field Marshal Lord Michael Carver, *A Policy for Peace* (London: Faber and Faber, 1982) or the views expressed in H. W. Tromp and G. R. LaRocque, eds., *Nuclear War in Europe* (Groningen, The Netherlands: Groningen University Press, 1982).

5. Caspar W. Weinberger, *Annual Report to the Congress, Fiscal Year 1984* (Washington, D.C.: GPO, 1983), p. 55.

6. Robert Jervis has commented extensively and incisively on the "illogic"— or, more accurately, the flawed logic—of U.S. deterrence strategy. See Jervis, *The Illogic of American Nuclear Strategy* (Ithaca: Cornell University Press, 1984), especially pp. 81-85.

7. John Lewis Gaddis, *Strategies of Containment* (New York: Oxford University Press, 1982), p. 148. For a brief but clear note on the failure of the Truman administration to move away from prenuclear conceptions of war in thinking about nuclear conflict, see Jerome H. Kahan, *Security in the Nuclear Age* (Washington, D.C.: Brookings, 1975), pp. 9-10. Freedman offers a good history of the period in *The Evolution of Nuclear Strategy*, pp. 47-56, 63-75. To be sure, the tremendous destructive power of nuclear weapons and the potential importance of these weapons in strategic operations were immediately clear; a few intellectuals—most

1. MAD AND THE NUCLEAR DETERRENCE PROBLEM

notably Jacob Viner and Bernard Brodie—even recognized the full revolutionary impact of nuclear weapons within a few months of Hiroshima. Brodie's views appear in Brodie, ed., *The Absolute Weapon* (New York: Harcourt, Brace, 1946). For an assessment of Viner's influence, drawing on the papers of Edward Meade Earle, see Kaplan, *The Wizards of Armageddon*, p. 27.

8. For example, a 1948 U.S. Air Force classified guidance entitled *Doctrine of Atomic Air Warfare* (December 30, 1948) noted: "Progression from the spear through the bow, musket, rifle and artillery to the weapons of World War II was simply a matter of ever-increasing firepower. . . . The atomic bomb does not appear to have deviated from this evolutionary trend." Quoted in Kaplan, *The Wizards of Armageddon*, pp. 181-82. For an excellent discussion of nuclear war plans, revealing their direct descent from World War II strategic bombing campaigns rather than from some new appraisal of the logic of nuclear war, see Desmond Ball, *Targeting for Strategic Deterrence*, Adelphi Paper no. 185 (London: International Institute for Strategic Studies, 1983), pp. 3-8.

9. For a discussion of the historic novelty of Eisenhower's New Look in terms of establishing a nuclear strategy, see Michael Mandelbaum, *The Nuclear Question* (Cambridge: Cambridge University Press, 1979), pp. 46-54.

10. Tactical nuclear operations, presumably involving smaller-yield, short-range nuclear systems, including nuclear-armed artillery and short-range rockets and aircraft, would seek to alter local battlefield conditions. Strategic nuclear operations, by contrast, would presumably employ larger-yield and longer-range weapons and seek to destroy Soviet political and economic capacity to wage war.

11. The Eisenhower administration also developed a distinctive policy on tactical nuclear weapons. Briefly summarized, the administration's policy was that tactical nuclear weapons would be used as a source of concentrated firepower in battlefield operations against Soviet forces. As part of its "New Look" in defense policy, designed to keep down the price of the American defense effort and build for an economically bearable "long haul," the Eisenhower administration moved in the mid-1950s to incorporate tactical nuclear weapons into American military units. The U.S. Army was reconfigured into "pentomic" divisions and U.S. military planning was based on the assumption that any war directly between the superpowers would be nuclear and that in such a conflict nuclear weapons would be available for battlefield use. For a good discussion of the incorporation of tactical nuclear weapons into U.S. forces and strategy, see Milton Leitenberg, "Background Materials in Tactical Nuclear Weapons (Primarily in the European Context)," *Tactical Nuclear Weapons: European Perspectives*, SIPRI (London: Taylor & Francis, 1978), pp. 9-40. NSC 162/2, signed by Eisenhower in October 1953, explicitly abandoned the planning assumption that either general or large-scale limited war might be waged without the use of nuclear weapons. See Samuel P. Huntington, *The Common Defense* (New York: Columbia University Press, 1961), p. 74. The U.S. advantage in nuclear weaponry was seen as a means of offsetting Soviet advantages in manpower; use of nuclear weapons on the battlefield was seen as a way of enhancing NATO's ability to slow a Soviet advance to the English Channel.

12. As Freedman suggests, "the 'New Look' uncoupled the response from the offending action. The West would not reply in kind to an Eastern invasion, but raise the stakes of war. Thereafter Western strategy would depend on convincing the Soviet leaders that it had the nerve to do this." *The Evolution of Nuclear Strategy*, p. 87.

13. Huntington, *The Common Defense*, p. 84.
14. Eisenhower, as quoted in Gaddis, *Strategies of Containment*, pp. 149-50. The basic statement of Massive Retaliation is John Foster Dulles' clarification of his January 12, 1954, "Massive Retaliation" speech to the Council on Foreign Relations in New York: Dulles, "Policy for Security and Peace," *Foreign Affairs* (April 1954), vol. 32, no. 3. There remains considerable debate about precisely what Massive Retaliation meant. It seems clear that some flexibility of response was envisioned by its authors. See Dulles, "Policy for Security and Peace," p. 358. But regardless of the intentions of its authors, as implemented by the military Massive Retaliation meant a risk of massive retaliation, not a certainty of a carefully graduated response: the actual U.S. operational strategy during the Eisenhower period was to view any direct conflict with the Soviet Union as inevitably nuclear, and any nuclear conflict as one in which the United States would use its nuclear forces in a massive, all-out strike, withholding no targets and keeping no nuclear forces in reserve.
15. Donald Snow, *The Nuclear Future: Toward a Strategy of Uncertainty* (University, Ala.: University of Alabama Press, 1983), p. 4. Emphasis added.
16. See Bernard Brodie, "Unlimited Weapons and Limited War," *The Reporter* (November 18, 1954), vol. 11, no. 9, p. 16. A second influential critique of Massive Retaliation was provided by William W. Kaufmann in *Military Policy and National Security* (Princeton: Princeton University Press, 1956). It should be noted that Brodie's view of the utility of the threat of unlimited war would change during the 1960s; this shift, however, reflected his understanding of the propensies of wars to escalate rather than a belated respect for Massive Retaliation's assumptions about the ability of the United States to make rational a decision to launch an all-out attack in response to a limited provocation. See Brodie, *Escalation and the Nuclear Option* (Princeton: Princeton University Press, 1966).
17. See Dulles, "Challenge and Response in United States Policy," *Foreign Affairs* (October 1957), vol. 36, no. 1; Dulles here hints at a move to a strategy of controlled and limited nuclear war by noting the growing possibility of battlefield use of nuclear weapons that would deny the Soviet Union its objectives on the ground while leaving homelands unscathed. Such a strategy would have differed from McNamara's Flexible Response strategy in that all-out tactical nuclear war was seen as a means of denying Soviet armies victory and therefore as an alternative to, not a foreshadowing of, strategic war.
18. Christian Herter, as quoted in Dean Acheson, "The Practice of Partnership," *Foreign Affairs* (January 1963), vol. 41, no. 2, pp. 251-52.
19. Mandelbaum, *The Nuclear Question*, p. 97.
20. The concepts of "punishment" and "controlled retaliation" as logically distinct modes of coercion will be developed more fully in chapter 3.
21. See, for example, Freedman, *The Evolution of Nuclear Strategy*, pp. 225-44; Kaplan, *Wizards of Armageddon*, pp. 258-85; or Bruce G. Blair, *Strategic Command and Control* (Washington, D.C.: Brookings, 1985), pp. 40-41.
22. Kaplan, *Wizards of Armageddon*, p. 269.
23. Robert S. McNamara, as quoted in William W. Kaufmann, *The McNamara Strategy* (New York: Harper and Row, 1964), p. 75.
24. Weinberger, *Annual Report to the Congress, Fiscal Year 1984*, p. 55.
25. Harold Brown, *Annual Report to the Congress, Fiscal Year 1980* (Washington, D.C.: GPO, 1979), p. 75

26. James R. Schlesinger, *Annual Report to the Congress, Fiscal Year 1975* (Washington, D.C.: GPO, 1974), pp. 37-38. Attention should be drawn to the significant discrepancy between the second and third sentences. Schlesinger first asserts that a massive nuclear attack would be folly except "where our own *or allied* cities were attacked." Without noting or attempting to explain the apparent contradiction, Schlesinger then states that a massive response appears increasingly incredible "in response to *anything less* than an all-out attack on the *U.S.* and *its* cities." Somewhere between the two adjacent sentences, the importance of European cities to the United States appears to have been substantially downgraded and the problem of coupling made much larger.

27. On the U.S. failure to distinguish between nuclear and conventional weapons in tactical operations, see Gaddis, *Strategies of Containment*, p. 149. The "Carte Blanche" NATO exercise of 1955 suggests the scale on which nuclear weapons might have been used to support military operations. Carte Blanche involved 335 NATO atomic detonations on over 100 targets in two days of simulated conflict. More notable, however, is that according to NATO calculations the tactical nuclear operations of Carte Blanche, even excluding the effects of fallout, would have killed 1.7 million Germans and wounded another 3.5 million. In the "Sage Brush" exercise conducted in Louisiana that same year, umpires ruled after some 70 "detonations" that all human life in the state had been destroyed. See Freedman, *The Evolution of Nuclear Strategy*, pp. 109–10.

28. For a good discussion, see Ball, *Targeting for Strategic Deterrence*, especially p. 17.

29. For a complete and authoritative account of the development of U.S. nuclear doctrine in the early 1960s, focusing particularly on Secretary of Defense McNamara's views and pronouncements, see Kaufmann, *The McNamara Strategy*. For a good secondary source, see Freedman, *The Evolution of Nuclear Strategy*, pp. 227–56.

30. See, for example, Freedman, *The Evolution of Nuclear Strategy*, p. 237.

31. This interpretation of McNamara's position draws on his Draft Presidential Memoranda of September 1961 and November 1962. See Kaplan, *The Wizards of Armageddon*, pp. 315–16.

32. John T. McNaughton, as quoted in Kaufmann, *The McNamara Strategy*, p. 145.

33. On this interpretation of the "damage limitation" element of U.S. strategy during the 1960s, see Kaufmann, *The McNamara Strategy*, pp. 74–75, 94–95; and Robert S. McNamara, *Fiscal Year 1969–73 Defense Program and 1969 Defense Budget* (Washington, D.C.: GPO, 1968), p. 47.

34. The misleading nature of the term "assured destruction" as a description of American strategy during the mid- and late 1960s is clearly revealed in a passage of the annual statement presented by Secretary of Defense Clark Clifford to Congress in January 1969: "our major hope for limiting damage if a nuclear war occurs is that it can be stopped short of an all-out attack on our cities. *We try to bring this about by providing our forces with characteristics that will permit them to be used effectively in a limited and controlled retaliation as well as for 'Assured Destruction', thereby being prepared for any type of Soviet attack.*" Clifford, *The 1970 Defense Budget and Defense Program for Fiscal Years 1970–74* (Washington, D.C.: GPO, 1969), p. 48. Emphasis added. See also, for example, the comments of Secretary of Defense Brown: "The need for flexibility and calibrating U.S. retaliation to

the provocation is not. . . a new discovery, whatever interpretation may have been placed on general statements of prior doctrines. It has never been U.S. policy to limit ourselves to massive counter-city options in retaliation, nor have our plans been so circumscribed. For nearly 20 years, we have explicitly included a range of employment options—against military as well as non-military targets—in our strategic nuclear employment planning." Harold Brown, *Annual Report to the Congress, Fiscal Year 1981* (Washington, D.C.: GPO, 1980), p. 66. For a good discussion of the continuity of U.S. nuclear employment strategy from the early Mc-Namara "No Cities" period through the "Assured Destruction" era to Schlesinger and beyond, see: Ball, *Targeting for Strategic Deterrence*, pp. 14–15 and Kahan, *Security in the Nuclear Age*, p. 105.

35. Blair, *Strategic Command and Control*, pp. 22–23.

36. Schlesinger, *Annual Report to the Congress, Fiscal Year 1975*, p. 4. Schlesinger's report makes clear that, in order to lay a foundation for future arms and command-and-control programs, he was deliberately and explicitly attempting to make public the case for controlled response and against "assured destruction" as a targeting policy. Unlike McNamara, whose wholehearted endorsement of limited options was somewhat obscured from the congressional and informed public eye by his "assured destruction" rhetoric, Schlesinger sought to provoke public debate on the idea of controlled nuclear war. Where McNamara had deliberately employed "assured destruction" rhetoric to hold down spending on strategic weapons programs, Schlesinger abandoned this rhetoric in order to create support for increased spending. As a consequence, it is Schlesinger rather than McNamara who is sometimes considered the father of controlled response. On the debate provoked by Schlesinger, see Robert J. Pranger and Roger P. Labrie, eds., *Nuclear Strategy and National Security* (Washington, D.C.: American Enterprise Institute, 1977). On Schlesinger's aims, see also, for example, Blair, *Strategic Command and Control*, p. 25.

37. On the distinction between countervailing and prevailing strategies, see Gray, *Nuclear Strategy and Strategic Planning*, p. 2.

38. Caspar W. Weinberger, *Annual Report to the Congress, Fiscal Year 1986* (Washington, D.C.: GPO, 1985), p. 46.

39. See, for example, Blair, *Strategic Command and Control*, p. 26.

40. Brown, *Annual Report to the Congress, Fiscal Year 1981*, p. 66.

41. Blair, *Strategic Command and Control*, pp. 26–28, 41–42.

42. Jervis, *The Illogic of American Nuclear Strategy*, p. 83.

43. *Ibid.*, p. 81.

44. Colin S. Gray, "Targeting Problems for Central War," *Naval War College Review* (January-February 1980), vol. 33, no. 1, p. 7.

45. Thomas C. Schelling, "Comment," in Klaus Knorr and Thornton Read, eds., *Limited Strategic War* (New York: Praeger, 1962), p. 255. This book, more than any other, developed and expressed the logic of controlled response in a full and formal manner.

46. More correctly, it is always possible to *attempt* to capitulate on the political issues rather than to prolong or escalate military hostilities. An opponent may, however, not hear or understand attempts to capitulate or may be unable to halt his military operations quickly. More interestingly, it may be impossible to arrest one's own military operations quickly. For an illustration of this, see Blair, *Strategic Command and Control*, p. 232.

47. Harold Brown, *Thinking About National Security* (Boulder, Colo.: Westview Press, 1983), pp. 274, 275.

48. Harold Brown, *Annual Report to the Congress, Fiscal Year 1979* (Washington, D.C.: GPO, 1978), p. 53.

49. For a discussion of some of the problems in keeping nuclear war limited, see Desmond Ball, *Can Nuclear War Be Controlled?*, Adelphi Paper no. 169 (London: International Institute for Strategic Studies, 1981); Ball, "U.S. Strategic Forces: How Would They Be Used?" *International Security* (Winter 1982–83), vol. 7, no. 3; Paul Bracken, *The Command and Control of Nuclear Forces* (New Haven: Yale University Press, 1983); John D. Steinbruner, "National Security and the Concept of Strategic Stability," *Journal of Conflict Resolution* (September 1978), vol. 22, no. 3; Steinbruner, "Nuclear Decapitation," *Foreign Policy* (Winter 1981–82), no. 45; Jervis, *The Illogic of American Nuclear Strategy*, pp. 106–7, 109–11. Not all analysts agree, of course. Edward Luttwak, for example, has stressed that the initial use of nuclear weapons is most likely to lead to immediate termination of the conflict: see "How to Think About Nuclear War," *Commentary* (August 1982), vol. 74, no. 2, pp. 25–26. Bracken has effectively rebutted Luttwak's line of argument, noting that nuclear escalation might occur during a conflict not because central authorities chose suicide over survival but because they had lost control and the commanders in the field found some "positive benefit" from firing nuclear weapons. Bracken, *Command and Control*, pp. 230–31. As we shall explore in more depth, it is also possible that central decision-makers may act irrationally and choose to escalate nuclear conflict.

50. Blair, *Strategic Command and Control*, pp. 77–78. Emphasis added.

51. Ball, *Can Nuclear War Be Controlled?*, p. 37. Emphasis in original. Logically, of course, Ball seems to go a bit too far here. Rationally or irrationally, it ought to be somewhat easier to envisage the use of nuclear weapons in a controlled fashion, since there is some chance, however unsatisfactorily small, that things will remain under control. The bottom line is the same, though: a rational decision-maker would be deterred from initiating nuclear strikes because of the difficulties of keeping a nuclear war controlled.

52. For this evaluation see, for example, McNamara, "The Military Role of Nuclear Weapons," pp. 71–72; or Brown, *Thinking About National Security*, p. 274. For a more thorough analysis of the difficulties of controlling tactical nuclear operations, see Bracken, *The Command and Control of Nuclear Forces*, pp. 158–78.

53. Brown, *Annual Report to the Congress, Fiscal Year 1980*, p. 75.

54. See, for example, Colin S. Gray, *Strategic Studies and Public Policy* (Lexington, Ky.: University Press of Kentucky, 1982), p. 159.

55. Colin S. Gray, "Presidential Directive 59: Flawed But Useful," *Parameters* (March 1981), vol. 11, no. 1, p. 33.

56. While not defining precisely what nuclear advantage would be necessary, Gray and Payne have claimed that "an adequate U.S. deterrent posture is one that denies the Soviet Union any plausible hope of success at any level of strategic conflict; offers a likely prospect of Soviet defeat; and offers a reasonable chance of limiting damage to the United States." Such a deterrent posture would require that the United States had developed "the targeting plans and procured the weapons necessary to hold the Soviet political, bureaucratic, and military leadership at risk" and "a combination of counterforce offensive targeting, civil defense, and ballistic missile and air defense . . . [to] hold U.S. casualties down to a level

compatible with national survival and recovery." Colin S. Gray and Keith Payne, "Victory Is Possible," *Foreign Policy* (Summer 1980), no. 39, pp. 25, 26–27.

57. Preemptive forces include: accurate missiles with hard-target kill capability necessary to destroy land-based missile fields and submarine pens as well as bomber bases; and naval forces able to locate and destroy Soviet ballistic missile submarines. Active defenses would include the shield against ballistic missiles envisioned in the Strategic Defensive Initiative as well as the kinds of air defense and anti-ballistic missile systems that the United States currently knows how to build. Passive defenses include the evacuation and/or sheltering of individuals and the dispersion and/or hardening of industry.

58. Brown, *Annual Report to the Congress, Fiscal Year 1980*, p. 80. Emphasis added. For a good nontechnical explanation of why mutual vulnerability is impossible to escape, see Spurgeon M. Keeny, Jr. and Wolfgang K. H. Panofsky, "MAD vs. NUTs," *Foreign Affairs* (Winter 1981–82), vol. 60, no. 2, pp. 298–304.

59. Brown, *Thinking About National Security*, pp. 57–58.

60. Certainly this would be the case if the Soviet Union attempted to gain nuclear superiority. Consider the role of the "Missile Gap" in the 1960 U.S. presidential election. An exact Soviet analogy is of course unlikely but one might intuitively suspect that a U.S. drive for superiority in the 1990s or beyond might indeed have some political impact within the Soviet Union.

61. See, for example, Arnold L. Horelick and Myron Rush, *Strategic Power and Soviet Foreign Policy* (Chicago: University of Chicago Press, 1966), especially pp. 126–40. Horelick and Rush write: "The Cuban missile episode was a bold effort to alter the unfavorable strategic environment in which the USSR found itself in 1962 as a result of the United States' intercontinental arms buildup and the collapse of the 'missile gap' myth" (p. 127). More recent discussions with Soviet decision-makers have suggested that at a basic emotional level, Khrushchev's sense of unilateral Soviet vulnerability and the unfairness of such a situation played an important role in prompting the decision to place missiles in Cuba.

62. For a good review of the discussion of the probable consequences of a limited nuclear conflict, see Pranger and Labrie, eds., *Nuclear Strategy and National Security*, pp. 85–188.

63. Donald Rumsfeld, *Annual Report to the Congress, Fiscal Year 1978* (Washington, D.C.: GPO, 1977), p. 73. Rumsfeld nonetheless argues for acquisition of a range of limited nuclear options as a prudential step.

64. Kaplan, *Wizards of Armageddon*, pp. 299–300. Kaplan goes on to argue that "if ever in the history of the nuclear arms race, before or since, one side had unquestionable superiority over the other, one side truly had the ability to devastate the other side's strategic forces, one side could execute the. . . counterforce/ no-cities option with fairly high confidence, the autumn of 1961 was that time. Yet approaching the height of the gravest crisis that had faced the West since the onset of the Cold War, everyone said, 'No' " (p. 301). Kaplan concludes of U.S. leaders that "even while they realized their own superiority they could find no practical way to exploit it"(p. 304).

65. *Ibid.*, p. 305.

66. The United States could, of course, reduce the utility the Soviet Union might derive from undertaking a limited attack on American territory. First, it could minimize the military consequences of an attack. The United States could reduce the vulnerability of targets (for example, by hardening or dispersing mili-

tary and key industrial facilities) or reduce the number of vulnerable targets (for example, by decreasing the number of land-based ICBMs and increasing the number of sea-based SLBMs). Second, the United States could reduce the political benefits likely to accrue to the Soviet Union from a limited attack by either reducing the threat these vulnerable assets pose to the Soviet Union or reducing the political friction between the superpowers that might lead the Soviet Union to contemplate war. By redefining its commitments to Western Europe, for example, the United States could sever the link between coupling and counterforce, reducing Soviet interests in destroying U.S. strategic forces. Ultimately, however, in an anarchic world self-protection depends on the existence of possible negative sanctions. It is difficult to imagine political, economic, or conventional military sanctions of sufficient magnitude to yield a high-confidence alternative to reliance on nuclear threats in deterring a limited Soviet attack on the United States.

67. Earl C. Ravenal, "Counterforce and Alliance: The Ultimate Connection," *International Security* (Spring 1982), vol. 6, no. 4, p. 34.

68. On this issue see, for example, the well-argued and provocative case presented by Josef Joffe on the essential stabilizing role of the U.S. presence in Western Europe in "Europe's American Pacifier," *Foreign Policy* (Spring 1984), no. 54.

69. Weinberger, *Annual Report to the Congress, Fiscal Year 1984*, p. 52.

70. Gray and Payne, "Victory Is Possible," p. 14.

71. Gray, "Presidential Directive 59," p. 32.

72. Bruce Russett, *Prisoners of Insecurity* (New York: W. H. Freeman, 1983), p. 161.

73. John Phelps, "On 'Firebreaks' to Inhibit Escalation," in John Phelps, Bruce Russett, Matthew Sands, and Charles Schwartz, eds., *Studies on Accidental War* (Washington, D.C.: Institute for Defense Analyses, 1963), p. I-18.

74. Alexander L. George and Richard Smoke, *Deterrence in American Foreign Policy* (New York: Columbia University Press, 1974), p. 54.

75. See Richard Rosecrance, *Strategic Deterrence Reconsidered*, Adelphi Paper no. 116 (London: International Institute for Strategic Studies, 1975), pp. 10–12 or Richard Rosecrance, "Deterrence in Dyadic and Multipolar Environments," in Richard Rosecrance, ed., *The Future of the International Strategic System* (San Francisco: Chandler, 1972), pp. 126–35.

2. RATIONALITY AND IRRATIONALITY

1. See Thomas C. Schelling, *The Strategy of Conflict* (Cambridge: Harvard University Press, 1960), p. 4.

2. Klaus Knorr, *The Power of Nations* (New York: Basic Books, 1975), p. 41.

3. Glenn H. Snyder, *Deterrence and Defense* (Princeton: Princeton University Press, 1961), p. 25. On this point see also Sidney Verba, "Assumptions of Rationality and Non-Rationality in Models of the International System," *World Politics* (October 1961), vol. 14, no. 1, especially pp. 95, 108. For a contrasting approach see John Harsanyi, "A Simple Probabilistic Model of Nuclear Behavior," in Richard Rosecrance, ed., *The Future of the International Strategic System* (San Francisco: Chandler, 1972), pp. 101–2. Harsanyi suggests that emotional, nonpragmatic values are *not* legitimate ends of "rational" policy.

4. Janice Gross Stein has demonstrated that it is possible in some cases to analyze convincingly the decision-making process itself. See Stein and Raymond Tanter, *Rational Decision-Making: Israel's Security Choices, 1967* (Columbus: Ohio State University Press, 1980). Stein's work reinforces the point, however, that it is extraordinarily difficult to obtain the sort of evidence necessary to make a convincing case about the rationality of a decision process.

5. Stephen Maxwell, *Rationality in Deterrence*, Adelphi Paper no. 50 (London: International Institute for Strategic Studies, 1968), p. 3.

6. *Ibid.*

7. See Philip Green, *Deadly Logic* (Columbus: Ohio State University Press, 1966), p. 216.

8. Maxwell, *Rationality in Deterrence*, p. 3.

9. See Patrick M. Morgan, *Deterrence* (Beverly Hills: Sage, 1977), p. 78. Morgan's concept of sensible decision-making also involves appreciation of uncertainty and of the possibility of miscalculation, accident, and irrationality. These features are not inconsistent with rational decision-making as we have outlined it.

10. Anthony Downs, *An Economic Theory of Democracy* (New York: Harper and Row, 1957), p. 5.

11. The terms are those of Alexander George and Robert Keohane. See Alexander L. George and Robert O. Keohane, "The Concept of National Interests: Uses and Limitations," in Alexander L. George, *Presidential Decisionmaking in Foreign Policy* (Boulder, Colo.: Westview Press, 1980), p. 221.

12. This is the simplest case. A situation in which the payoffs themselves—the *costs and benefits* of possible outcomes—are not known with certainty can also be described as decision-making under uncertainty. For example, if I know that the coin is fair but am unsure what I win if it comes up heads or what I lose if it comes up tails, my decision whether to bet still involves uncertainty.

13. Knorr, *The Power of Nations*, p. 41. Morgan has introduced a logically different, though semantically similar, notion of "perfect decision-making," by which he appears to mean something roughly akin to the notion of objectively rational decision-making that we will discuss below. Morgan, *Deterrence*, pp. 78–82.

14. Herbert A. Simon, *Administrative Behavior*, Third Edition (New York: The Free Press, 1976), p. 76. To be slightly more precise, we shall say that it is (subjectively) rational to take the medicine if, *on the basis of an intelligent use of the information available,* one believes it will cure the disease.

15. Downs, *Economic Theory*, p. 6. Emphasis added.

16. See, for example, James G. March and Herbert A. Simon, *Organizations* (New York: John Wiley, 1958), pp. 137–38.

17. The reader familiar with the work of John Von Neumann and Oskar Morgenstern will recognize that the whole notion of surprise aversion violates two of the axioms involved in their expected utility hypothesis—those on monotonicity and compound lotteries. The theoretical implications of this intuitive and seemingly innocuous notion are therefore significant and the reader is advised to proceed cautiously.

18. March and Simon, *Organizations*, p. 138.

19. *Ibid.*

20. See Anatol Rapoport, *Fights, Games, and Debates* (Ann Arbor: University of Michigan Press, 1960), pp. 200–1. We shall look more closely below at what is

involved in a "rational" use of information such as that required for rationally calculating a subjective probability assessment.

21. See, for example, March and Simon, *Organizations*, pp. 140–41.

22. March and Simon, *Organizations*, p. 141. Janis and Mann have argued that empirical psychological evidence suggests that while decision-making on minor problems is more appropriately thought of as satisficing, decision-making on major issues is generally better modeled as optimizing. See Irving L. Janis and Leon Mann, *Decision Making* (New York: The Free Press, 1977), pp. 40–41.

23. John D. Steinbruner, *The Cybernetic Theory of Decision* (Princeton: Princeton University Press, 1974).

24. *Ibid.*, p. 86.

25. Harold Brown, *Annual Report to the Congress, Fiscal Year 1980* (Washington, D.C.: GPO, 1979), p. 75

26. *Ibid.*, pp. 14–15.

27. Steinbruner, "Beyond Rational Deterrence," *World Politics* (January 1976), vol. 28, no. 2, p. 239.

28. *Ibid.*, p. 241.

29. Jack L. Snyder, "Rationality at the Brink," *World Politics* (April 1978), vol. 30, no. 3, p. 349.

30. *Ibid.*, p. 365.

31. See, for example, Thomas C. Schelling, *Arms and Influence* (New Haven: Yale University Press, 1966), pp. 151–68, 234–38, 244–51, 256–59.

32. It is not entirely apparent that Steinbruner himself would disagree. See his warnings about attempting to use cybernetic analysis in a prescriptive framework, in "Beyond Rational Deterrence," pp. 235, 242.

33. Knorr, *The Power of Nations*, p. 44.

34. Mancur Olson, "How Rational Are We?" (A Review of *Choice and Consequence* by Thomas C. Schelling), *The New York Times Book Review* (July 1, 1984), vol. 133, no. 46,092, p. 10.

35. Downs, *Economic Theory*, p. 9.

36. See, for example, Steinbruner, "Beyond Rational Deterrence," p. 235.

37. Downs, *Economic Theory*, p. 215. Though their concept of "vigilant" information processing does not reflect this trade-off, Janis and Mann recognize that it may not be rational to be as vigilant as possible. See *Decision Making*, pp. 10–14, for this alternative approach.

38. Downs, *Economic Theory*, p. 215. I am indebted to Avinash Dixit for originally directing my attention to this infinite-regress problem; I regret that I cannot advance a more elegant solution.

39. Janis and Mann have formulated seven procedural criteria for judging the quality of decision-making which focus on the use of information. Though more demanding—because of its requirements about evaluating the utility of further information and about belief systems (see below)—our concept of intelligent information processing is consistent with their concept of vigilant information processing. See Janis and Mann, *Decision Making*, pp. 10–14.

40. Glenn Snyder, *Deterrence and Defense*, p. 25.

41. Rapoport, *Fights, Games, and Debates*, pp. 200–1.

42. Downs, *Economic Theory*, p. 9.

43. Alexander L. George and Richard Smoke, *Deterrence in American Foreign Policy* (New York: Columbia University Press, 1974), p. 74.

2. RATIONALITY AND IRRATIONALITY

44. See, for example, George, *Presidential Decisionmaking in Foreign Policy*, pp. 28–35.

45. Schelling, *The Strategy of Conflict*, p. 4. See also Rapoport, *Fights, Games, and Debates*, pp. 107–08.

46. Again, for this assumption to be plausible we must assume that the consumption of decision resources has a cost and that the rational decision-maker takes this cost into account. Rational value maximization thus may yield a satisficing decision criterion, where the standard is set rationally. See Richard Cyert and James March, *A Behavioral Theory of the Firm* (Englewood Cliffs, N.J.: Prentice-Hall, 1963), pp. 10ff; and March and Simon, *Organizations*, pp. 140ff.

47. For a discussion that suggests this typology, see Knorr, *The Power of Nations*, pp. 42–43. See also Jack Snyder, "Rationality at the Brink," p. 347.

48. Jack Snyder, "Rationality at the Brink," p. 347. Snyder has in mind behavior such as that identified by Alexander L. George and Juliette L. George in *Woodrow Wilson and Colonel House* (New York: Dover, 1956).

49. Downs, *Economic Theory*, p. 9.

50. *Ibid.*, pp. 9–10.

51. Verba, "Assumptions of Rationality," p. 94.

52. *Ibid.*, p. 108.

53. For example, it may be rational for a chess player to rely on a belief system that holds it is imperative to control the center of the board: given limited time to identify and assess options, the player thus focuses on those that do not leave his pieces in the periphery. From experience he knows that moves toward the center of the board are likely to be effective ones.

54. This discussion builds on Robert Jervis' notion of "irrational cognitive consistency." See Jervis, *Perception and Misperception in International Politics* (Princeton: Princeton University Press, 1976), pp. 17–42. See also Richard Ned Lebow, *Between Peace and War* (Baltimore: Johns Hopkins University Press, 1981), pp. 102–7.

55. Knorr, *The Power of Nations*, p. 42.

56. Though my approach differs, I am indebted to the discussion in Jack S. Levy, "Misperceptions and the Causes of War: Theoretical Linkages and Analytical Problems," *World Politics* (October 1983), vol. 36, no. 1, pp. 76–82. The useful literature on perception and misperception is extensive and growing rapidly. See especially Jervis, *Perception and Misperception;* and Klaus Knorr, "Threat Perception," in Klaus Knorr, ed., *Historical Dimensions of National Security Problems* (Lawrence, Kans.: University Press of Kansas, 1976).

57. See, for example, Ole R. Holsti and Alexander L. George, "The Effects of Stress on the Performance of Foreign Policy-Makers," in Cornelius P. Cotter, ed., *Political Science Annual* (Indianapolis: Bobbs-Merrill, 1975), especially p. 257. See also Janis and Mann, *Decision Making*.

58. Janis and Mann, *Decision Making*, p. 50.

59. *Ibid.*, p. 51.

60. The discussion of decision-making under conditions of stress by Janis and Mann is incomparable. See *ibid.*, pp. 45–133.

61. The approach to "national interests" developed by George and Keohane differs fundamentally from the approach to the interests of state decision-makers developed below; nonetheless, their observation appears relevant. See George and Keohane, "The Concept of National Interests," pp. 234–35.

62. Lester Grinspoon, "Crisis Behavior," *Bulletin of the Atomic Scientists* (April 1984), vol. 40, no. 4, pp. 27–28. Daniel Frei's discussion of the stress-related problems of nuclear decision-making during crisis is also excellent; it should be clear, though, that much of his discussion is related to the synergistic effects between stress, cognitive failure, and organizational dysfunction. See Frei, *Risks of Unintentional Nuclear War* (Totowa, N.J.: Rowman & Allanheld, 1983), pp. 109–53.

63. Lebow, *Between Peace and War*, pp. 283–85. See also Richard Ned Lebow, *Nuclear Crisis Management: A Dangerous Illusion* (Ithaca: Cornell University Press, 1987), for a discussion of the problems for rational decision-making likely to be created by an acute superpower crisis.

64. See Irving L. Janis, *Victims of Groupthink* (Boston: Houghton Mifflin, 1972).

65. Frei, *Risks of Unintentional Nuclear War*, p. 92.

66. See Robert Jervis, "Deterrence Theory Revisited," *World Politics* (January 1979), vol. 31, no. 2, pp. 289–90, for an insightful discussion of the connection between deterrence theory and realism.

67. George and Smoke, *Deterrence in American Foreign Policy*, p. 72. There is, of course, no reason to accept the contention of George and Smoke that one must coerce a *majority* of the relevant participants. Clearly, one must coerce some sufficient subset of the participants but the smallest sufficient subset may comprise more or less than a majority, since there is no reason to expect either that decision will be by simple majority vote or that participants will have an equal vote.

See also Morgan, *Deterrence*, pp. 49–75. Morgan has noted that conclusions about the deterrence process depend very much on "the level of analysis"—the level of organization at which one assumes decision-making takes place. Morgan himself cursorily examines three levels of analysis—the individual level, "the group/organization level," and the national level—without coming to any conclusion about which level or levels are particularly useful or about how one might combine them.

The principal criticism of the rational unitary actor model has come from observers of bureaucratic and organizational behavior, most notably Graham Allison. See Graham T. Allison, *Essence of Decision* (Boston: Little, Brown, 1971). This critique has been essentially one of the appropriate level of analysis. As Steinbruner has pointed out, the bureaucratic and organizational politics critiques of the rational-actor model do not question the intelligent attempt to maximize expected utility but only the level of disaggregation necessary in order to witness it. See Steinbruner, "Beyond Rational Deterrence," p. 226.

68. This approach to understanding the decision-maker is similar to the one suggested by Cyert and March in *A Behavioral Theory of the Firm*, p. 27.

69. While this analysis differs from the one George offers, there is clearly an intellectual debt to be acknowledged. See George, *Presidential Decisionmaking in Foreign Policy*, pp. 1–14.

70. Donald W. Taylor, "Decision-making and Problem Solving," in James G. March, ed., *Handbook of Organizations* (Chicago: Rand McNally, 1965), p. 63.

71. See Cyert and March, *A Behavioral Theory of the Firm*, pp. 27–28.

72. The extent to which values *do* vary between participants and the extent to which this variance does in fact lead to inconsistent ordering of preferences has been debated. See—on the one side of the debate—Allison, *Essence of Decision*, and Morton H. Halperin, *Bureaucratic Politics and Foreign Policy* (Washington, D.C.: Brookings, 1974); or—on the other—Stephen D. Krasner, *Defending the Na-*

tional Interest (Princeton: Princeton University Press, 1978). The amount one worries about collective decision-making, therefore, depends on the extent to which one assumes that a commonly shared perception of the "national interest" dominates individual preference functions.

73. The presumably typical B-52 crew—for whom the moral, legal, and military sanctions available to the national command authorities are effective—will of course not represent an *independent* decision center at all.

74. Simon, *Administrative Behavior*, p. 76.

75. Robert S. McNamara, "Speech Delivered at Commencement Exercises, University of Michigan, Ann Arbor, MI, June 16, 1962," as published in Robert J. Art and Kenneth N. Waltz, eds., *The Use of Force*, Second Edition (Lanham, Md.: University Press of America, 1983), p. 149. Emphasis added.

76. Matthew Sands, "Information Exchange and Inadvertent War," in John Phelps, Bruce Russett, Matthew Sands, and Charles Schwartz, eds., *Studies on Accidental War* (Washington, D.C.: Institute for Defense Analyses, 1963), p. II-5.

77. Klaus Knorr, *On the Uses of Military Power in the Nuclear Age* (Princeton: Princeton University Press, 1966), pp. 90, 91–92. For a different interpretation of the Cuban missile crisis—explaining Khrushchev's actions as irrational, rather than inadvertent, behavior—see Richard Ned Lebow, "The Cuban Missile Crisis: Reading the Lessons Correctly," *Political Science Quarterly* (Fall 1983), vol. 98, no. 3.

78. Maxwell, *Rationality in Deterrence*, p. 11.

79. Schelling, *The Strategy of Conflict*, p. 188.

80. Maxwell, *Rationality in Deterrence*, p. 11.

3. COERCIVE POWER AND COERCIVE STRATEGIES

1. Klaus Knorr, *The Power of Nations* (New York: Basic Books, 1975), p. 4.

2. The best discussion of compellence and deterrence remains Schelling's. See Thomas C. Schelling, *Arms and Influence* (New Haven: Yale University Press, 1966), pp. 69–78. Additional distinctions are possible. Alexander George, for example, also makes the insightful analytical distinction between compellence (in his terms, "coercive diplomacy") aimed at making an opponent stop and compellence aimed at making him go back. George also distinguishes between offensive and defensive uses of coercive diplomacy—perhaps a more difficult distinction to make objectively and empirically. See Alexander L. George, "The Development of Doctrine and Strategy," in Alexander L. George, David K. Hall, and William R. Simons, *The Limits of Coercive Diplomacy* (Boston: Little, Brown, 1971), pp. 22–24.

3. For criticism of the failure of theorists and practitioners of "pure coercion" to take the possible role of positive sanctions into account, see George, "The Development of Doctrine and Strategy," pp. 25–26. For a good discussion of the importance of and theoretical problems with the notion of positive sanctions, see Knorr, *The Power of Nations*, pp. 7–8.

4. Knorr, *The Power of Nations*, p. 5. Emphasis added. For a discussion of the nature of power resources see, for example, *ibid.*, pp. 6, 9–17.

5. In game theoretical modeling a case of this sort is known as "Big Bully." Studying "Big Bully" games in international affairs, Snyder and Diesing have concluded: "In Big Bully. . . B is again in Chicken, but A prefers no agreement and

probably war not only over any conceivable compromise but also over B's total capitulation. This distinguishes the game from Bully, where A, though unwilling to compromise, would accept B's yielding to his (A's) demands rather than no agreement or war. A is a 'big bully' because his demands on B are intended only as a pretext for the use of force." Glenn H. Snyder and Paul Diesing, *Conflict Among Nations* (Princeton: Princeton University Press, 1977), pp. 46–47.

6. For an examination of the relationship between direct power and coercive power and an unparalleled discussion of the nature of coercive power, see Schelling, *Arms and Influence*, pp. 1–34.

7. In his study of U.S. coercive diplomacy, for example, George identifies eight conditions:

1. Strength of United States motivation
2. Asymmetry of motivation facing the United States
3. Clarity of American objectives
4. Sense of urgency to achieve the American objective
5. Adequate domestic political support
6. Usable military options
7. Opponent's fear of unacceptable escalation
8. Clarity concerning the precise terms of settlement

Alexander L. George, "Comparisons and Lessons," in George, Hall, and Simons, *The Limits of Coercive Diplomacy*, p. 216.

8. We use the term "strategy" in its game theoretic meaning. A decision-maker's strategy represents a description of his behavior in all possible contingencies. For a fuller explanation see, for example, Morton Davis, *Game Theory* (New York: Basic Books, 1970), p. 10.

9. On the notion that irrationality may lead to yielding when rationality would not, Robert Jervis has perhaps summed the situation best: "Irrationality could also lead to a state of passive acquiescence, while a rational grasp of the situation could lead to belligerence." See Jervis, "Deterrence Theory Revisited," *World Politics* (January 1979), vol. 31, no. 2, p. 299. For an illustration of this situation, see Jervis, "Deterrence and Perception," *International Security* (Winter 1982–83), vol. 7, no. 3, pp. 14–17.

10. See Glenn H. Snyder, *Deterrence and Defense* (Princeton: Princeton University Press, 1961), p. 12.

11. See chapter 2 for a discussion of the concept of surprise aversion.

12. See Schelling, *Arms and Influence*, pp. 69–86.

13. Robert Jervis, "Deterrence and Perception," pp. 14–17. See also Barry R. Posen, *The Sources of Military Doctrine* (Ithaca: Cornell University Press, 1984), pp. 145–46, 160.

14. For a discussion of pure and mixed strategies, see R. Duncan Luce and Howard Raiffa, *Games and Decisions* (New York: John Wiley, 1957), p. 70.

15. The distinct meanings of "contingent" and "mixed" should be clear. In a contingent strategy the imposition of pleasure or pain depends on the behavior of the opponent. In a mixed strategy, *given* the behavior of the opponent, the imposition of pleasure or pain will be probabilistic rather than certain. As it turns out, while most coercive strategies can be described as contingent and mixed, *neither* quality is a necessary condition for an effective coercive strategy. Noncontingent coercive strategies—for example, a strategy in the game of "Chicken" of driving

straight down the middle of the road regardless of what the other driver does—may have implict in them the necessary "assurance" or positive sanction: the opponent can be "assured" of surviving by swerving. Thus, an effective coercive strategy may involve a threat to behave in the same fashion regardless of whether or not the opponent modifies his behavior: a coercer need not have a contingent strategy for the opponent to have a contingent strategy. This said, however, it should be clear that all the nuclear threats explicitly or implicitly issued to date have involved contingent coercive strategies.

16. The term is Schelling's. His discussion, while unparalleled, is only suggestive when it comes to explaining why chance may exist and, logically, how a threat that leaves something to chance may be structured and made credible. See Thomas C. Schelling, *The Strategy of Conflict* (Cambridge: Harvard University Press, 1960), pp. 187–204.

17. In other words, if both the costs of being deterred and surprise aversion are assumed to be zero, a rational opponent will be coercible in this simple example if $-(x-y)U_p>U_t$, where x is the probability of the imposition of the threatened pain given execution of the threat; y is the probability of the imposition of pain given execution of the promise rather than the threat; U_p is the (negative) utility to the opponent of the pain; and U_t is the utility to the opponent of the trespass. Even apart from the assumptions about the costs of being deterred and about surprise aversion, this example is simplistic because it implicitly eliminates the risk that the opponent will not achieve his objectives given the coercer's response (factor 2 in our list) and the risk in or uncertainty about the coercer's strategy (factor 4 in our list).

18. Schelling, *Arms and Influence*, pp. 107–9.

19. Similarly, an opponent may be *compelled* to undertake an action desired by the coercer—such as a return to some status quo ante—because of the coercer's credible commitment to achieve his desired goal through the direct application of power if coercion fails. Thus there exists a logically parallel notion of *"affirmation"* as a mode of compellence.

20. See Glenn Snyder, *Deterrence and Defense*, pp. 31–32. Snyder distinguishes between intrinsic, strategic, deterrent, and political values. See Chapter 4 for a more detailed discussion of the nature of values.

21. The illustration is not intended to be politically provocative. If, for some reason, this example seems unrealistic, the reader is invited to substitute "United States" for "Nicaragua" and "Afghan" for "Salvadoran."

22. See, for example, Mohamed Heikal, *The Road to Ramadan* (New York: Times Newspapers, 1975), pp. 20–45, 204–6.

23. Michael Howard has made this point eloquently in presenting his argument for conventional deterrence as a supplement to increasingly incredible nuclear deterrence in Europe. See Howard, "Comment and Correspondence: The Issue of No First Use," *Foreign Affairs* (Fall 1982), vol. 61, no. 1, p. 212.

24. For an exploration of the concept of, and the requirements for, a strategy of nuclear retaliation, see Klaus Knorr, "Limited Strategic War," in Klaus Knorr and Thornton Read, eds., *Limited Strategic War* (New York: Praeger, 1962), pp. 16–27; and Morton A. Kaplan, "Limited Retaliation as a Bargaining Process," in *ibid.*, pp. 142–62.

25. Increasing marginal costs from retaliation may not be as implausible in real life as this somewhat strained example suggests. It may be that the Soviet

Union is willing to tolerate a limited number of blows against military bases or industrial capacity which cut into the "fat" or excess capacity of the system but is unwilling to tolerate blows that cut deeper and begin to threaten the continued functioning of the Soviet state and economy. Even if the flow of benefits from aggression remains undiminished, in this situation the Soviets might choose to yield to coercive pressure.

26. As we have noted, in making utility calculations it is necessary to allow for surprise aversion as well as risk aversion. See Chapter 2.

27. Perhaps the most notable is Robert Jervis. See Jervis, *The Illogic of American Nuclear Strategy* (Ithaca: Cornell University Press, 1984), p. 20. Jervis is driven to this error by his reliance on a mistaken dichotomy between denial and punishment. Since he can envision only one type of retribution—namely, punishment—then every strategy for inflicting pain that is is not a punitive one (as Countervailing certainly and obviously is not) must by definition and elimination be one of denial.

28. Obviously, if the United States does proceed to deploy a partially effective anti-ballistic missile (ABM) system as part (or all) of a strategic defense initiative, then a new "denial" thread would have been woven into the Countervailing strategy. An ABM system would complicate a Soviet attack, forcing the Soviet Union to expend an increased fraction of its nuclear force in a limited attack. At some point, denial logic suggests, the effort might cease to be worth the prize.

29. Caspar Weinberger, *Annual Report of the Secretary of Defense to Congress, Fiscal Year 1986* (Washington, D.C.: GPO, 1985), p. 46.

30. Perhaps a more perfect analogy would be to liken the situation to a neighbor who, having been implicitly threatened by my brickpile, undertakes to smash my bricks. My countervailing strategy does not involve making such an undertaking overwhelmingly difficult; rather it protects my brickpile by creating a threat that if my neighbor does attempt to destroy my bricks, I will begin to throw bricks and stones at targets in my neighbor's yard until he concludes that he would be better off stopping.

31. Schelling, *The Strategy of Conflict*, pp. 187–204.

32. Eduard Beneš, as quoted in A. J. P. Taylor, *The Origins of the Second World War* (New York: Atheneum, 1964), p. 185.

33. Given the long history of a prosperous but nonindependent Czech nation— and the understanding by state leaders of both the durability of Czech society in the absence of a Czech state and the dangers of attempting to pursue an independent policy in conflicts with more powerful neighbors—this was, in retrospect, hardly a surprising conclusion. The lesson of the Battle of White Mountain in 1618, and of the three centuries of history as a nonindependent people that followed it, had been thoroughly learned by the Czech leadership.

34. Richard Rosecrance, "Deterrence in Dyadic and Multipolar Environments," in Richard Rosecrance, ed., *The Future of the International Strategic System* (San Francisco: Chandler, 1972), p. 125. More recently Rosecrance appears to have modified his thinking: "Each [nation-state] seeks to ensure its own persistence, cultural and political. But this does not mean that it fights each time its autonomy is impinged upon." Richard Rosecrance, *The Rise of the Trading State* (New York: Basic Books, 1986), p. 49. Consider some of the many cases in which resistance did not occur: in twentieth century European history alone, we find the Czechs in 1938, 1939, and 1968; the Estonians, Latvians, and Lithuanians in 1939; and arguably

the Austrians in 1938. It would also be incorrect to conclude simply that Rosecrance's generalization fails in those cases where a small state faces an overwhelming opponent. For example, the Czechs in 1938 were capable of offering not inconsiderable resistance. By contrast, in an objective international situation not altogether dissimilar from that of the Baltic states, the Finns resisted in 1939. Similarly, there was some significant Hungarian resistance in 1956, despite the fragmented political leadership, while there was none to speak of in Czechoslovakia in 1968. The occurrence or nonoccurrence of resistance thus appears not simply a result of the military realities, but of values at stake and the likelihood of preserving those values given various courses of action.

35. In terms that we will develop in the following chapter, these three reasons involve, first, the intrinsic value associated with punishment; second, the strategic value associated with it; and, third, the deterrent and political value associated with it. This draws upon Glenn Snyder, *Deterrence and Defense*, pp. 31–32.

36. I am indebted to Barry Posen for his criticism of my attempts to avoid coming to grips with this point.

37. This idea harks back to the periodically rediscovered concept of establishing a public "price list" for Soviet transgressions: for an invasion in the periphery the Soviets might have to "pay" one major city; for aggression in Europe, a dozen cities; for any attack on the United States, all their major cities. This retribution would be carried out without any expectation that it would cause the Soviet Union to cease the particular transgression, but simply to establish a reputation for sticking to our outrageously priced "price list."

4. CREDIBLE COMMITMENT AND MODES OF COMMITMENT

1. In fact, as a practical matter, coercive strategies will never be certain, but always probabilistic. After all, as we have noted, weapons do not work with certainty, only probabilistically.

2. See, for example, Thomas C. Schelling, *The Strategy of Conflict* (Cambridge: Harvard University Press, 1960), pp. 36–37.

3. As we observed in passing in Chapter 3, while all coercive strategies involve "giving an opponent a choice," not all effective coercive strategies involve contingent behavior on the part of the coercer. There is a difference between contingent imposition of costs or benefits (something necessary for coercion) and contingent behavior by the coercer (something logically unnecessary for coercion). The contingency of pain or pleasure may result from the opponent's actions, not the coercer's. In the game of Chicken, for example, the coercer does not threaten to behave in a contingent fashion: quite to the contrary, he threatens to drive straight down the middle of the road regardless of what the opponent does. The imposition of pain, however, is certainly contingent. As this suggests, an opponent may have a contingent strategy as a result of some *noncontingent* pattern of behavior by the coercer. Indeed, this is frequently the case in relations between the very strong and the very weak. An Israeli military demolition team, sent to destroy the home of a Palestinian engaged in terrorism, will behave in a noncontingent fashion—it will follow its orders to destroy the home whether the family removes its belongings or not—but it is likely to succeed in coercing the family into leaving. It gives the occupants

a choice, but—unlike a threat, say, to shoot them if they refuse to leave and to give them bus fare if they agree to go—the actual actions of the team do not vary according to whether or not the family alters its behavior. I have developed the distinction between "active," contingent coercive strategies and "passive," noncontingent ones elsewhere. See Edward Rhodes, *Nuclear Weapons, Irrational Behavior, and Extended Deterrence* (Ann Arbor: University Microfilms, 1985), appendix 4–1. Schelling offers a different approach, noting correctly that all coercive strategies can be rephrased as contingent ones. See Thomas C. Schelling, *Arms and Influence* (New Haven: Yale University Press, 1966), p. 74.

4. Glenn H. Snyder, *Deterrence and Defense* (Princeton: Princeton University Press, 1961), p. 13.

5. The notion of surprise aversion is developed in chapter 2.

6. See Glenn Snyder, *Deterrence and Defense*, pp. 31–32. Although Snyder explicitly focuses on the values involved in *deterrence* situations, this typology works equally well for compellence situations. "Deterrent value" as defined by Snyder is simply reputational value *with the opponent* and as such it is equally relevant to compellence and deterrence.

7. *Ibid.*

8. Or, for a more interesting example, burning down my neighbor's house in response to his trespass will have strategic value because it eliminates his source of shelter and sustenance, thus reducing his ability to carry out further forays.

9. See, for example, Graham T. Allison, *Essence of Decision* (Boston: Little, Brown, 1971), pp. 187–200.

10. *Ibid.*, p. 194.

11. The Carte Blanche exercise provides an interesting baseline illustration of this point. Obviously, to the extent that the strategic value of Western Europe is a purely negative one to the United States—that is, to the extent that Western Europe has strategic value only because it would convey military advantage to the Soviet Union if it fell under Soviet control and not because Western control over it yields any military benefit to the United States—the destruction of Europe would preserve its strategic value.

12. Consider, for example, former Secretary of Defense Robert S. McNamara's comment: "It is inconceivable to me, as it has been to others who have studied the matter, that 'limited' nuclear wars would remain limited—any decision to use nuclear weapons would imply a high probability of the same cataclysmic consequences as a total nuclear exchange. In sum, I know of no plan which gives reasonable assurance that nuclear weapons can be used benefiically in NATO's defense." McNamara, "The Military Role of Nuclear Weapons," *Foreign Affairs* (Fall 1983), vol. 62, no. 1, p. 72. How seriously McNamara's statement should be taken and whether it reflects his true views have been questioned. In addition, McNamara is obviously playing fast and loose with the English language. If nuclear use has "a high probability" of leading to escalation, then it is conceivable, not "inconceivable," that nuclear war would remain limited. Nonetheless, problems of controlling escalation are real and it seems likely that decision-makers have information on this point.

13. To say that the strategy is "in part" *ex post* irrational is to say that either the positive sanction (the assurance or reward) or the negative sanction is *ex post* irrational, but not both.

14. Stephen Maxwell, *Rationality in Deterrence*, Adelphi Paper no. 50 (London: International Institute for Strategic Studies, 1968), p. 2. Emphasis added.

15. *Ibid.*, p. 18.

16. To be sure, making the claim that "I have denied myself choice" increases the cost of not carrying out the threatened coercive strategy (by increasing the deterrent and political value at stake), just as making the public claim that "I will carry out my threat" would. Thus, claiming to have denied oneself choice—whether or not one actually succeeds in doing so—may make it *ex post rational* to carry out the coercive strategy and create a commitment-through-rationality.

17. For a simple mathematical illustration, suppose exactly two policies, a_1 and a_2, are available to the coercer and suppose a_1 would rationally be chosen. Now suppose the coercer has a probability x of being rational (and $1-x$ of being irrational); suppose further that if the coercer is irrational he will behave irrationally and choose a_1 with probability y (and a_2 with probability $1-y$). Given this rational policy preference and this decision-making structure, the coercer is committed to a mixed strategy that plays a_1 with probability $x+y-xy$ and a_2 with probability $1-x-y+xy$. Even if the opponent has perfect knowledge of the coercer's values and decision-making process—that is, the opponent has no problem of uncertainty—the opponent is faced with a *risk* of $1-x-y+xy$ that the coercer *will choose to play* a_2.

18. Klaus Knorr, *The Power of Nations* (New York: Basic Books, 1975), p. 9.

19. For an early insightful exposition of the twin problems of communication and credibility, see William W. Kaufmann, "The Requirements of Deterrence," in William W. Kaufmann, ed., *Military Policy and National Security* (Princeton: Princeton University Press, 1956), pp. 17–20. This essay originally appeared in 1954 as Princeton University Center for International Studies memorandum no. 7.

20. Snyder, *Deterrence and Defense*, pp. 27–28.

21. *Ibid.*, p. 28.

22. Obviously, an actor may also lie about the existence of capabilities necessary for an effective coercive strategy rather than simply about the existence of commitment to it. I may try to deceive my neighbor that my can of gasoline is full when in fact it is empty, or that I have matches when in fact I have run out. In this case, not only am I not actually committed to an effective coercive strategy, but I do not in fact *possess* an effective coercive strategy to which I can be actually committed. In the nuclear case, if an effective coercive strategy required the ability to target Soviet political leadership cadres in hidden, hardened bunkers and the United States did not in fact possess the information necessary to destroy these bunkers, the United States might still attempt to deceive the Soviet leadership that it had such a capability. To use an actual historic example of this sort of deception about capabilities: in the late 1950s and early 1960s, the Soviet Union deliberately undertook to deceive the United States about Soviet intercontinental nuclear capabilities. See, for example, Arnold L. Horelick and Myron Rush, *Strategic Power and Soviet Foreign Policy* (Chicago: University of Chicago Press, 1966), pp. 58–70. By contrast, Soviet threats during the Berlin crisis that "our missiles will fly automatically" (Nikita Khrushchev, as quoted by Averill Harriman in his June 23, 1959, *Life* interview; see *ibid.*, p. 120) represented a bluff simply about commitment. The missiles actually existed.

23. See, for example, Schelling, *The Strategy of Conflict*, p. 36.

24. Again, Schelling has noted this relationship in *ibid.*, p. 23.

25. Snyder, *Deterrence and Defense*, p. 25.

5. NUCLEAR WEAPONS AND CONFLICT LIMITATION

1. Thomas C. Schelling, *Arms and Influence* (New Haven: Yale University Press, 1966), pp. 19, 21.

2. Morton Kaplan, "Limited Retaliation as a Bargaining Process," in Klaus Knorr and Thornton Read, eds., *Limited Strategic War* (New York: Praeger, 1962), p. 144.

3. See, for example, Bernard Brodie, *The Atomic Bomb and American Security* (New Haven: Yale University, 1945 [Memorandum no. 18]) and Bernard Brode, ed., *The Absolute Weapon* (New York: Harcourt Brace, 1946).

4. Schelling, *Arms and Influence*, pp. 21–22.

5. *Ibid.*, p. 20. Schelling hints, however, that even without nuclear weapons and their speed, wars may persist long after it might be rational to terminate them or may result in irrational conclusions: "There is no guarantee, of course, that a slower war would not persist. The First World War could have stopped at any time after the Battle of the Marne. There was plenty of time to think about war aims, to consult the long-range national interest, to reflect on costs and casualties already incurred and the prospect of more to come, and to discuss terms of cessation with the enemy. The gruesome business continued as mechanically as if it had been in the hands of computers (or worse: computers might have been programmed to learn more quickly from experience). One may even suppose it would have been a blessing had all the pain and shock of the four years been compressed within four days. Still, it was terminated. And the victors had no stomach for doing then with bayonets what nuclear weapons could do to the German people today." *Ibid.*, p. 21.

6. Perhaps a fairer measure of the concentration of power achieved with nuclear weapons is a comparison of the Tokyo and Hiroshima bombing raids of World War II. The former raid involved more than 300 bombers, the second only one.

7. Desmond Ball, *Can Nuclear War Be Controlled?*, Adelphi Paper no. 169 (London: International Institute for Strategic Studies, 1981), p. 36. See also John D. Steinbruner, "National Security and the Concept of Strategic Stability," *Journal of Conflict Resolution* (September 1978), vol. 22, no. 3, and Steinbruner, "Nuclear Decapitation," *Foreign Policy* (Winter 1981–82), no. 45.

8. Bernard Brodie, *Strategy in the Missile Age* (Princeton: Princeton University Press, 1959), pp. 305–6. Emphasis added.

9. *Ibid.*, p. 309.

10. See Richard Smoke, *War: Controlling Escalation* (Cambridge: Harvard University Press, 1977), p. 14.

11. These three approaches to understanding the limitation of war—in terms of war's ends, means, and consequences—parallel the three common approaches to judging the morality of war—again in terms of ends, means, and consequences.

12. General Sir John Hackett et al., *The Third World War: A Future History* (New York: Macmillan, 1978), pp. 313–30.

13. Interestingly, in some situations temporal limitation may be objectively *irrational* for precisely the same reason. The legitimacy of the Syrian state in the 1970s and 1980s, for example, was to some significant degree built on a pan-Arabist ideology involving continued hostility toward Israel.

14. See Schelling, *Arms and Influence*, pp. 1–25.

15. The Iran-Iraq war illustrates both developments. Compared even to the Arab-Israeli clashes of earlier decades, the lack of restraint in its vertical dimension (and, for a long time, in its temporal one) is apparent.

16. As Schelling has noted: "That nuclear weapons make it *possible* to compress the fury of global war into a few hours does not mean that they make it *inevitable*. We still have to ask whether that is the way a major nuclear war would be fought, or ought to be fought. Nevertheless, that the whole war might go off like one big string of firecrackers makes a critical difference between our conception of nuclear war and the world wars we have experienced." Schelling, *Arms and Influence*, pp. 20–21. Emphasis in original.

17. For an elegant exposition of the logic that might lead to this conclusion, see Schelling's discussion of salient points in *ibid.*, pp. 131–41.

18. See the distinction drawn by George and Keohane between other-regarding, collective, and self-regarding benefits in Alexander L. George and Robert O. Keohane, "The Concept of National Interests: Uses and Limitations," in Alexander L. George, *Presidential Decisionmaking in Foreign Policy* (Boulder, Colo.: Westview, 1980), p. 221.

19. The National Conference of Catholic Bishops, *The Challenge of Peace: God's Promise and Our Response* (Washington, D.C.: United States Catholic Conference, 1983); George F. Kennan, *The Nuclear Delusion* (New York: Pantheon, 1982).

20. An attempt might be made to portray this limitation as contingent (on the Soviet Union's willingness to similarly limit its actions) but to the extent that the Soviets had perfect information and understood U.S. antipathy to destroying Soviet cities under any circumstances, the contingent linkage would be recognized as a bluff, and any threat to respond to an attack on American cities by attacking Soviet cities would not be credible. In general, *nonlimitation* in some or all dimensions may also be a dominant strategy, even for a rational actor. In the U.S.-Soviet case, to be sure, nonlimitation in *all* dimensions is unlikely to be a dominant strategy. Although possible, it is improbable that the United States could come to hate, fear, or mistrust the Soviet Union so much that the urge to inflict all possible damage on it would rationally outweigh all moral and practical arguments for withholding some attacks—at least so long as the Soviets still held important U.S. targets hostage. But the United States may rationally conclude that nonlimitation in *some* dimension is rational regardless of Soviet behavior. The United States might, for example, conclude that the destruction of all Soviet ICBMs (nonlimitation in depth) was rational regardless of Soviet behavior.

21. Bruce G. Blair, *Strategic Command and Control* (Washington, D.C.: Brookings, 1985), p. 233. Emphasis added.

22. *Ibid.*, p. 239.

23. Paul Bracken, *The Command and Control of Nuclear Forces* (New Haven: Yale University Press, 1983), pp. 232–33.

24. *Ibid.*, p. 177; the discussion commences on p. 164.

6. DOOMSDAY MACHINES

1. See Herman Kahn, *On Thermonuclear War* (Princeton: Princeton University Press, 1961), pp. 148–50.

2. See, for example, *ibid.*, p. 145.

3. That is, even given the embarrassment of being revealed as bluffers, the Soviets would rationally prefer that their Machine *not* work if the Americans failed to be deterred.

4. See Kahn, *On Thermonuclear War*, pp. 145–52. Kahn distinguishes between a Doomsday Machine and a Homicide Pact Machine—the latter does not threaten the survival of third parties. The distinction is an interesting one, but does not seem necessary for our basic discussion here.

5. For a discussion of the concepts of punishment, retaliation, and denial, see Chapter 3. Briefly, punishment involves retribution imposed without any aim of impelling compliance; retaliation involves retribution aimed at coercing compliance; and denial involves preventing the opponent from achieving his objectives at an effort justified by the gains.

6. The punishment aspect is essential to a Doomsday Machine: the United States could build a black box that destroyed only Germany instead of everyone involved. If the Soviet objective were (the unlikely one of) exploiting German industry and technology, such a black box might serve to deny and deter. It would not, however, be a Doomsday Machine.

7. I.e., some probability of doomsday is imposed each time period in which the opponent fails to yield to the coercer's demand. The opponent is forced to keep on playing Russian roulette (with a loaded chamber resulting in doomsday rather than just a messy death for the gambler) until he finally yields to the coercer's wishes.

8. For a good discussion of this point, see Paul Bracken, *The Command and Control of Nuclear Forces* (New Haven: Yale University Press, 1983), pp. 158–78.

9. *Ibid.*, p. 164.

10. *Ibid.*, pp. 158–70.

11. A caveat about the necessity of U.S. reliance on Doomsday Machines needs to be made here. Although doomsday clearly has a larger negative utility, any irrational U.S. nuclear use, even one that does not trigger doomsday, will have some negative utility for the Soviets; conceivably, Soviet aggression will be objectively irrational even if it triggers only the lesser use and not doomsday. It is logically conceivable, therefore, that the Soviet Union might be deterred by a commitment-through-irrationality to limited nuclear use even though, because the probability of doomsday is made slight, it is not deterred by the Doomsday Machine. That is, the Soviets might be deterred by the greater probability of the lesser harm even though undeterred by the smaller probability of the larger one.

12. Indeed, we must assume that doomsday does *not* have an infinitely negative utility. Since, any policy the United States selects (even nuclear disarmament) carries with it some *risk*, however small, of leading to doomsday, all policies would be equally unacceptable; after all, infinity multiplied by any probability equals infinity, and the expected utility of *every* policy would be negative infinity.

13. Blair's discussion is excellent. See Bruce G. Blair, *Strategic Command and Control* (Washington, D.C.: Brookings, 1985), especially pp. 287–89.

14. Examples of the literature I have in mind are: John D. Steinbruner, "Nu-

clear Decapitation," *Foreign Policy* (Winter 1981–82), no. 45; John D. Steinbruner, "National Security and the Concept of Strategic Stability," *Journal of Conflict Resolution* (September 1978), vol. 22, no. 3; Paul Bracken, *The Command and Control of Nuclear Forces;* and Carl Sagan, "Nuclear War and Climatic Catastrophe," *Foreign Affairs* (Winter 1983–84), vol. 62, no. 2.

15. Richard M. Nixon, *The Real War* (New York: Warner Books, 1980), p. 255. For a fuller discussion in the context of the Vietnam War, see, for example, John Lewis Gaddis, *Strategies of Containment* (New York: Oxford University Press, 1982), pp. 299–301.

16. Thomas C. Schelling, *The Strategy of Conflict* (Cambridge: Harvard University Press, 1960), p. 18.

17. *Ibid.*

7. COERCION AND CONTINGENTLY IRRATIONAL BEHAVIOR

1. This is distinct from a "rationally unneighborly homeowner"—a homeowner who is vicious toward his neighbor all or some of the time because he intelligently calculates he will "get something out of it" and evaluates that "something" as being worth the effort of unneighborliness.

2. On reflection, it should be obvious that commitment-through-irrationality does not always involve *contingently* irrational behavior. In some coercive situations *both* the positive sanction and the negative sanction of the effective coercive strategy are irrational to carry out. The commitment-through-irrationality in such a situation must be to *noncontingently* irrational behavior.

3. Again, the reader should recall that this denial may be a probabilistic one. The Soviet Union need not be threatened (or see itself threatened) with the *certainty* of irrational action—only with some increase in the probability of irrational action, an increase that is unacceptably large given the incentive for transgression.

4. Obviously, irrational behavior may also occur contingently as a result of the opponent's *yielding*, as opposed to *not* yielding. We focus discussion on the case in which irrational behavior occurs contingently upon the failure of the opponent to yield because it is the one relevant to the problem of nuclear coercion, not because it is logically unique.

5. Some predelegation of nuclear decision-making authority appears to have existed in the past. A 1957 memo from Air Force Chief of Staff Thomas White to Strategic Air Command (SAC) commander Tommy Power, for example, noted that Power's "plans provide for assumption of authority by your Air Force commanders under specified circumstances. This can be construed as at least an element of the delegation we would prefer." Memo from White to Power, November 22, 1957; Thomas D. White Papers, Box 41. The overall record, however, seems to suggest that the U.S. posture fell far short of one of unreasoned choice. The situation, as McGeorge Bundy was to inform an incoming President Kennedy three years later, was one "in which a subordinate commander faced with a substantial Russian military action could start the thermonuclear holocaust on his own initiative if he could not reach you (by failure of communication at either end of the line)." Bundy Memo to the President, January 30, 1961; John F. Kennedy Library, National Security Files, Box 313. Such potential for organizational dysfunction raised seri-

ous dangers of nonintelligent calculation of cost and benefits and of inconsistent evaluation of utility, but hardly seems describable as unreasoned choice. The danger in such a situation was that the commander would be unable to calculate consequences intelligently or would evaluate costs and benefits differently than central decision-makers would.

6. Thomas C. Schelling, *Arms and Influence* (New Haven: Yale University Press, 1966), pp. 166–84.

7. There would be some precedent for this. Lebow has noted the incapacitation of leaders who, following psychological attempts to shield themselves from unpleasant information, were confronted with an unpleasant and psychologically inescapable reality. His examples include Kaiser Wilhelm II at the outbreak of World War I, Stalin at the German invasion, and Nasser in the wake of the Israeli preemptive attack that opened the Six Day War. See Richard Ned Lebow, *Between Peace and War* (Baltimore: Johns Hopkins University Press, 1981), pp. 283–85. Lebow has gone on to explore the relationship between efforts at psychological shielding from unpleasant realities, psychological collapse, and miscalculated escalation in *Nuclear Crisis Management: A Dangerous Illusion* (Ithaca: Cornell University Press, 1987), pp. 104–53.

8. Indeed, this is likely to be easier to imagine than an organization that suffers from a continuous inability to use information intelligently. After all, such an organization is likely to be put out of business by a more effective organization in the long run.

9. See Chapter 2 for a brief discussion of value extension. This notion draws on work by Alexander L. George, *Presidential Decisionmaking in Foreign Policy* (Boulder, Colo.: Westview Press, 1980), chs. 2, 13.

10. Or, by contrast, we may now listen to my father-in-law, who always said that if we were not more neighborly we would be asking for trouble, and who is willing to donate a plate of homemade cookies to solve our problems. While the contingency may be more likely to cause a shift in membership and power within family councils in one direction rather than another, which direction is not *a priori* certain.

11. This is quite apart and analytically distinct from the change in behavior that may result because the outbreak of war provides new information about the nature of the opponent and hence about the steps that might be taken to protect one's interests. I may be quite happy to adopt a live-and-let-live attitude toward my neighbor until he trespasses. His trespass—and the evidence it provides me about his hitherto unknown propensity to trespass—may lead me rationally to abandon my live-and-let-live behavior and to continue to harass him until he is forced to leave the neighborhood entirely. The fact that the status quo *ante* is no longer acceptable once war has begun—and that after war has begun I am willing to pay staggering costs to achieve outcomes I would not previously have considered to be worth the cost of a single life—does not in itself suggest an inconsistent evaluation of utility or indeed any form of irrational decision-making.

12. In developing his cognitive/cybernetic model of decision-making, John D. Steinbruner examines U.S. policy regarding a multilateral nuclear force; this seems a good example of a historical case in which the state decision-maker appears to have been unable to form a consistent utility function. See Steinbruner, *The Cybernetic Theory of Decision* (Princeton: Princeton University Press, 1974), pp. 153–326.

13. Obviously, history does provide examples of apparently manifestly psycho-

pathological leaders retaining power for protracted periods despite the harm their leadership caused their societies. Amin in Uganda and Bokassa in the Central African Empire come to mind. Stalin in his later years is another possible, though less clear-cut, example. The relationship between state and society in the United States is, however, fundamentally different, making the relevance of these examples dubious.

14. It was widely reported, following the final days of the Nixon presidency, that Secretary of Defense James Schlesinger had discreetly taken steps to further restrict the president's control over nuclear weapons.

15. Glenn H. Snyder, *Deterrence and Defense* (Princeton: Princeton University Press, 1961), p. 26.

16. To say that a strategy is an effective coercive one is to say that (if commitment is credible) it leads the opponent to alter his behavior in the desired fashion. An effective coercive strategy of course may be a probabilistic rather than certain one. See Chapter 3 for a discussion of coercive strategies.

17. Obviously, intention is not altogether unimportant to the problem. If intention is observable, my action will provide my neighbor with further information that may be important to him in assessing risks of various courses of action.

18. See *Field Manual 100–5*, July 1976 edition (Washington, D.C.: GPO, 1976), pp. 10–5 – 10–9. The discussion and diagrams are obviously somewhat dated: nuclear land mines, for example, have since been entirely retired from NATO's arsenal, and presumably from its war plans. The 1982 edition of this manual, which superseded the 1976 edition, deleted all description of nuclear-use packages. The point remains valid, however, that effective tactical use of nuclear munitions is likely to require extensive coordination of operations.

19. A complicating problem is that an effective NATO denial effort might well have to involve substantial and coordinated nuclear use by the forces of a number of the allied nations. The various NATO members might thus have to acquiesce in American irrational behavior if denial is to be successful.

20. See for example Glenn Snyder's musings on the possible irrational use of nuclear weapons under Eisenhower's "New Look" in *Deterrence and Defense*, p. 26. See also Fred Kaplan, *The Wizards of Armageddon* (New York: Simon and Schuster, 1983), pp. 245–47.

21. The distinction between punishment and retaliation is not whether the retribution is large or small, in relative or in absolute terms; rather, it is whether or not the sanction provides intraconflict compellent power. While this implies that retaliatory actions can be neither all-out nor total, it does not suggest that punitive ones need to have either of these qualities.

22. Bruce G. Blair, "Solving the Command and Control Problem," *Arms Control Today* (January 1985), vol. 15, no. 1, p. 7.

8. THEORY AND POLICY

1. See Chapter 3 for a discussion of credible commitment and coercibility as necessary and sufficient conditions for the existence of coercive power.

2. Colin S. Gray, *Nuclear Strategy and Strategic Planning* (Philadelphia: Foreign Policy Research Institute, 1984), pp. xviii-xix.

3. Robert Jervis, *The Illogic of American Nuclear Strategy* (Ithaca: Cornell University Press, 1984), p. 170.

4. Though the context and policy conclusions are somewhat different, one cannot help but be reminded of Christ's rhetorical inquiry: "For what shall it profit a man, if he shall gain the whole world, and lose his own soul." Mark 8:36.

5. The reader is invited to recall the discussion in Chapter 3 of the necessary and sufficient conditions for deterrence. The typology presented there suggested that deterrence requires the *existence* of an effective coercive strategy and *credible commitment* to that strategy. An effective coercive strategy might not exist either if the coercer lacked sanctions of sufficient magnitude to induce a rational preference to yield or if the opponent were unable to act, *ex post*, on a rational preference to yield.

6. See John D. Steinbruner, "National Security and the Concept of Strategic Stability," *Journal of Conflict Resolution* (September 1978), vol. 22, no. 3; John D. Steinbruner, "Nuclear Decapitation," *Foreign Policy* (Winter 1981–82), no. 45; Paul Bracken, *The Command and Control of Nuclear Forces* (New Haven: Yale University Press, 1983); Bruce G. Blair, *Strategic Command and Control* (Washington, D.C.: Brookings, 1985).

7. Bracken represents a significant exception here. See *Command and Control of Nuclear Forces*, pp. 163–65. Bracken does not, however, pursue this point.

8. "Report of the President's Commission on Strategic Forces, 11 April, 1983" (Scowcroft Commission Report), as published in "Documentation," *Survival* (July/August 1983), vol. 25, no. 4, p. 181.

9. This observation is particularly relevant since proposed C^3 improvements are not aimed at the problem of preventing unauthorized peacetime use—a problem the United States feels it has largely under control—but rather at the problem of maintaining tight central control during a nuclear war, even one of protracted duration.

10. For a good summary of the arguments on the negative effects of time pressure on nuclear decision-making, see Daniel Frei, *Risks of Unintentional Nuclear War* (Totowa, N.J.: Rowman & Allanheld, 1983), pp. 133–37. On the importance of time pressures in decision-making, see also Ole R. Holsti, *Crisis, Escalation, War* (Montreal: McGill-Queens University Press, 1972), and Alexander L. George, "Adaptation to Stress in Political Decision Making," in G. V. Coelho, David A. Hamburg, and J. E. Adams, eds., *Coping and Adaptation* (New York: Basic Books, 1974).

11. Richard Ned Lebow, *Between Peace and War* (Baltimore: Johns Hopkins University Press, 1981), p. 110. Lebow draws on Irving L. Janis and Leon Mann, *Decision Making* (New York: The Free Press, 1977). For a brief discussion of hypervigilance, the reader is advised to review Chapter 2.

12. See Graham T. Allison, *Essence of Decision* (Boston: Little, Brown, 1971), pp. 124–26. It may, however, be necessary to reconsider Allison's analysis in light of declassified information. His emphasis on the failure of military staff work does not square entirely with McNamara's notes of the October 21 meeting with the president. These notes suggest that a larger problem was the real inability of the Air Force and intelligence services to locate all of the missiles. A high-confidence disarming attack may, in fact, have been impossible. See Robert S. McNamara, "Notes on October 21, 1962 Meeting with the President," John F. Kennedy Library, Box 313.

13. Quite apart from damage to radio antennae, satellite ground terminals, and terrestrial communication lines from nuclear blasts aimed at military bases, electromagnetic pulse generated by nuclear detonations is likely to destroy much ordinary ground communication, while scintillation of the atmosphere may interfere with radio communication. See, for example, Bruce G. Blair, "Solving the Command and Control Problem," *Arms Control Today* (January 1985), vol. 15, no. 1, p. 7; or Desmond Ball, *Can Nuclear War Be Controlled?*, Adelphi Paper no. 169 (London: International Institute for Strategic Studies, 1981). For a fuller discussion, see Blair, *Strategic Command and Control*.

14. Tommy Power, as quoted by Fred Kaplan in *The Wizards of Armageddon* (New York: Simon and Schuster, 1983), p. 246. This is not to suggest that military officers are by birth or training more likely to suffer from cognitive rigidity than are civilian National Command Authorities. But the NCA may have spent comparatively less time studying traditional ways of thinking about war and comparatively more time thinking about the horrible implications of "pushing the button." Beyond this, simple mathematics also becomes involved: in the event of decentralization of control, there are likely to be many independent military secondary decision centers (as compared with the single decision center of the NCA), thus multiplying the possibilities of cognitive failure affecting collective U.S. behavior.

15. Obviously, even if it is not the physical survival of the NCA that is at stake but their ability to command U.S. forces, perceived time pressure may induce hypervigilance.

16. Blair, "Solving the Command and Control Problem," p. 7.

17. Logically, a third scenario might exist: nuclear escalation might occur because of cognitive failure by the NCA. National political leaders might view nuclear escalation in Europe in inappropriate, inaccurate prenuclear terms. If, however, one accepts former Secretary of Defense Robert McNamara's view that U.S. presidents have accepted his advice that the United States under no circumstances (rationally) choose to initiate a nuclear war, this scenario ceases to be a plausible one. See McNamara, "The Military Role of Nuclear Weapons," *Foreign Affairs* (Fall 1983), vol. 62, no. 1.

18. On this last point, it is useful to remember President Reagan's oft-quoted public musings on the conceivability and controllability of tactical nuclear war. See Gregory F. Treverton, "Managing NATO's Nuclear Dilemma," *International Security* (Spring 1983), vol. 7, no. 4, p. 94.

19. Deployment of U.S. nuclear forces abroad creates a risk not only of an irrational *U.S.* use when U.S. fundamental interests have not been attacked, but of seizure and use of U.S. weapons by foreign states or political groups. The history of the postwar period indicates that local instability has indeed on occasion posed a threat to rational U.S. control over U.S. nuclear forces. See Milton Leitenberg, "Background Information on Tactical Nuclear Weapons," *Tactical Nuclear Weapons: European Perspectives*, SIPRI (New York: Crane, Russak, 1978), pp. 42–49; see also Bracken, *The Command and Control of Nuclear Forces*, pp. 170–72. This suggests not only that the United States should avoid deployments in exceptionally unstable locales, such as Southwest Asia (unless, of course, the United States concludes that its interests there have become fundamental), but also that it should not be complacent about current deployments in South Korea, Turkey, Greece, Italy, and even the Netherlands and Belgium.

20. That is, the Countervailing strategy implies a requirement for C^3 that would,

at an absolute minimum, continue to function reliably after the U.S. had been subjected to a nuclear attack and would ideally continue to function in a nuclear environment throughout the hours, days, weeks, or months that hostilities lasted.

21. The choice of the word "permit" is a careful one. It is not being suggested that an explicit shift in strategy would either necessarily or immediately result in the curtailment of the current U.S. strategic modernization effort. It would be ridiculous to ignore the bureaucratic and political momentum propelling the programs involved. Only the naive or optimistic would expect a perfect (or even substantial) congruence between what could be done and what will be done. There does appear to be some reason for optimism that procurement items that lack strategic justification or run counter to official strategy *can* be eliminated, however. The supercarriers in 1949, the intermediate-range nuclear forces in the early 1960s, and the ABM system in the late 1960s and the early 1970s provide interesting, if mixed, evidence. Particularly if programs are expensive or otherwise politically vulnerable, elimination of the rationale for any given program may provide an *opportunity* to cut it.

22. For the justification of these programs see, for example, Caspar W. Weinberger, *Annual Report to Congress, Fiscal Year 1985* (Washington, D.C.: GPO, 1984), pp. 186–89. With the exception of the Stealth bomber, these programs have been justified in terms of their capacity to put hardened targets at risk; the Stealth bomber has been justified in terms of maintaining the capability for manned-bomber penetration of Soviet airspace—a capability required only because of demands for flexibility in targeting and intrawar reconnaissance.

23. Steven Kull, "Nuclear Nonsense," *Foreign Policy* (Spring 1985), no. 58, pp. 47–48.

24. See, for example, Samuel P. Huntington, "Conventional Deterrence and Conventional Retaliation in Europe," *International Security* (Winter 1983–84), vol. 8, no. 3.

25. Of the Army's 14 active and reserve "heavy" (tank or mechanized infantry) divisions, for example, 10 are currently based entirely or principally in the United States, not in Europe. U.S. plans are to have 6 of the Army divisions and 60 of the Air Force tactical squadrons that are based in the United States transported to Europe within 10 days; cuts could be made among these forces rather than among those based in Europe.

26. Ronald Reagan, as quoted in Treverton, "Managing NATO's Nuclear Dilemma," p. 94. For a good sketch of the difference in interest between America and Europe regarding how to deter the Soviet Union, see pp. 93–94.

27. Bracken, *The Command and Control of Nuclear Forces*, p. 176.

28. Ronald Reagan, as quoted in Weinberger, *Annual Report to the Congress, Fiscal Year 1985*, p. 38.

29. Thomas C. Schelling, "Comment," in Klaus Knorr and Thornton Read, eds., *Limited Strategic War* (New York: Praeger, 1962), p. 243.

30. Klaus Knorr, "Limited Strategic War," in Knorr and Read, eds., *Limited Strategic War*, p. 30.

INDEX